The Promise of Paradise

The
Promise
of
Paradise

Utopian Communities in B.C.

WHITECAP BOOKS
Vancouver/Toronto

for Shiane

The information in this book is true and complete to the best of our knowledge. All recommendations are made without guarantee on the part of the author or Whitecap Books Ltd. The author and publisher disclaim any liability in connection with the use of this information. For additional information please contact Whitecap Books Ltd., 351 Lynn Avenue, North Vancouver, BC V7J 2C4.

Edited by Elizabeth McLean
Proofread by Lisa Collins
Cover and interior design by Tanya Lloyd
Cover photograph courtesy of BCARS (C-07803)
Printed and bound in Canada

Canadian Cataloguing in Publication Data
Scott, Andrew, 1947–
    The promise of paradise

    Includes bibliographical references and index.
    ISBN 1-55110-622-1

    1. Utopias—British Columbia—History. 2. Collective settlements—British Columbia—History. I. Title.
    HX659.B7S36 1997   335'.02'09711   C97-910658-3

The publisher acknowledges the support of the Canada Council for the Arts for our publishing program and the Cultural Services Branch of the Government of British Columbia in making this publication possible.

For more information on titles from Whitecap Books,
visit our web site at www.whitecap.ca

CONTENTS

ACKNOWLEDGEMENTS

Many people helped with this book. I'd like to thank the staffs at the B.C. Archives and Records Service (BCARS) in Victoria, Special Collections at the Vancouver Public Library and Special Collections at the University of British Columbia library. I fondly remember the company of my deceased wife Shiane Scott on an early visit to Sointula. Katherine Johnston, who came with me on several later journeys of research and discovery, offered much encouragement. I'm very grateful to the Canada Council, without whose financial support the project could not have been completed.

The following people all provided assistance. The list is alphabetical, and I apologize in advance if I've left anyone out. Thank you all so much: Anne Blaney, 100 Mile House; Vivien Bowers, Nelson; James Bowman, Calgary; George Brandak, Special Collections, UBC Library; Kate Brauer, formerly of Sointula; Liz Bryan, Rock Creek; Jan and Tom Bulman, Vancouver and Langley; Maureen Butler, Langley; Alan Carpenter, Langley; Dawn Child, Cedar-by-the-Sea; Wilf Christensen, Bella Coola; Sue Collerman, Langley; Maureen Cumming, BC Ferries, Victoria; Susan Davidson, Aldergrove; Kathy Day of Bernholz & Graham, Anchorage; Wallace Dergousoff, Grand Forks; Simon Dick, Mitchell Bay; Larry Ewashen, Castlegar; Leslie Field, Special Collections, UBC Library; Laura Fisher, Bradner; Merrolly Frostrup, Bella Coola; David Gluns, Nelson; Peter Gritchen, Grand Forks; Gwen Hanson, Quatsino, who kindly gave me a tour and put me in touch with many old-timers; Ralph Harris, Sointula; Hugh and Agnes Herbison, Argenta; Fred Horkoff, Grand Forks; Jack Howich, Quatsino; Jack Hudson, Metlakatla, Alaska; Steven Hume, Saturna; Nora Johnson, Quatsino; Don and Marian Knoerr, who helped track down utopian communities in the Smithers area; Len Laurance and Taquan Air, for generously flying me from Prince Rupert to Ketchikan and over to Metlakatla and back; Patti Mackey, Ketchikan Visitors Bureau; Michael Marrapese, Vancouver; Stewart Marshall, formerly of Sointula; John Masters, Vancouver; Mark Mealing, of Castlegar's

Selkirk College, for reading the chapter on the Doukhobors; Nan Meister, for helping me develop patience and trust; Bob Mercer, Vancouver; Linda Mickle, Alaska Marine Highway System, Juneau; Anna and Robert Miles, Aiyansh; Alvin Nelson, Kincolith; Carl and Doreen Nelson, Sointula; Chief Harry Nyce, Gitwinksihlkw; John Oliphant, Vancouver; Willie Olney, Sointula; John Pearson, who showed me around Metlakatla, Alaska (and mayor Jack Booth for letting us use his car); Eli Popoff, Grand Forks; Annette Island School District superintendent Bob Pratt; Heather Pringle, Vancouver; Gary and Anita Raaum of Innside Passage Bed & Breakfast, Ketchikan, for hosting above and beyond the call of duty; Fran Reece, band manager at Metlakatla, B.C.; Cathy Ringham, Langley; Tauno and Ruth Salo, Sointula; Lynn Sherrill, Smithers; Peter and Barbara Solyell of Hagensborg for their hospitality; John and Helen Stevenson, Nelson; Kaz Takahashi, Vancouver; Betty Tillotson, Argenta; Catherine Traer, Victoria; Richard Van Cleave at Ketchikan's Tongass Historical Museum; John Verigin, Jr., Grand Forks; Lillian Weedmark at the Bulkley Valley Museum, Smithers; Al Whittaker, for letting me camp at Quatsino Lodge; Gloria Williams, Sointula; Doris Wold, Quatsino; and Daniel Wood, Vancouver, for suggesting the original idea.

British Columbia

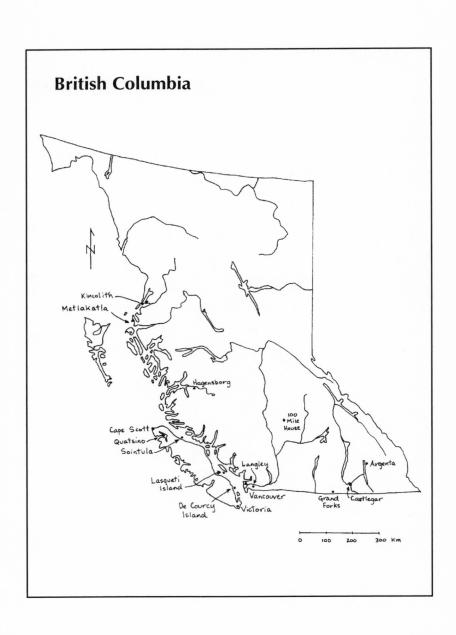

Kincolith
Metlakatla

Hagensborg

100
Mile
House

Cape Scott
Quatsino
Sointula

Langley

Argenta

Lasqueti
Island

Vancouver

Grand
Forks

Castlegar

De Courcy
Island

Victoria

0   100   200   300 km

INTRODUCTION
Promised Lands

A map of the world that does not include Utopia
is not worth even glancing at, for it leaves out the one
country at which Humanity is always landing.
—Oscar Wilde, *The Soul of Man Under Socialism*

In the last 150 years, British Columbia has attracted more than its fair share of experimental communities. The model villages of the missionaries, designed to transform the bodies and souls of the province's aboriginal inhabitants, were in full sway by the 1870s. Before and after the turn of the century, idealistic Scandinavian and Russian immigrants established significant colonies. The early 1930s saw the titillating, far-reaching scandals associated with Brother XII and his cult. The back-to-the-land movement of the 1960s led to a grand blossoming of communes. And in the 1990s, B.C. is home to Canada's first cohousing projects.

British Columbia is not unique as a proving ground for quixotic ideas. Cults, colonies and communes have come and gone elsewhere in North America and around the world. But no other region can outdo B.C. for its abundance of alternative, utopian settlement attempts in as short a time frame. This book examines some of the most significant communities and the impulses that inspired them.

Why was Canada's westernmost province blessed with this rich history? I believe the reasons stem from the fact that B.C. is Europe's youngest child, the last hospitable corner of the world to be explored and colonized by the representatives of western civilization. To the European mind, preoccupied with the noble tasks of improving the human condition and getting rich, the province was a vast empty space on the map, a blank slate where any number of ambitious schemes might take root and flower. The age of exploration—at least for the temperate regions—ended here.

The Pacific Northwest attracted visionaries and schemers from around the world. Those who would not remain satisfied with the familiar and routine frequently ended up in B.C. Those who were used to moving on and starting anew stopped here as they searched for the kingdom of their dreams—and found they could move no further. British Columbia was the end of the road. And still the dreamers come to B.C. Where else should they go?

The Tsimshian village of Metlakatla, and others like it, were founded during a period of great colonial expansion. William Duncan, his missionary brethren and the English church societies that financed them were products of Victorian prosperity and moral certitude. But the resources of the frontier, which kept British mills running and made money available for missionary work, were extracted at a terrible cost to aboriginal people. The degradation of the Tsimshians, which caused Duncan to come to B.C.'s north coast in 1857, had direct links to commercial avarice and corrupt trade practices. Ironically, the kind of community sought by many of those described in this book—one characterized by simplicity, harmony with nature, spiritual cohesion and a high degree of communal activity—was one that First Nations groups have had much experience with. They may yet lead us forward to a revised version of this ancient form of existence.

A depression in the United States in the early 1890s prompted the arrival in British Columbia of groups of Danes and Norwegians, who formed agricultural colonies in remote parts of the province. The Finns who followed at the end of the century were also economic migrants. All three groups chose to stay in B.C. because the government of the day offered them free land and other incentives.

The Doukhobors did not head west for economic reasons but because they felt betrayed by the Canadian government over the final settlement of land granted them in Saskatchewan. They were able to develop their remarkable communal empire in British Columbia largely because of their agribusiness success before, after and during World War I. The same forces that caused their collective enterprise to decline during the Depression-era 1930s, and eventually fail, also attracted Brother XII and his disciples to B.C. These Aquarians intended to hole up and wait out the coming global collapse, then emerge from the ruins and establish a new civilization.

After World War II, North America enjoyed an era of unprecedented peace and plenty, and the formation of utopian communities surged. Starting with the Emissaries of Divine Light in the late 1940s, the Quakers at Argenta in the '50s and some early countercultural experiments in the '60s, the wave of naive, optimistic activity reached a peak in the 1970s, when America's children of affluence, the hippies, reached adulthood.

And today? As the second millenium and twentieth century race to a finish, clouds of economic fear cast familiar shadows on the psychological landscape. The service sector is shrinking under the onslaught of technology; dwindling natural resources put other jobs at risk. Yet our human population grows and grows. Globe-spanning corporations and giant bureaucracies grapple impotently with an ever-lengthening list of social and environmental problems.

In response to these threats, another cycle of utopian community-making is taking shape in British Columbia. Innovative living arrangements such as cohousing, where bands of people circumvent the traditional market to build their own custom-designed habitations, are just a beginning. The next stage in this progression is something called an ecovillage: a small, planned settlement where human activities enhance nature rather than harm her. Ecovillages are springing up around the world; it is only a matter of time before they appear in B.C. as well.

Facing the inevitability of change, many groups and individuals have turned quietly away from the dominant culture and its unfulfilling, wasteful emphasis on consumption. Some are thinking small, designing local land-use systems that integrate food production, housing, wildlife habitat and appropriate technology—a process called permaculture. Some are thinking large, applying the permaculture approach to bioregions. All are searching for enduring, decentralized alternatives that celebrate diversity and human co-operation. The future may depend on their efforts.

Before proceeding further, it may be helpful to clarify a few terms and sketch in some background. What are utopian communities, anyway, and how did they get started? No universal standards exist for classifying such settlements. A number of adjectives are commonly used to describe them, including alternative, experimental and intentional. They are also called colonies, communes, collectives, co-operatives and cults. The places described in this book were all created with deliberate intent; none was accidental or haphazard. They were not necessarily isolated. They had a common purpose of some kind and were established as alternatives to the surrounding society. These criteria do not define them, though, but merely bring an illusion of order to bear on a changing social phenomenon.

The phrase "intentional community," which originated in the United States in the late 1940s and is now in widespread use, refers to a group of people who live together by choice, have collective goals, and co-operate to create a way of life that reflects their shared values. Monasteries and ashrams, student housing co-operatives, communes—all are intentional communities. The term "commune" had a slightly sinister connotation twenty years ago; today it designates an intentional community where income and assets are shared. Some degree of authoritarian control or manipulation is implied by the word "cult," however; at the very least, the free will of a cult member may be restricted or interfered with.

It is the concept of utopia that gives the most trouble. Each person's vision is different. Those who have this dangerous word's uncertain drift applied to their community unfailingly reject it. There is a world of difference, apparently, between "utopian," a useful term describing the intention to achieve a better society, and "utopia," the improved society itself, which is imaginary and can never be achieved, except in books. These days, "utopian" is often misinterpreted as "naive and impractical," and "utopia" can mean just about anything. A recent advertisement in the *Vancouver Sun* defined it as "a place where the sun always shines, where Mother Nature teaches surfers who's boss, where a slice lands your ball in the ocean, and where Alaska Airlines gives you Double Miles."

The word was coined, of course, by Sir Thomas More in *Utopia.* Published in 1516, it is both a political essay and a fictional account of travel in a communistic island state where all men and women received an education and religious freedom was tolerated. The title is taken from the Greek *outopos,* or "nowhere," though it also plays on the word *eutopos,* or "good place." *Utopia* is short but multilayered: a satire on English laws and social conditions, a discourse on effective government, a parody of the explorer's journal and a futuristic fantasy. It gave birth to a new narrative form—the "utopian" novel.

But other writers before More had described ideal societies.

Biblical interpretations of paradise on earth, from the Garden of Eden to the prescriptive visions of such Hebrew prophets as Amos and Ezekiel, have influenced Judeo-Christian thinking. One early utopian author was Plato, whose blueprint for an alternative society, *The Republic,* was published in the fourth century B.C. Plato's plan was far from egalitarian, and outlined instead a rigid class system ruled by a caste of benevolent philosopher kings who owned no property, lived together in spartan unity and participated in a selective breeding program designed to encourage intellectual rigour.

A number of historic utopian communities are known to have existed. The Essenes, an ascetic Jewish sect that inhabited the western shores of the Dead Sea in the first century B.C., dwelt communally, sharing possessions, agricultural production and meals. Biblical scholar Barbara Thiering has suggested that Jesus Christ may have grown up in an Essene settlement. After Christ's death, his persecuted followers formed countercultural communes based on the principles of equality, common ownership of goods and shared work, food and ritual. These groups were the forerunners of the monastic movement.

As the Christian church grew rich and powerful, its communal foundations began to weaken. But hundreds of groups of heretics, disillusioned with ecclesiastic excess, broke away from the main body of the church and sought renewal in Christ's teachings and a simple, co-operative way of life. A tradition of dissent was started that would eventually include the Hutterites, Mennonites and Doukhobors.

Several communes in the eastern United States became famous in the nineteenth century. Shaker villages flourished, their inhabitants dedicated to lives of simplicity and celibacy. New Harmony in Indiana, originally established by German Lutherans, was purchased in 1825 by a Welsh social reformer and industrialist named Robert Owen, who tried unsuccessfully to turn it into a showcase of co-operative business and social practices. The Christian socialist collective of Oneida achieved notoriety for rejecting exclusive sexual relationships in favour of "complex marriage." Echoing Plato's Republic, it endorsed what was known as "stirpiculture," a form of eugenics where a committee decided who should procreate. The founders of British Columbia's utopian settlements later in the century would have been aware of these experiments or others like them.

Elsewhere in Canada, many co-operative immigrant colonies were springing up in the nineteenth century, especially on the Prairies, which needed farmers. A range of ethnic groups was involved: Manitoba's New Iceland dates from 1876, while New Jerusalem and New Hungary were founded in Saskatchewan in the 1880s. In 1887, the first Mormon settlers established Cardston in Alberta.

Mennonite and Amish groups had emigrated to Ontario even earlier, starting in 1786. Another forty thousand Mennonites moved to the Prairies in the 1870s and 1920s, and large numbers of Hutterites arrived in 1918 from the U.S. These Protestant sects, born of the sixteenth-century Anabaptist movement, were systematically harassed for their beliefs, which were based on early Christian teachings. Only the Hutterites, with over 280 colonies in Alberta, Saskatchewan and Manitoba, still maintain a comprehensive communal lifestyle.

You will not find every commune in British Columbia listed in the following chapters; I do not pretend that this book is comprehensive. I've chosen some fifteen settlements I feel are representative of the utopian movement in British Columbia and described them in detail.

I've tried to make each chapter a journey of discovery, visiting the places in question, talking to inhabitants or their descendants and incorporating archival research into the narrative. My intent to write only profiles of individual settlements broke down slightly when faced with the 1970s. There were such marvellous sources and so many groups at play that I felt compelled to include a mini-overview.

If you start to dig into B.C.'s history, you find traces of utopian communities just about everywhere. There were unsung Icelandic colonies on the B.C. coast, for instance—at Hunter Island near Bella Bella and at Osland near Prince Rupert—that surely shared the idealism of their better-known Scandinavian brethren. Many settlements based on agricultural co-operation and asset sharing were ventured—including late-1940s experiments at Colebrook in Surrey and Kitseguecla near Smithers—but all were short-lived.

A truly socialistic venture did take place in 1896 at Ruskin, also in the Fraser Valley. The name alone waves a red flag for utopia hunters. John Ruskin, the Victorian art and social critic, was involved with several communitarian efforts in England, including an attempt to revive the handmade linen industry. Ruskin's writings and philanthropic example appealed to wealthy, altruistic men such as Charles

Whetham, former principal of Vancouver's Whetham College, a forerunner of the University of British Columbia. Whetham admired Thoreau's writings also, and started a Ruskin discussion circle at Walden, his fine Fraser River estate, where a group of young Christian idealists gathered.

Ruskin was opposed to mechanized industry. Nevertheless, the Walden circle, most of whom lived in the area, decided to build a communally owned sawmill where the nearby Stave River joined the Fraser. The Canadian Co-operative Society was incorporated, equipment purchased and set up, and logs began floating down the Stave to the mill. Whetham persuaded the group to name their settlement after the great reformer. The women ran a communal garden, a small store and a school, which the noise of the mill forced them to move. The colonists made contact and bartered with another similar community named Hamona in Saskatchewan's Qu'Appelle Valley, exchanging flour and butter for salmon and lumber.

The flow of the Stave, unfortunately, was so deficient after the hot, dry summer of 1898 that the mill could not be supplied with timber. The society ran into financial problems. In 1899 they were forced to hand over all their assets to E. H. Heaps, the prominent local forestry company that had sold them their machinery. Heaps made Ruskin the headquarters of its empire, and planned a network of logging railroads and B.C.'s first all-electric mill. John Ruskin must have been rolling in his grave.

Finally, other than in passing, I have not examined the historic village systems of B.C.'s First Nations. (A look at contemporary community-making by the Nisga'a people in northern B.C. forms part of the final chapter.) First Nations settlements, although communal, could not really be called experimental, as they were not established as alternatives to some dominant culture. Utopian concepts did not seem to apply to aboriginal people. They really had little need for them—despite the best efforts of missionaries such as William Duncan. The world was one; man, god, earth, plants, animals—all was unified and coherent. Utopia was superfluous.

The idea of a utopian community could only have come to us from Renaissance Europe. Before Sir Thomas More and his fellow humanists, medieval society prevailed. Everyone subscribed to the medieval world view, which was framed by the great corporate mono-liths of church and state. Everything had its place, even poverty and war. There were schisms within the church, but all agreed on the primacy of Christ and his teachings. Then along came *Utopia* and described an alternative form of existence—one not based on Christian doctrine but on how men and women might improve the social contract that bound them together in everyday community life.

Christianity, however, continued to have a powerful effect on utopian thinking. Many idealistic sects subscribed to the belief that the kingdom of God would shortly be established on earth and that those who passed the entrance requirements would enjoy a thousand-year interval of peace and prosperity. These groups, which are described as millenarian or chiliastic, did not try to form deliberate utopias—that would come naturally in due course. Their Christian duty, as they saw it, was to follow simple, communal routines and prepare themselves for the joyous day.

Age-old millenarian convictions have been curiously mirrored by more modern, secular ones. Brother XII, for instance, thought that a two-thousand-year period of tranquil, universal co-operation would follow the dawn of the Aquarian Age. In the 1970s, some of B.C.'s back-to-the-landers shared similar views of the future. The Texas Lake Community felt itself to be "a part of the plan which will bring about the New Age on Earth." The Marxist Ochiltree Commune considered that the province's hippie settlements should protect themselves "against those that would try to divert us from our destination—the creation, ultimately, of a new society."

Other groups were sure that the kingdom of God already ex-isted—within the human heart. The Doukhobors, Quakers and Emissaries, who founded some of B.C.'s longest-lasting settlements, adhered to this belief, which may have allowed them to survive and succeed. When each member of a group can find, within himself or herself, the utopian principles that guide and energize the community, there need be less reliance on an eloquent chief. The truth is no longer invested in just one individual. While many early communities in B.C. depended on charismatic leadership, those that lasted found a way to democratize the ideals that inspired them. The Doukhobors are a good example; the role of the divine leader has dwindled in importance, replaced by the raised consciousness of the fellowship as a whole.

British Columbia has been fertile ground for idealistic seekers. Its vast spaces, which newcomers have wrongly seen as empty, are still a perfect location for attempting to bring utopia—or "nowhere"—to life. Because many people fear communal modes of living, and because North American society is hostile to anything that threatens privacy and private property, early utopian communities were forced to B.C.'s margins. Today, we are slightly more comfortable with alternative lifestyles, and current intentional communities have become more mainstream and urban.

Businesses, in fact, are beginning to manufacture and market intentional communities like any other commodity. But these commercial creations—such as the village of Celebration, a new fantasy from the Walt Disney Company, now playing in Florida—are not genuine communities, designed and brought into existence by those who will be part of them. With their emphasis on "family values" and old-fashioned small-town life, they harken back to a nostalgic past, when life was safe and predictable, rather than forward into the unknown. Utopian communities are true celebrations—of human diversity and ingenuity, and of democratic, egalitarian principles.

These past two years, as I meandered contentedly down the dusty corridors of B.C.'s history, poking into archival attics and cul-de-sacs, I was struck by the powerful quality of faith that the early utopians possessed. They travelled to the human periphery, to the physical and psychological edge, and often truly did not know where their next meal would come from. As I met today's communitarians and visited their homes, what touched me most was the trust they had—in themselves and each other, in the future, in life itself. They inspired me with hope.

Ultimately, all utopias are doomed. The goal is unattainable, but also strangely irrelevant; only the journey towards the "good place" has true value. We have outgrown the medieval view of the world and almost destroyed the aboriginal view. Yet we must find a new view, one that allows us to control the damage we are causing to ourselves and to the earth. Today's pioneers are working to turn sustainable visions—ecovillages, permaculture and bioregionalism—into reality. Utopian communities are living laboratories, places where we keep trying to invent improved versions of ourselves so we can survive and evolve as a species.

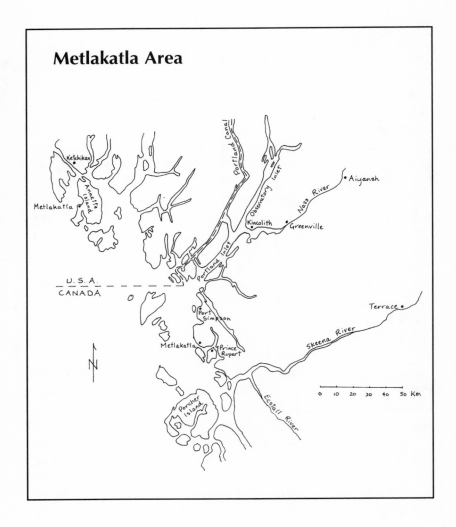

Metlakatla Area

Ketchikan

Metlakatla

Annette Island

U.S.A.
CANADA

Portland Canal

Observatory Inlet

Ness River

Aiyansh

Kincolith

Greenville

Portland Inlet

Port Simpson

Metlakatla

Prince Rupert

Porcher Island

Skeena River

Terrace

Ecstall River

N

0   10   20   30   40   50 Km

A BEACON OF LIGHT
William Duncan and Metlakatla

*Thus the surrounding tribes have now a model village
before them, acting as a powerful witness for the truth of the
Gospel, shaming and correcting, yet still captivating them . . .*
—William Duncan, letter to Church
Missionary Society, 1863

To everyone's surprise, a prolonged spell of early May sunshine has settled over British Columbia's north coast. On the steps of the Metlakatla band office, we bask in the unaccustomed warmth and look out towards the village beach. Further west, a cluster of tiny islands at the entrance to Chatham Sound interrupts the horizon. The citizens of Prince Rupert, eight kilometres away across the harbour, are shucking raincoats and boots and searching for sunblock. In Metlakatla, people have been taking advantage of the weather to dry a papery black seaweed that they first soak in clam juice. I tried some and it's good: salty and crisp.

With only forty-five homes and 130 inhabitants, this Tsimshian First Nations village is a small and sleepy place. No road connects it to the wider world. Each morning, school kids head to Prince Rupert on the *Sisayda Lady,* one of several powerful boats owned by the community. Metlakatla controls Rupert's water-taxi business and operates a regular passenger service to Lax Kw'alaams, also known as Port Simpson (and, a century ago, Fort Simpson), further up the coast. A herring roe-on-kelp aquaculture operation lies just offshore, and a dozen gillnetters are tied up snugly at Metlakatla's new marina. The youngsters' return from school in the afternoon is about as exciting as things get.

Next to the band office, a dilapidated picket fence encloses two eighty-year-old cypress trees and the toppled gravestone of an Anglican missionary. Nearby stand other stone markers: one in the form of a totem pole, another dated 1884. Looming over them hangs a placard, one of those familiar green and gold "place of interest" notices that the government has scattered all over B.C. in order to get travellers to stop their cars and absorb a little history. Only here, 760 kilometres northwest of Vancouver, where there are neither highways nor tourists, it looks a little out of place.

The sign's bald description hardly does justice to Metlakatla's peculiar heritage. In the 1870s and 1880s, well before Prince Rupert was even a gleam in a railroad baron's eye, it was a key spot on the north coast: a self-sufficient "model Indian village," complete with Victorian-style houses, streetlamps, sawmill, cannery, school, jail, store and one of the largest churches in North America. Metlakatla had its own ships, a uniformed Tsimshian constabulary and a fine brass band.

This unusual nineteenth-century community was the utopian vision of an Anglican lay missionary named William Duncan. By our standards, Duncan was an autocrat—paternalistic, manipulative, even cruel. But by the standards of the day, he was a huge success. He became a celebrity, the subject of several books. Government native affairs departments frequently copied his methods. For a few years, Metlakatla was the world's most famous example of how Christianity could supposedly transform and elevate aboriginal people.

Times changed. Duncan quarrelled with both church and state, and moved his mission to Alaska in 1887. In 1901, the original model village burned to the ground. "It all seems like ancient history now," band manager Fran Reece had told me earlier. "The story of the original mission was never passed down to us. People here have divided opinions about Duncan."

Other Metlakatlans are less diplomatic about their past. "I don't think you'll find too many Duncan fans here any more," says band councillor Carol Beynon. She and fellow councillor Susan Yorke are sitting beside me on the band office steps, both wearing green and black Volunteer Firefighter team jackets. I've been asking them about the community's attitudes towards its famous former patron.

"Duncan had a very negative influence on residential school development in B.C.," Beynon explains, referring to an education process that separated aboriginal children from their families and punished them for following native customs. "The schools were all based on the Metlakatla model. But the perfect little world Duncan created turned out to be not so perfect after all. In the longhouse tradition, there was little abuse. In the schools…" Her voice tapers off, but she doesn't need to finish. We are all familiar with the grotesque catalogue of social and sexual misdeeds that the residential system had engendered, its legacy of lost and damaged lives. "Probably the only thing we didn't lose," she continues, "was the preparation and gathering of traditional foods."

"We're even losing that now," responds David Nelson, the band's youth worker, who has joined the conversation. "If Duncan hadn't come to this community, we'd still be practising our Indian ways. It's difficult for our young people to revive traditional practices because of how far we have moved away from them. This is because of Duncan."

Blamed and reviled by many, revered and imitated by others, the missionary's bequest to succeeding generations was complex and controversial. Anthropologist Philip Drucker claimed that Duncan left a deeper mark on north Pacific native history than any other single person. The story of this strong-willed, energetic man and the two idealistic communities he helped create is one of the most compelling tales the west coast has to offer.

William Duncan was twenty-four when he was chosen as the Anglican Church Missionary Society's first emissary to the wilds of British Columbia. Born in 1832 near Beverley in Yorkshire, he abandoned a promising career as a salesman with a local tannery after deciding that what he really wanted to do was missionary work. He applied to the society, was accepted and went off for two years to the teacher-training facility of Highbury College. When the call came in late 1856, he packed up his missionary kit—blacksmithing and carpentry tools, shovels and rakes, medical supplies, prayerbooks—and set off on the six-month journey around Cape Horn to Fort Victoria.

Duncan may have seemed an improbable candidate for the important new post. In fact, he was fairly representative of the young men England was sending out to bring civilization and Christianity to her colonial subjects. According to the *Christian Missionary Intelligencer,* the society's newsletter, someone of "undaunted courage, of well-nigh indomitable determination and will-power, of unlimited faith in God, and of good, sound judgement" was sought, "as the entire management of the mission would practically depend on him alone, without the aid and direction of the society." Duncan fit the job description well. Although he was never ordained as a priest, he was tough, tireless and brave—a dedicated teacher with a practical background.

At the helm of the Church Missionary Society in the mid-nineteenth century was an influential figure named Henry Venn. Venn believed that the aim of missionary work was to improve the lives of aboriginal people, not just to accumulate large numbers of converts. He expected the society's agents to help their charges achieve economic self-sufficiency. Industrial and commercial skills were to be imparted as well as the gospel. Then, after native leaders and pastors were installed, missionaries were to move on and conquer fresh territory.

Missionary societies were at the peak of their popularity in England in the 1850s. There was great curiosity about exotic cultures. Bold explorers such as Richard Burton and famed missionary David Livingstone became culture heroes. Donations poured in to support the societies, and many young people offered their services to the cause. Mission jobs were considered glamorous—a chance for tradesmen and artisans, in particular, to break free of the class system and rise in status.

Duncan's choice of vocation may well have been prompted by feelings of social inadequacy. He never revealed much about his origins, but thanks to the exhaustive research of Peter Murray, whose *The Devil and Mr. Duncan: A History of the Two Metlakatlas* is the most authoritative source on the subject, we know that he was born out of wedlock and raised by working-class grandparents. The fatherless boy came under the spell of a Beverley clergyman, Reverend Anthony Carr, who filled him with religious zeal. Duncan's journals reveal a maelstrom of conflicting emotions: shame about his family origins, contempt for those who lacked his piety, anger at his own shortcomings. Perhaps it's not surprising that, after listening to a lecture on the Church Missionary Society, the exciting overseas life of an evangelical teacher began increasingly to appeal to him.

A short, stocky figure whose trademark features later in life would be a thick beard and a receding hairline, Duncan arrived at the small Hudson's Bay Company fur-trading post of Fort Victoria in June 1857. A year later, the great Fraser River gold rush would transform the entire region, but in 1857 Victoria was a quiet spot, with a non-native population of only about two hundred. It was the undisputed domain of James Douglas, chief factor of the company and governor of the crown colony of Vancouver Island. Douglas fully expected to decide on the location of Duncan's mission.

The Anglican church, however, had already chosen a mission site. James Prevost, captain of a Royal Navy sloop based on the west coast, had been appalled by the lawless scenes he'd observed at Fort Simpson, a Hudson's Bay post in northern B.C. He appealed to the church to establish a presence there. Douglas didn't really want a mission on the north coast. He feared—rightly, as it turned out—that Duncan might disrupt the profitable fur trade, and told him the area was too dangerous. But the church and navy insisted, and Douglas acquiesced. Until passage became available, Duncan moved in with Reverend Edward Cridge, Fort Victoria's chaplain. The young missionary spent the summer studying Chinook, the regional trade jargon, and Tsimshian, the north-coast native language.

When he finally reached Fort Simpson in October, more than nine months after leaving England, Duncan found a tidy, fifty-metre-square log palisade, painted white with bright red trim, surmounted by two gun bastions and eight cannons. The Hudson's Bay Company would provide him with room and board there for the next four years. After running a gauntlet of curious aboriginals, the self-conscious Duncan joined eighteen post employees and their families behind the wooden pickets; outside, a native encampment of more than 2,300 souls occupied about 140 traditional longhouses.

The fort had been built in 1834 between the mouths of the Nass and Skeena rivers, about 850 kilometres northwest of Victoria. It lay in the heartland of the Tsimshian people—avid middlemen in the fur trade—who bought skins from neighbouring tribes and sold them at the fort. Entire bands had left their villages and moved their longhouses to Fort Simpson to be close to the action. By the 1850s, it had become one of the largest permanent settlements on the west coast of North America.

Duncan was understandably apprehensive about the task before him. "I feel almost crushed with my sense of position," he wrote in his journal. "My loneliness, the greatness of the work, which seems ever increasing before me . . . together with deepening views of my utter weakness: these indeed at times seem ready to overwhelm me, but the Lord is my refuge."

The new arrival began his duties by conducting church services and school lessons for the fur traders and their children. He engaged as a language tutor a bright young Tsimshian named Clah. The fluency that Duncan eventually achieved with the local language was fundamental to his success; most other missionaries in British Columbia, despite genuine efforts, were unable to master a native tongue. With no alphabet or dictionary to help him, Duncan compiled a list of fifteen hundred common English words and, through a combination of Chinook and charades, he managed to learn their Tsimshian equivalents.

He also visited each longhouse and studied native customs. Although clearly impressed with Tsimshian craftsmanship in wood and other natural materials, Duncan managed, simultaneously, to abhor their "garish" house and body decorations. He primly refused to take any pleasure in ceremonial dancing and viewed potlatch habits, where chiefs gained status by giving away goods, as a barbarous waste. He was also horrified, though with more reason, by the casual Tsimshian cruelty to slaves, the endemic drunkenness and prostitution, and the murders that regularly occurred beyond the walls of the fort. "Intoxicating drink," he felt, was the root problem. Although supposedly illegal as a trade medium, alcohol was widely available—and the cause of much grief—on the coast.

Duncan's journal reveals a high regard for the intelligence and industry of the people he had come to convert, though he soon grew doubtful about his mandate, which was to turn them into farmers, following the example of successful missionaries elsewhere in the world. On the north Pacific coast, where the great coniferous forests stretched to the ocean's edge and the annual rainfall often exceeded four metres, large-scale agriculture was a fantasy. The Tsimshian had no need to farm, in any case; they had built a rich, stable, complex culture from the abundant resources of land and sea.

The inhabitants of Fort Simpson showed great interest in the intense young missionary, who was unlike any foreign intruder they had yet encountered. They assumed that his role was not unlike that of their own shamans. The Tsimshian were intent on acquiring and converting to their own use the various and singular powers that the white strangers seemed to possess, and they were open to hearing this newcomer's message.

During his first winter, Duncan restricted his activities to starting a modest school for Tsimshian children and evening classes for adults. He translated hymns, conducted drills and marches, and introduced the concept of writing. He visited the sick and the elderly and tried to dispense a little preventative medical advice.

By the summer of 1858, Duncan felt comfortable enough with the Tsimshian language to begin sermonizing in the village. He started in the longhouse of Neyahshnawah, the friendliest chief. "My heart quailed greatly," he confided to his journal. "I knelt down to crave God's blessing, and afterwards I gave them the address. They were all remarkably attentive." He repeated the procedure at the house of Legaic, the most powerful chief, who was not so friendly but couldn't appear to be less hospitable than his rivals. By day's end, he had delivered simple explanations of the Bible and Christian purpose to nine longhouses and nine hundred individuals. It was the first time that B.C.'s aboriginal people had been preached to in their own tongue.

Over the next two years, Duncan went on teaching and preaching, and gathered a group of fifty or more adherents. In "Bringing the Indians to their Knees," a *Raincoast Chronicles* essay, Howard White looks closely at these early days, noting that Duncan's followers were mostly young and low-born, people on the fringes of Tsimshian society. He was making little serious headway with the chiefs and shamans, several of whom were implacably opposed to him. Others seemed polite and even captivated by Christian ways, says White, but had a blithe and irritating tendency to continue traditional practices. The winter ceremonies of dancing and potlatching were as popular as ever—and so was alcohol.

In 1860, Duncan visited Nisga'a villages on the Nass River, then spent the summer in Victoria. He discussed with James Douglas a momentous idea he had been mulling over: moving the mission. He had written to his superiors in England, suggesting that "a colony ought to be established in some spot where industry would be taught and rewarded; and where intoxicating drinks would be excluded." He believed that "no real or permanent good, in my humble opinion, can be effected" at Fort Simpson, but that "we might reasonably expect the Gospel tree to take root" at some other location. Douglas supported the plan and agreed to reserve any necessary lands.

The governor was pleased with Duncan's progress, and asked for his advice on controlling Victoria's growing native encampments. Duncan came up with a list of regulations for the rowdy suburbs and recommended that his rules be enforced by aboriginal constables, with troublemakers punished or sent away. Douglas ignored his proposals, but Duncan's ideas were not wasted, as he would adopt a similar style of village governance when he left Fort Simpson.

The next eighteen months were lonely ones for Duncan. He had one notable success—the baptism of the first Tsimshian Christians—but Fort Simpson's chronic violence depressed him. His health was sabotaged by a severe bronchial infection, and he barely escaped death in several terrifying confrontations with native opponents. To sustain him, he had only his dream of "a model Christian village, reflecting light and radiating heat to all the spiritually dark and dead masses around us." The location of the new colony had been chosen: twenty-five kilometres south, at an important former winter village site named Metlakatla, or "a passage connecting two bodies of salt water." The move was set for spring.

In May of 1862, while an advance party was cutting timbers and planting potatoes at Metlakatla, alarming news arrived from Victoria. Another smallpox epidemic was at large on the coast. Using the dreaded plague as a stimulus, Duncan exhorted his followers to quickly dismantle the combined mission and schoolhouse that had been erected the previous year and flee. About seventy Tsimshians paddled to their new home, set up camp and began the exhausting work of rebuilding a community.

A week later, three hundred more natives arrived. They were accepted at Metlakatla only if they agreed to abide by Duncan's fifteen commandments. A complete change of lifestyle was required: no more shamanism, gambling, potlatching, face-painting, "deviltry" and, of course, drinking. Prospective Metlakatlans had to rest on Sunday, attend church, send their children to school, be industrious, peaceful, clean and "liberal and honest in trade." They had to "build neat houses" and pay a village tax.

By July, the plague reached Metlakatla. Duncan had managed to secure a shipment of vaccine from Reverend Cridge in Victoria, and he worked frantically to inoculate his flock. By some estimates, the 1862 epidemic killed one-third of the coastal population; Fort Simpson alone saw over five hundred deaths. But only five Metlakatlans were lost, and the village's reputation as a holy sanctuary was born. By August, Duncan estimated that six hundred people were living there. The vaccine had proven stronger than the shamans' medicine; resistance to Duncan's way of doing things diminished. The Tsimshian spirit had been subdued, if not crushed, by the holocaust of disease. And the word of the tenacious little missionary became law.

By the end of 1862, Duncan and the villagers had erected about thirty houses in Metlakatla, plus a church and school that could seat six hundred. Most people spent the winter in bark-covered huts. Duncan convened a village council consisting of himself, the hereditary chiefs and twenty people elected from the community at large. A corps of constables and a group of church elders were also elected. The community was organized into companies, each led by three councillors, two elders and two constables. Company leaders were given eighteen specific instructions to follow; among other responsibilities, they were to visit the sick, consult together, raise money and admonish backsliders.

The firm hand of the schoolteacher is evident in this village plan, yet it seems to have worked. The Tsimshian may have accepted the new social structure because of its vague similarity to the crest or phratry divisions of the coastal tribes. It also solved, at least temporarily, one of the largest problems Duncan faced: how to avoid alienating the chiefs. Social rank was of great importance to Tsimshian society. By involving the chiefs, who had lost much authority in the move to Metlakatla, in major decisions, Duncan hoped to avoid their disaffection. Leaders received badges of office, to be worn on special occasions. On New Year's Day, the proudly emblazoned chiefs led their companies to the main square for speeches and celebration.

Duncan moved quickly to introduce industry and trade to his new realm, to help it become self-sufficient and fulfill the expectations of Henry Venn and the Church Missionary Society. Foremost in his plans were a sawmill, a fish processing plant and a store. Duncan modelled his approach on self-supporting villages that the society had established in Africa, India and New Zealand, and on an English co-operative village scheme, which never came to much, promoted by the Anglican church as a "practical demonstration of Christian brotherhood and unity."

So that his mission should not be at the mercy of the Hudson's Bay trading posts, Duncan purchased a fifteen-metre schooner. The *Carolena* took Metlakatla's furs, salted and smoked fish, oolichan oil, dried berries, lumber, cedar shingles, mats and native handicrafts directly to Victoria, the most competitive market on the coast, and returned with a wide assortment of manufactured goods. A store was opened, which outbid the Bay for skins and sold merchandise at lower prices. To the chagrin of established traders, Metlakatla soon began to monopolize the regional fur business.

In 1863, Douglas appointed Duncan a magistrate, and the missionary turned his attention to the illegal traffic in alcohol, which continued in his area. Metlakatla's native constables participated in "sting" operations, first posing as buyers and then arresting the whiskey dealers. Heavy fines were imposed and boats were impounded. Corrupt traders had been the bane of Duncan's existence for years, and he went a bit overboard in his pursuit of justice, nabbing several likely parties on insufficient evidence. Victoria's upright citizens were outraged at the prospect of aboriginal authorities apprehending and punishing white criminals. Duncan was reprimanded and the charges dropped. Alcohol sales continued.

Duncan had always been strong on law. He was proud of Metlakatla's lack of crime. The villagers were free to leave or stay, but if they stayed they obeyed the rules. Metlakatla had a jail as well as a police force, and offenders were disciplined by flogging, incarceration and fines. Bonds might be posted to ensure good behaviour. Persistent transgressors were shamed with a black flag hung outside their door. Corporal punishment for children, both boys and girls, was frequent.

Metlakatla flourished and grew stronger as the 1860s progressed. More missionaries joined Duncan from England. Some soon faltered and returned to familiar terrain or, like Robert Cunningham, left Christian service altogether and metamorphosed into Hudson's Bay Company traders. Others, like Arthur Doolan, Robert Tomlinson and

William Collison, became trusted Duncan aides, later going on to found or supervise miniature versions of Metlakatla at Kincolith on Nass Bay, Massett in the Queen Charlottes and Alert Bay to the south.

By 1870, Duncan had enough confidence in his helpers to return to England where, as well as raising funds for the mission, he researched several cottage industries that he wished to introduce on his return: weaving, rope-making and the manufacture of shoes, clogs and brushes. He purchased a weaving machine. He also studied music, so that a donated brass band set might be put to good use. Upon arriving back in Metlakatla thirteen months later, he handed out the instruments and told the Tsimshians "to go out in the bushes and blow." The results, he noted in his journal, were at first pure "bedlam," but his followers became accomplished musicians, and the village band was a byword up and down the B.C. coast.

The construction, in 1874, of St. Paul's Church launched Metlakatla into its golden age. With a vestibule, gallery, belfry and spire, groined arches and solid timber frame, this Gothic cathedral—reportedly the largest church west of Chicago and north of San Francisco—could accommodate twelve hundred. Although it had an organ and a hand-carved pulpit, and sported stained-glass windows and Brussels carpet in the aisles, the interior was otherwise simple. In keeping with Duncan's belief that ritual or symbol might incite Tsimshian emotions, there were no crosses or altars.

By the late 1870s, Metlakatla could boast soap and textile factories, a tannery, cooperage, guesthouse, fire hall and dog pound. Villagers lived in two-storey single-family residences with enclosed flower gardens; pairs of houses were linked with one-storey common areas. According to White's "Bringing the Indians to their Knees," people

William Duncan, shown here at about the age of forty, would lose even more hair later in life, and his bushy beard would turn snow-white. (BCARS A-01175)

wore European clothes and dressed "very tastefully." One visitor was "not sure but that they have the latest fashions." They promenaded after work along a three-metre-wide macadamized sidewalk that ran the length of the village. Oolichan-oil street lamps hung in front of each home. The thirty-man police force had boots and caps, and brass buttons on their uniforms.

Work and worship were the primary village activities, but Duncan made sure that there was leisure time as well. Soccer matches were held on two playing fields; a choir practised regularly, as did, of course, the band. There was a museum and reading room, a bandstand, a printing press and a playground with climbing bars and merry-go-round. The Tsimshian love of potlatching was redirected towards other forms of communal festivity: Christmas, New Year's, Victoria Day, birthdays and house-raisings were all marked by celebrations.

Metlakatla became a destination: a state-of-the-art Christian colonial outpost. Rich tourists on round-the-world expeditions were astonished at how well the village mimicked English Victorian reli-

St. Paul's, Metlakatla's great church, was constructed of red cedar and could seat twelve hundred. The building was finished in 1874 and burned to the ground in 1901. (BCARS B-03572)

gious and social values. Government officials and other missionaries dropped by in order to learn the latest techniques for turning unruly aboriginals into exemplary citizens. Lord Dufferin, Canada's governor-general, paid a vice-regal visit in 1876. He had high praise, reported the Victoria *Daily Colonist,* for "the neat Indian maidens, as modest and as well-dressed as any clergyman's daughter in an English parish." At about the same time, in a report to his superiors, Bishop George Hills was able to write that Metlakatla "has now grown to one thousand people, forming the healthiest and strongest settlement on the coast."

Magazine and newspaper articles were especially effusive, portraying Duncan as a brilliant, divinely inspired figure who was single-handedly civilizing the native people of the west coast. In his 1909 book, *The Apostle of Alaska,* John Arctander called the missionary an extraordinary leader and claimed that he had "fewer faults than any man I ever met." But all was not quite as well at Metlakatla as these glowing reports led readers to believe. Duncan did have faults. Even if he'd had none, disruptive external forces were also beginning to shake his pedestal.

At the heart of the changes that were about to sweep down on the model village were growing rifts between William Duncan and his superiors. One of these superiors was Bishop Hills, who was based in Victoria and whose diocese comprised the entire province. Hills was not a typical frontier churchman. His tastes, both personal and liturgical, were far from simple and direct. Patrician in manner, the son of an admiral, he was "high church," and Duncan took an immediate dislike to him.

Hills wanted Duncan to be ordained. Metlakatla had become important, and the bishop felt a clergyman should be in charge. Duncan, somewhat mysteriously, resisted taking holy orders all his life. He did not feel "called," he said, and worried that ordination would interfere with his secular duties. Hills was also concerned about Duncan's refusal to offer the Eucharist at his church services. But how, argued the missionary, could you serve communion wine to people who were sworn not to consume alcohol? The austere Metlakatla church, the lack of priestly vestments, the total absence of pomp and pageantry—these things distressed Bishop Hills, for ceremony was at the core of his version of Christianity.

Back in England, the Church Missionary Society was displeased with Duncan, as well. Officials there expected him to groom native clergymen. They wanted more of the day-to-day operations of the mission turned over to Tsimshian leaders. Ironically, Duncan's efforts had produced potential leaders—articulate, capable men such as David Leask and Robert Hewson—but he always seemed to have some excuse for why Metlakatla was not yet ready for independence. Duncan often claimed that he was willing to move on and prepare new ground for God, but this next, supposedly obligatory stage in his career never seemed to arrive.

In 1877, an incident occurred that gave Duncan a convincing reason to stick around. He left the mission in the care of a new arrival, a young minister named James Hall, and went to Victoria. Hall's passionate, near-hysterical style of preaching, as opposed to Duncan's low-key approach, resulted in an unexpected wave of religious frenzy. Some congregation members heard divine voices; others saw angels. A group of girls discovered a mystical cross in the woods. Several dozen men set off in canoes to take the news to Fort Simpson. Hall was panic-stricken at this turn of events.

Duncan rushed home and managed, with difficulty, to settle everyone down. It was just as he had predicted; the Tsimshian were too childlike to be left to their own devices. They required more training. They needed him, and he could not leave. The incident revealed the community's fatal flaw: Duncan needed Metlakatla as much as it needed him. He and his model village were like co-dependants in an unhealthy marriage. He had created this beacon of light and defended it against detractors, and now he was unable to surrender control.

Although Metlakatla appeared outwardly to possess a degree of self-governance, everything important depended on Duncan's initiative and authority. The Tsimshian village council held lengthy discussions and made community decisions, but Duncan was always there in the background, subtly guiding the meetings so that the decisions made were the ones he wanted. His view of the mission was paternalistic; he could not allow his children to grow up and live their own lives. He couldn't let go.

At first, Duncan had been keen to translate religious texts so that villagers could worship in their own tongue. But his efforts in that department began to flag; village church services were soon held exclusively in English. Duncan justified this change by saying that since English would surely become dominant on the British Columbia coast, everyone might as well get used to it. But this reliance on the language of the colonizer also increased his level of control.

In 1879, Hills persuaded church authorities to split his domain in three—partly, it is difficult to avoid thinking, so that he would no longer have to deal with Duncan. A new diocese of Caledonia, covering northern B.C., was formed, with Metlakatla as its headquarters. A new bishop, William Ridley, was appointed and soon arrived, with his wife Jane, to take up residence. Bishop Ridley had a history of health problems and an undistinguished past; he was an odd choice for the wilderness posting. He agreed with Hills on matters ecclesiastical and was horrified that a mere lay missionary should possess such freedom and authority. The scene was set for a rapid escalation of the conflicts simmering between Duncan and the church.

Ridley, backed by the missionary society, began to pressure Duncan to offer Holy Communion and conduct services in Tsimshian. Duncan countered by suggesting a modified Eucharist; his version

In this 1880s view of Metlakatla, the industrial buildings are on stilts over the beach, the mission house is at the far right beside St. Paul's Church and the residents' homes start at the upper left. (BCARS G-04699)

would include a symbolic communal meal but avoid wine and any reference to consuming Christ's body. He feared the natives might interpret the sacrament as an endorsement of cannibalism, and the possible consequences alarmed him, especially after the Hall fiasco. The bishop rejected this compromise.

The society's officers agreed with Hills and Ridley that an ordained minister must run the mission. Duncan could be moved elsewhere, they thought, or forced into a subordinate role. The missionary tried to negotiate around this impasse by proposing that England cease to fund Metlakatla. It would serve as a lay example of self-sufficiency—a model industrial village, which it already was. This suggestion was also rebuffed.

Realizing that a showdown was probably at hand, the society had sent a letter of dismissal for Bishop Ridley to give Duncan if an understanding could not be reached. Neither party was willing to make concessions, and the fateful letter was delivered in the spring of 1882. Duncan, in a fury, immediately moved out of the mission house. The great campaign for Metlakatla was now reaching its final stages.

When Duncan informed the Tsimshian that he was unemployed, they quickly rallied round him and prepared a house for his use. A small group of disgruntled chiefs and their families, about fifty in all, who saw this latest development as a chance to unseat Duncan, declared their support for Ridley. The bishop, greatly outnumbered, decided that the wise course of action might be to absent himself temporarily. He sailed off to London to explain the situation, leaving an uncomfortable William Collison in theoretical charge.

The villagers decided they would establish an independent Christian church with Duncan and carry on as usual. Metlakatla's latest project—and a major new business venture—was a cannery, and that kept people busy. But Bishop Ridley went on the attack. On his return to B.C., he wrote and circulated a sensational pamphlet accusing Duncan of cruelty, and sexual and financial misconduct. Duncan certainly employed corporal punishment at the mission, but no hint of moral impropriety ever attached itself to him over the course of a long career, and his financial record was brilliant. Ridley's charges were probably based on little else than his deep dislike for his competitor. Victoria, though, was suitably amazed and entertained by this latest scandal.

Things got worse. While Duncan and the bishop were exchanging insulting letters, the two factions at Metlakatla exchanged threats. A small piece of land, less than a hectare, had been reserved in the name of the missionary society. The mission house stood there but not the church or the school or most of the businesses, which were located on the larger native reserve. No one was certain which reserve Duncan's store was on, so his followers dismantled and moved it, much to Ridley's anger. The bishop, in turn, announced that the school, which had been built with society money, would be turned into another church, but he was prevented from making any changes. Then Ridley got into a punch-up with a group of natives over the ownership of a drum. He sent an urgent message to Victoria suggesting that lawlessness and chaos prevailed in the community and that lives—his, in particular, and that of his wife—were in danger.

The government had no choice but to respond. Ridley was a bishop, after all. No navy ship was available, and a U.S. cutter, the *Oliver Wolcott,* had to be called in. Several dignitaries, including Indian superintendent Dr. Israel Powell and the head of the provincial police, piled aboard, and the *Wolcott* raced north to protect Metlakatla's beleaguered minority. They found the village tense but in no danger of civil war, handed out ten-dollar fines to two native men for assault and left, no doubt shaking their heads over the strange behaviour of clerics. Even though the *Wolcott's* services were provided for free, this little escapade cost the province $7,000, a pretty sum in 1883.

The following year, after further incidents and a general state of native unrest on the north coast, the government decided to launch an official enquiry into Metlakatla's problems. As the core issues concerned property ownership, the hearings quickly focused on the question of aboriginal land rights, which B.C.'s bureaucrats had been infamously unsympathetic to over the years. In their report, the enquiry commissioners reinforced old attitudes, which basically held that native people had no land rights whatsoever. The reserves set aside for them were perfectly adequate, and the Crown, not aboriginal people or their missionary advisors, would determine the uses those reserves could be put to.

Duncan, anxious that the Metlakatlans should own their land or at least have substantial control over the village, took his fight to Ottawa. He felt that aboriginal people should receive individual title to individual plots of reserve land. He wanted guarantees that federal reserves would not be sold or altered. He disputed the right of the Church Missionary Society to any mission property, arguing that the land had merely been reserved in trust. Now that the majority of villagers wished to form an independent church, it should be handed over to them. Prime Minister John A. Macdonald, who was also superintendent-general of Indian affairs, slyly agreed with Duncan but authorized no change in policy. After lobbying by church officials, though, he decided to award the disputed reserve to the missionary society.

This last betrayal started Duncan thinking about moving his operation. A missionary society commission descended on Metlakatla and wrote a report criticizing his leadership. In 1886, disputes arose over Ridley's attempts to survey church land in Metlakatla, and that fall, in a related trespassing case, B.C. chief justice Matthew Begbie reiterated that the villagers had no legal rights to the land. The Tsimshian village council finally consented to have Duncan go to Washington and ask for permission to emigrate. There he met Henry Wellcome, a young pharmaceutical magnate and one of his most influential supporters.

At first, U.S. government officials were oblivious to Duncan's appeals. The last thing the Bureau of Indian Affairs wanted was responsibility for another eight hundred people. Then Wellcome, a human publicity dynamo, went to work. For the next four months, Duncan addressed associations and boards, preached in the best and biggest churches and received countless column inches of newspaper coverage. Wellcome formed a committee of twenty-five prominent men to work behind the scenes. His 1887 book, *The Story of Metlakahtla,* created a huge, appreciative audience for Duncan's plans.

Duncan even met President Grover Cleveland, who supported the move but was anxious to avoid an international incident. Eventually, U.S. officials confirmed that if the missionary and his followers would select a site and move of their own accord, the government would recognize them and grant them squatters' rights after they were settled. Duncan sent a message to Metlakatla, and in March 1887 a Tsimshian party set off by canoe. Within two weeks, the group had decided that uninhabited Annette Island, just over 110 kilometres north, fit their needs.

In August, Duncan, along with thirty tonnes of supplies and a portable sawmill, arrived via northbound steamer at Port Chester, a bay on the west side of the island where New Metlakatla was to be established. An advance guard from the old village was waiting, and U.S. flags flew on improvised poles. Speeches were made on the beach, and the passengers and crew of the steamship joined the villagers in celebration. Over the next two weeks, despite Ridley's opposition, buildings were dismantled and as much of Metlakatla as possible went on an ocean voyage. An enormous motley flotilla—canoes, rafts, fishing boats and virtually every vessel on the north coast that could be borrowed or chartered—ferried back and forth between the two sites. Eight hundred people travelled north. It was one of the largest human exoduses that Canada had known.

Down at the longhouse, eleven decades later, the descendants of those early émigrés are ready for the tourists. The men and women of the Fourth Generation Dancers—clad in red and black button blankets, fringed tunics, beaded moccasins and exotic ermine-skin headgear—launch into the welcome song. As it ends, they blow eagle down over their visitors' heads, then segue to a salmon dance, in which some performers are fish and the rest act as a human seine net. Metlakatla, which dropped "new" from its name long ago, is busy

The fish plant at Metlakatla, Alaska, now packs smoked-salmon souvenirs for its gift shop as the village moves from a traditional logging- and fishing-based economy to cautiously embrace tourism. (Andrew Scott)

attracting some of the half-million cruiseship passengers who spend a day at nearby Ketchikan each summer.

Outside, in the fresh May sunshine, a "chain gang" is hard at work, clearing away garbage, cleaning, painting. Miscreants are allowed to work off fines for minor offences by helping prepare for the tourist season, and community members get a kick out of seeing their wrong-doers do right. Nearby, Tim Gilmarten and his partner are finishing a salmon bakehouse. "Tourism means development, which allows people like us to continue working," says Gilmartin, a carpenter and former council member and definitely not a miscreant. "It also gives our young people something to do—and perhaps something to look forward to in the future."

Metlakatla's newfound interest in tourism is partly dictated by the economy. Up and down the Alaska coast, traditional forest and fishing industries are depressed. Though the village's two sawmills keep busy, the band has logged most of its Annette Island reserve. Its heritage cannery, now used only for cold storage, is being remodelled as a gift shop and retooled to produce smoked-salmon souvenir packs. Perched on the ocean's edge, surrounded by islands and lush mountain wilderness, Metlakatla feels that its physical assets and native culture should be of interest to travellers. And the community can always play its trump card: history.

Although this vigorous Tsimshian village of eighteen hundred people is not, geographically speaking, within the scope of this book, I cannot allow William Duncan and the Metlakatlans to disappear from these pages as abruptly as they did from British Columbia. The Alaskan community has its own lengthy history, but a brief overview will have to suffice.

As with the first Metlakatla, the second one prospered, despite the difficulties of starting over in a wilderness region. An immense church was erected, plus a cannery and a sawmill. Architectural oddities appeared in the landscape, including an octagonal guesthouse and a twelve-sided community hall. Wooden boardwalks led between tree stumps to gingerbread-trimmed houses. The band and police force still had their brass-buttoned uniforms and, in honour of its new country of residence, the community formed a baseball team and celebrated the fourth of July. Today, there are few signs of the nineteenth-century village remaining; only four original houses are left, plus William Duncan's cottage, which is now the museum.

But Metlakatla also brought old problems to its new location. Duncan, sadly, grew more and more intransigent as he got older. With the help of Henry Wellcome and several U.S. investors, he organized the colony's financial and business affairs as a private company, over which he had complete and rigid control. He was inflexible about education, refusing to provide any kind of advanced or vocational training. In 1908, over one hundred villagers complained about Duncan's policies and petitioned for a government school. Five years later, one was authorized.

As it had been in B.C., the community once again became divided. Many individuals had been with Duncan from the beginning and remained his staunch supporters. Others felt it was time the village ran its own affairs. Conflicts grew common once more; this time they were usually between Duncan and the government teacher or various Tsimshian leaders. When the missionary seized control of the village water supply and closed off the wharf, people began to wonder if perhaps he was suffering from a form of dementia.

Despite the urgent pleas of the Metlakatla village council, U.S. officials were loath to remove Duncan. "This old man is a good man," wrote interior secretary Franklin Lane, "and has led a life of great usefulness, and I don't believe in taking harsh measures with him excepting as a very last resort." Finally, in 1915, Lane wrenched control from

This old postcard reveals William Duncan's stubborn, unyielding personality as he stands in front of his cottage at Metlakatla, Alaska, a few years before his death in 1918 at age eighty-six. (Author's collection)

Duncan by deciding that the government—which had set Annette Island aside as a native reserve in 1891, "subject to such restrictions as may be prescribed from time to time"—could, if it wished, manage the island's facilities on behalf of its inhabitants. Today, those inhabitants manage their own affairs, but still operate under the terms of the 1891 agreement; they are the only First Nations group in Alaska not to have concluded a land-claims agreement, and Annette Island is the state's only native reserve.

Duncan continued to live at Metlakatla, embittered and broken in spirit. He had become a truly tragic figure: his self-sacrifice, endless labour, innovative methods and unselfish, humanitarian goals were, in the end, sabotaged by a stubborn, unyielding personality. He told Henry Wellcome, who would spend the next two decades defending the missionary's reputation, that he and his supporters were being treated "much worse" in the U.S. than they had been in B.C. He died in the village in 1918, aged eighty-six, and was given an elaborate funeral.

Duncan is buried in front of his church, and many Metlakatlans continue to revere him. His old cottage has been preserved almost exactly the way he left it. Above the narrow bed, his hats and black suits still hang on the wall. His huge old Bible is on the table, his books stacked along the shelves. Part of the cottage was a clinic, and bottles of saccherated pepsin, Break-up-a-Cold tablets and C & W worm syrup line the cabinets. Since Duncan's death, however, his church has been joined by seven others, including Evangelical, Presbyterian and Mormon houses of worship. The community is no longer solely Christian, either. Traditional ways are slowly returning.

At the high school, for instance, noted Tsimshian artist Jack Hudson teaches painting and sculpure to eager students, several of whom have gone on to professional art careers. New totem poles adorn the townsite. At a 1987 potlatch celebrating the centennial of the move to Annette Island, neighbouring First Nations groups gave the Metlakatlans a number of traditional songs and dances to replace the ones they had lost as a result of Duncan's zeal. Now, native performers entertain tourists.

Secular problems such as alcohol abuse and petty crime have crept back into Metlakatla's social life, but they haven't destroyed the fabric of the community or its friendly, open atmosphere. Even the members of the work crew cleaning up garbage to settle their debts to society seem happy. Back at the band council offices at the end of the day, they laugh and joke as they wipe the sweat from their brows and punch out their time cards. William Duncan, I can't help but feel, would have approved.

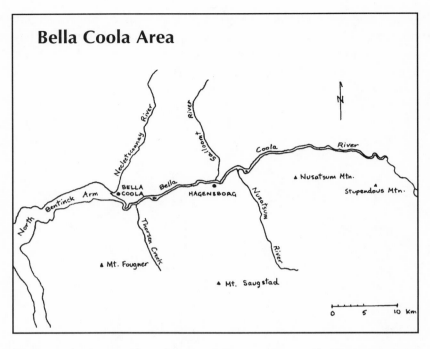

Bella Coola Area

Neeletsconnay River
Salloomt River
Coola River
Nusatsum Mtn.
Stupendous Mtn.
Bentinck Arm
BELLA COOLA
Bella
HAGENSBORG
North
Nusatsum River
Thorsen Creek
Mt. Fougner
Mt. Saugstad

0 5 10 Km

N

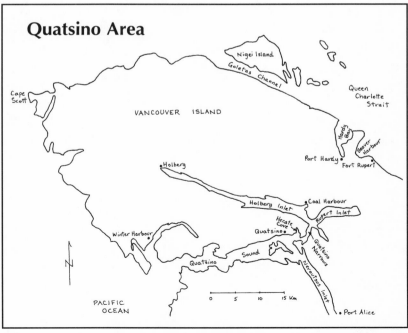

Quatsino Area

Nigei Island
Goletas Channel
Queen Charlotte Strait
Cape Scott
VANCOUVER ISLAND
Hardy Bay
Beaver Harbour
Port Hardy
Fort Rupert
Holberg
Coal Harbour
Holberg Inlet
Rupert Inlet
Hecate Cove
Quatsino
Winter Harbour
Quatsino Narrows
Quatsino
Sound
Neroutsos Inlet
Port Alice
N
PACIFIC OCEAN

0 5 10 15 Km

NEW FJORDLAND
The Norwegian Colonies of Hagensborg and Quatsino

My mind is now on Canada bent....On Bella Coola
River is very likely my future home. There will latent
powers possessed by me come forth, and the air castles
of youth become a reality.
—Ivar Fougner, diary

The walls of the valley rise steeply to a cap of grey clouds, which parts from time to time to reveal snowy highlands. A grey river races through lush, lowland forests. Dozens of icy, long-tailed waterfalls course down the granite flanks of the surrounding mountains. Yet the mouth of the valley is at sea level, and the climate, influenced by an ocean fjord that burrows deep into British Columbia's central coastline, is fairly mild. The name of this remote place does not derive from Spanish or Italian, as many have assumed, but from a neighbouring tribe's description of the aboriginal inhabitants. Still, the words—Bella Coola—have a mellifluous lilt.

It's early June, and the weather is cool and wet, as it has been all along the coast this year. Peter Solhjell is showing me the sights. His great-grandparents, Ole and Johanna Gaarden, colonized the valley in the mid-1890s, along with more than two hundred fellow Norwegians. The Gaardens emigrated twice—once from Norway, and then again from Minnesota—enticed by an "immigration lease" offered by the B.C. government. Free land was the main attraction. Provided they lived in a remote part of the province and met certain conditions of settlement, members of select foreign groups could, with five years of back-breaking labour, each claim a complimentary quarter-section of 160 acres (about 65 hectares).

Today, the Bella Coola valley reflects the perseverance of those early settlers. The region remains isolated, and the countryside is as rugged as ever, yet the valley bottom has been transformed into a patchwork quilt of fields, fences and neat homesteads. Many older log cabins survive, often with crisp window-curtains and blooming flower boxes. Vegetable gardens flourish and horses graze in sweet-smelling meadows. In the past, grain and cattle were raised, as well as cabbages, root vegetables and other crops. Bella Coola potatoes, says Solhjell, are famous far and wide for their flavour. Now, only a few people farm on a large scale, having turned to logging and other trades. But the valley maintains a rare air of rural contentment.

There are many reminders of the first Norwegian colonists. In the graveyard, a large granite stone commemorates their leader, Reverend Christian Saugstad. On a clear day, you can look up from his grave and see the peak and glacier named after him. At 2,908 metres, Mount Saugstad is the highest in the region. And if you arrive at the Bella Coola dock and glance at the big Shell Oil tanks, Saugstad is the first name to greet you: his great-grandchildren, Gerrald and Merroly, own the local fuel agency.

Reverend Saugstad gathered the original colonists. He searched out the valley and inspected it personally in advance of the move. He drew up idealistic laws to govern his disciples, whose behaviour was stalwartly co-operative and, in many respects, communal. Only "moral, industrious and loyal Norwegian farmers, mechanics and business men" would be accepted, according to the colony's constitution. More importantly, the rules prohibited, on pain of expulsion, "the use of intoxicating drinks."

Bella Coola's remoteness did not bother Saugstad, as he had in mind a place where upright Christians could grow in spirit and virtue, far from the evils of the world. His own devout faith carried him through the hard early years, and his tireless example and personal charisma carried the rest of the colonists. But the Lutheran preacher paid a high price for setting his utopian goals in motion: he was among the first to die in the new land, in 1897, aged only fifty-eight. His family flourished, though, and his dream lived on, even if it never quite gained the momentum Saugstad had originally hoped for, and veered towards cultural assimilation rather than spiritual refinement.

Nevertheless, all up and down the valley, Norwegian names prevail: Brekke and Brynildsen, Frostrup and Fredriksen, Harestad and Hansen, Knudsen and Nygaard. Few Norwegian descendants still speak their native tongue, but most continue to take pride in their heritage and customs. "My mother always used to say that you're in this country now and that's the way to go," explains Merroly Frostrup, born a Saugstad. "It was hard enough eking out a living without worrying about your culture. As long as we had flatbread at Christmas, that was good enough."

"And lutefisk," adds her brother Gerrald, referring to another much-loved Norwegian snack: cod preserved by soaking it in lye.

The Saugstads do business where the Bella Coola River reaches saltwater. Most of the river mouth is a maze of grassy mudflats, but on the south bank is a good flat area, and trading posts operated there since the 1860s. Now this spot is home to the unusual community of Bella Coola. The village site is right up against the main reserve of the Nuxalk people, which extends to the east several kilometres. A picturesque old church sits beside a ceremonial longhouse, while derelict grave markers peek from a snarl of brambles along the river bank.

The villages of the Nuxalk—who are more closely related to the Coast Salish, far to the south, than to any of their First Nations neighbours—once extended the length of the valley. The largest one was twenty-five kilometres upriver. The valley had a strategic location: the trails that allowed B.C.'s coastal tribes to trade oolichan grease with those of the interior terminated there. (By following those trails, Alexander Mackenzie reached Bella Coola—and the Pacific Ocean—in 1793, the first European to cross Canada by land.) The Nuxalk were friendly towards the Norwegian settlers and welcomed them to the valley. The relationship between the two groups has always been cooperative; without Nuxalk help the colony might not have survived.

Due east of the reserve stand a handful of pioneer homesteads where enterprising white settlers put down roots in the 1880s: men such as Tom Draney, founder of the cannery town of Namu, and young Fillip Jacobsen, who combed British Columbia collecting curios for European museums. For the next thirty kilometres or so, one passes the tidy farms of the former Norwegian colonists. A focal point for their strung-out community was established about fifteen kilometres east of Bella Coola and named Hagensborg, after Hagen Christensen, who built an early store there. The entire sixty-five-kilometre-long valley has a current population of about 2,500.

We stop at Hagensborg to tour an ancient farmhouse, which the local Sons of Norway branch is helping restore and furnish as a typical turn-of-the-century valley home. The weathered building, constructed of massive, hand-trimmed ten-by-fifty-centimetre logs, had belonged to Andrew Svisdahl, another Norwegian pioneer. In 1988, with funding from several community groups, the house was purchased from the Svisdahl family and skidded three kilometres down the highway to its present location.

Inside, the great Majestic stove, antique butter churns and simple period furniture re-create a pleasant atmosphere, but it's the exterior walls that impress me most. Each giant slab of red cedar has been hewn into shape with nothing more than a broad-axe, then connected to its corner-mate with a wonderful dovetail joint. Each dovetail has a little extra notch or groove to keep the joint from slipping—an unusual touch but characteristic of valley workmanship. The logs are rounded at top and concave at bottom, and fit snugly against each other. Even after nearly a century, scarcely any chinking is necessary to keep the house warm in winter.

As I explore the valley and meet a few of its inhabitants, I begin to understand how well that farmhouse represents Bella Coola and its pioneers. The simple, strong construction, so purposeful and dignified, is a symbol of self-sufficiency. This region wasn't connected to the rest of the province by road until 1953—and that was more to allow outsiders in, I sense, than to let the locals out. Today, vehicles and their occupants can leave Bella Coola by ferry, visit Vancouver 425 kilometres to the southeast, and return across the Chilcotin plateau from Williams Lake via dusty, scenic Highway 20. The increased access is appreciated, no doubt, but visitors to Bella Coola may get the feeling that, if the highway suddenly vanished, the residents of the valley would still be perfectly comfortable.

The colonization of the Bella Coola valley really started with Adrian and Fillip Jacobsen, two Norwegian brothers who gathered enormous collections of aboriginal artifacts in the 1880s, mainly for Berlin's

Royal Ethnological Museum. They left gripping accounts of their individual journeys to remote British Columbia inlets and villages, usually made with a single native guide. Besides buying artifacts, the Jacobsens were commissioned to hire a group of west-coast native people willing to take part in one of the circus-style ethnic expositions organized by Hamburg impressario Carl Hagenbeck.

In 1885, the Jacobsens persuaded nine men from Bella Coola to sign up. This troupe sang and danced its way through Germany's main cities, performing "games and recreations" and "showing the habits, manners and customs of the Indians." They influenced Franz Boas, who studied them while working temporarily at the Berlin museum and decided to pursue the career in Northwest Coast anthropology that would make him world-famous. The Nuxalk entertainers were, by all reports, treated well; accompanied by Fillip, they returned to Victoria a year later in good health. One participant subsequently built a longhouse in Bella Coola topped with cedar-shingled spires and carved gargoyles, supposedly modelled after Cologne cathedral.

Fillip took a particular liking to Bella Coola. In 1887, he talked the B.C. government into surveying the valley and starting construction of a trail. Next year, he pre-empted a quarter-section beside the Nuxalk

The village of Bella Coola, at the mouth of the Bella Coola River, is dwarfed by the valley's high mountain walls in this postcard of the region, probably taken in the 1940s. (Author's collection)

reserve. Convinced that there was enough good land in the valley to support an agricultural colony—and hoping to act as an agent for prospective settlers—he wrote letters describing Bella Coola's potential to Norwegian-American newspapers in Seattle, Tacoma and Iowa. Norwegian immigrants, he promised, would find this northern coastal valley very similar to their own beloved homeland.

At the time Jacobsen was writing, over 300,000 of his compatriots had emigrated to North America. Most settled in the north-central United States, especially Wisconsin and Minnesota. They left Norway because of poverty and lack of opportunity; a rapidly expanding population at home was putting intolerable pressure on arable land, which had always been in short supply. The New World, supposedly blessed with endless quantities of rich soil, had a near-hypnotic appeal, for the dream of poor Norwegians was to free themselves from wage slavery by cultivating a modest piece of private property.

By the late 1930s, when the great trans-Atlantic migrations had essentially ended, Norway had lost a higher percentage of its population than any other European country except Ireland. In 1830, Norway had just over one million inhabitants; during the course of the next century, more than 750,000 emigrated. Those who left were mainly landless peasants: farm and forestry workers, servants, fishermen, labourers. In America, they typically worked for wages for several years, saving money to buy land and set themselves up as farmers. And they succeeded. Determined, uncomplaining, energetic and tough—most Norwegians made superb pioneers.

Jacobsen received several enquiries about Bella Coola from the mid-west, and Reverend Saugstad, who lived in the Red River valley, near Crookston, Minnesota, probably saw or heard about his letters. The Red River farmers were hardy folk, practised at scratching a living on the margins of civilization. Many of them were from the far north of Norway—places such as Tromsö, the Lofoten Islands and the Bardu valley—all located well above the Arctic Circle. But some had become disenchanted with life in America. The treeless landscape depressed them, as did the locusts, floods, prairie fires and alternately scorching and freezing climate. The land was fertile, but the Norwegians were used to a combination of farming, fishing and logging, not the tyrannical monoculture of wheat. An economic collapse in 1893, which sent grain prices plummeting, was the final insult.

Rumours were circulating—that new lands had opened for settlement in Washington and British Columbia, that a life more to the liking of Norwegian farmers might be possible, in more familiar surroundings. A few were tempted to raise money to leave by selling their land. They were scorned by their fellows, who saw them as dupes of settlement agents and railway companies. But change was in the wind. One group from the Red River area made plans to decamp, and in May of 1894 they headed off, not for the coast but for central Alberta, where they founded Bardo (which still exists), named after their home valley.

Saugstad had an additional reason for making a fresh start. The Lutheran church in America was in disarray, embroiled in doctrinal disputes and split into at least half a dozen factions. Saugstad, for example, was a Haugean: a follower of Hans Nielsen Hauge, whose "born-again" puritanism and excoriating attacks on the state church earned him a lengthy prison sentence and great fame in Norway. Saugstad had already come into conflict with other Lutheran groups in Crookston and elsewhere. The pious immigrants, for whom religion was inextricably woven into everyday life, were caught up in the discord. Saugstad longed to lead his supporters to a place where they could practise their own particular beliefs undisturbed.

Idealistic communities of disaffected Lutherans were not unknown in North America. The most famous were the Amana villages in Iowa, founded in 1855 by German pietists. Amana had a communal economy, producing high-quality woollen goods, cloth, lumber and agricultural products. The villagers were mystics, inspired through divine revelation to migrate from Germany. The villages exist today. Although the Amana economy is now structured in the form of a corporation, rather than as a commune, the villagers still refuse to give oaths of allegiance or perform military service.

Another well-known colony was Bishop Hill in Illinois, founded by Eric Janson in 1846 in an attempt to recapture the simplicity and sincerity of early Lutheranism. This was a Swedish community, where all farmland was held communally and everyone worked for the common good. Although Bishop Hill flourished for many years, it eventually disintegrated in a welter of debt, lawsuits and internal strife. A short-lived Norwegian communistic settlement was established at Green Bay, Wisconsin, in the 1850s. Saugstad may well have been aware of some of these efforts.

A group of Red River Norwegians appointed Saugstad and Anders Stortröen to head west and look for new land. They left in June 1894, investigated the Yakima and Willamette valleys in Washington and Oregon, and then made the steamer trip north to Bella Coola. Walking fifteen kilometres upriver, they examined soil and vegetation and were pleased to find another Norwegian family there, that of Captain Thor Thorsen, a friend of Fillip Jacobsen's. Jacobsen had recently married Thorsen's eldest daughter and was managing a store at Clayoquot on the west coast of Vancouver Island (where he also tried to start a Norwegian colony). He would later return and live at Bella Coola.

When he arrived home from the coast, Saugstad held several meetings in the Crookston area. The minister was a stocky, powerful figure with a long beard and a fiery, eloquent manner of speaking. He soon had a number of dissatisfied farmers eager to follow him into the unknown. Encouraged, he started a correspondence with Colonel James Baker, B.C.'s provincial secretary and minister of mines, education and immigration.

The B.C. government was eager to develop the province's resources, including agriculture. Wealthy industrialists, whose interests were well represented by Premier Theodore Davie and his ministers, benefited greatly from increased immigration. New settlements needed railway and steamship connections, and healthy profits could be made from freight and passenger operations. In addition, new transportation schemes often attracted huge land grants and subsidies, and opened up additional territory for mines, lumber mills and canneries.

In the Okanagan and elsewhere in the interior, well-heeled gentlemen farmers, mostly of British origin, were snapping up the better ranch and orchard lands. At the Chicago world exposition of 1893, a B.C. exhibit lured potential U.S. immigrants with maps, brochures and giddy descriptions of the future. The Victoria *Daily Colonist* described the fair as "little more than a giant advertising scheme." In 1894, Colonel Baker championed a special type of land grant as a method of persuading groups of settlers to clear and farm more remote areas, especially on the coast: the immigration lease.

The terms by which such a lease might be obtained were still vague when Saugstad first approached the B.C. government in August 1894. His group from Minnesota turned out to be the first suitable applicants. Their exchange of letters was a form of negotiation—

exploratory on Baker's part, deferential on Saugstad's. The initial missive seems to have been lost, but most of the correspondence survives in the B.C. Archives. Saugstad apparently asked for land in the Bella Coola valley to be put aside for three years to allow his followers time to get fair prices when selling their U.S. properties.

Colonel Baker, who considered the Norwegians a "most desirable class of immigrants," wrote back that the land could only be reserved for three months. At least twenty families would be required for a free grant, he added, and declared that "it would have to be shewn that they possessed sufficient means of their own to make them useful settlers." He ended his letter by saying that "if the settlement was of an advantageous character to the Provincial Government, the Government would no doubt assist the settlers by the construction of a waggon road."

Had the equivocating tone of Baker's final statement rung warning bells for Saugstad, he might have saved himself a lot of letter-writing later on: most archival correspondence from B.C.'s early colonies consists of complaints about the government's promises to build roads. But the pastor was more concerned with Baker's "sufficient means" remark. "We have never intended to bring paupers into your Province to make a burden," he wrote back. His group intended to support itself until "we, with honest work, can raise the means from the land we occupy." He also tried politely to discover whether the eventual Crown grant would give his settlers clear title to their land or if hidden strings might not be attached.

By September, Baker had worked out the details of the proposed lease: the land would be reserved for six months; a minimum of thirty families or mature adults were required; each would receive a quarter-section and must have $300 in cash; settlers had to occupy their lands for five years, with only minor absences tolerated, and increase them in value by five dollars per acre. At the end of that period, Crown grants would give clear title to each property. If the conditions weren't met, the land might be reclaimed or the settlers might purchase it at five dollars per acre. Immigration leases did not actually become law until late October, at which time the Norwegians were already in Victoria preparing to head north. They were discontinued in 1899, when a new administration came to power.

In the meantime, the colonists were getting organized. Saugstad drew up a constitution and a set of by-laws for his group, which he named the Bella Coola Colony of British Columbia, and started signing up members. At a meeting in September, the members adopted Saugstad's rules, elected him president and also elected a five-person managing committee. Saugstad and colony secretary Hagen Christensen were authorized to negotiate with the B.C. government. Anyone wanting to join the colony had to be screened by the managing committee, "which must be furnished satisfactory evidence of a good moral character, working ability, and possession of necessary means to cover travelling expenses and provisions for one year."

On October 17, 1894, about eighty Norwegians, mostly men, left Crookston for Winnipeg, where they changed trains and continued their westward journey. Saugstad brought along his young daughter, Gea; his wife and other children would join him the following year. At Sicamous, in central B.C., the immigrants were visited by Lord Aberdeen, the governor-general of Canada, and his wife. Aberdeen owned the Coldstream Ranch fifty kilometres to the south. His palatial coach was joined to the train, and he welcomed the newcomers, urging them "to hold fast to the fine religious principles which have brought you together."

Five colonists from Seattle joined the group in Vancouver, and a steamship carried them all to Victoria, where they spent a week buying supplies. Ivar Fougner, the colony's articulate school teacher—whose diary and magazine articles are a useful early source of information— noted that 147 sacks of flour were purchased, plus coal oil, soap, sugar, tobacco, tools, stoves and "Japan tea." A number of custom-made tents were run up. A major expense, at $62.64, was coffee; 332 pounds of the wilderness-enhancing stimulant were required. The Norwegians' patron, Colonel Baker, met them, gave a speech and passed out "indenture forms" to be signed, setting out the terms of the lease.

The immigrants received Victoria's stamp of civic approval. "Scandinavians make good settlers," the *Daily Colonist* informed its readers on October 25. "They are intelligent, sober, pious, industrious and self-reliant. They do not expect too much. They come from a country where nature is not very generous—where men have to work hard and continuously to gain a comfortable livelihood, and they therefore will not be discouraged when they are required to face the difficulties and endure the hardships and privations incident to pioneer life."

The newspaper report was not entirely accurate. One colonist, for instance, flagrantly abused the rule against alcohol consumption by going on a substantial bender in Victoria. A hastily convened meeting condemned the unfortunate fellow and he was left behind. The rest of the Norwegians, along with government surveyor Peter Leech ("an old man of seventy," according to Fougner), boarded the *Princess Louise* and made their way slowly up the coast. En route, they formed into parties of four individuals or four families, with each party drawing a section, or square mile, of land by lot. This was done in order to avoid conflicts, and also to share the work of home-building, as four men could erect one shelter fairly quickly, then live in it while other houses were being built. Each party would subdivide its land as it saw fit.

The colonists' first impression of Bella Coola was "not encouraging," wrote Fougner: "Out of the sea rose the almost perpendicular mountains dark with evergreens, their tops hidden by fog; to eastward we could see the valley, which seemed like a mere fissure in the immense mountain masses." Colonel Baker had recommended that the settlers not arrive in winter. "It seems to me that you have chosen

Andrew Svisdahl, left, and Mathis Hammer, photographed squaring timber for construction, were two of the original Norwegian settlers. (Ivar Fougner; BCARS G-00977)

a bad time of the year," he wrote to Saugstad. "Would it not be better to wait until the Spring?...Think well over it before starting." But Saugstad was adamant. "Hope we will stand the hardships as well in your province as we have done it here," he replied.

The initial hardship was to get ashore. The steamer's lifeboats leaked so badly that the colonists had to wait for canoes from the nearby Nuxalk village to ferry them and their possessions to dry land—a service for which they were later charged over $100. The only highlight of day one at Bella Coola was the presence of Thor Thorsen and his family. His young blonde daughter, Bertha, seemed "an apparition from another and better world," Fougner recalled, "sent to bid the strangers welcome." Even so, to the eighty-five strangers putting up their tents in a winter rain that now fell in earnest, the whistle of the departing *Princess Louise* must have made a mournful sound.

Saugstad and his fellow Lutherans were not the only Norwegians to attempt to set up a colony in British Columbia that year. A small group from Fargo, North Dakota—also in the Red River valley, and not far from Crookston—had heard great things about Canada's west coast, as well. This company, which styled itself the Nova Co-operative Society, was less cohesive than Saugstad's following. It lacked a charismatic leader and was not united by intense religious beliefs. But the community founded by the Fargo colonists—Quatsino, on northern Vancouver Island—has managed to retain a rare air of rugged pioneer independence.

The original impetus for the colony of Quatsino—the name is a Kwakwaka'wakw word for the area's original inhabitants—came from a Swede, Christian Nordstrom. He had attended the 1893 Chicago exposition and met an Englishman there named Jobe Leeson. Leeson, one of Quatsino Sound's first settlers and a bit of a promoter, had a trading post at Winter Harbour, near the stormy west coast of Vancouver Island. He wanted to turn his remote sanctuary into a metropolis called Queenstown by selling lots to immigrants such as Nordstrom.

Nordstrom visited Victoria and liked what he saw of B.C. He heard about Colonel Baker's proposed immigration leases and, returning to North Dakota, convinced nine other families and single adults— about twenty people in all, mostly Norwegians—to emigrate. He and his fourteen-year-old son George quickly headed back to Victoria in the fall of 1894. Almost seventy-five years later, George Nordstrom would recall in a *B.C. Outdoors* interview with Will Dawson that his father's "big argument was that the States was getting too crowded. British Columbia sounded just right." By November, in collaboration with Leeson and another Quatsino Sound pioneer and trader named Edward Frigon, the hardy band chartered the steam-schooner *Mischief* and set off to look for a place to live.

Queenstown did not suit their needs, nor did Koprino Harbour, where Frigon's post was situated. Captain Foote of the *Mischief* suggested that the group spend the fast-approaching winter at Coal Harbour, near the head of Quatsino Sound, where they could stay in some empty mining cabins and explore the surrounding coves and channels by renting canoes from the local native people. It seems incredible that these recent prairie farmers, with minimal supplies and tools, could adapt to such a wet, swampy, rocky place. Yet, by mid-December, they were writing to Colonel Baker, cheerfully asking him to set aside a stretch of shoreline between Quatsino Narrows and Drake Island and also to cut a trail to the east coast of Vancouver Island, so that the potential colony could have access to shipping routes.

Baker was supportive but noncommittal. He didn't want to lose the new settlers. "It is important to make things go as smoothly as possible for them," he wrote to a fellow politician, "as other Scandinavian colonies are to be encouraged to settle in other portions of the Province, and they make the best of immigrants." But at the same time, the magic number of adults and families required to secure a lease had been pegged by the government at thirty, and the Nova Co-operative Society had not reached that mark.

Several more prospective colonists arrived over the next few months. In March 1895, Nordstrom travelled to Victoria with a letter appointing him as the colony's official representative. It bore twenty-three signatures, including those of the caretaker of the Coal Harbour mine and the captain of the *Mischief*. Eleven of the names were distinctly non-Scandinavian, giving the impression that the Nova group was becoming somewhat of a ragtag assembly in its increasingly desperate quest for a quorum.

Colonel Baker, perhaps feeling that twenty-three settlers, with more on the way, was a good start, allowed the colonization attempt to proceed. Nordstrom returned in triumph with a government surveyor, Hugh Burnet, who spent the next three months laying out thirty half-quarter sections (of eighty acres, or thirty-three hectares) around Hecate Cove and westwards along the north shore of Quatsino Sound. As a result of constant entreaties by Nordstrom and Halvar Bergh, the colony's main spokesmen, Baker directed Burnet to stay on an additional four months and survey a road between Coal Harbour and Hardy Bay on Queen Charlotte Strait. Many colonists earned two dollars a day over the summer working on this fourteen-kilometre link.

The rest of their energy they put into cabin construction. Distrustful of tides, and all too familiar with the Red River's frequent floods, they built well back from the shoreline. They shuttled back and forth between Coal Harbour and Quatsino by canoe, chancing the risky currents of Quatsino Narrows on each trip. By the fall of 1895, the settlers were permanently installed at Scandia Settlement, as they called Quatsino. They cleared land for vegetable gardens, brought in poultry and livestock, and hunted and fished to supplement their modest food stocks. A sawmill was erected and, in December, a merchant named Thomas Nogar arrived with a boatload of goods. His waterfront store soon expanded to include a post office and government wharf, and became the hub of the new-found community.

In 1896, Scandia suffered a setback in its drive to attract more members. Great Britain and the U.S. were threatening to go to war with each other over a minor South American border dispute; although the disagreement was short-lived, it discouraged prospective American settlers from joining former neighbours in a British colony. Halvar Bergh wrote articles singing the praises of Quatsino for Norwegian-language newspapers in Iowa and Washington, and pleaded for more colonists. Colonel Baker had given the group until the end of June 1897 to attract the thirty families and single adults it would need to receive the land for free. He warned Nordstrom that if the magic number was not reached, he and his compatriots would either have to leave or pay five dollars an acre for their property.

The looming deadline hung like a raincloud over the embryonic village. Its residents continued to work on the wagon road to Hardy Bay, which they considered essential for bringing in cattle. They managed to process and export to Victoria several shiploads of salted salmon. Friendly relations were maintained with aboriginal neigh-bours. A school was built (which still stands), and the region's rich mineral resources were explored. Across the sound at Comstock Mountain, for instance, Nordstrom, Bergh and another colonist staked the initial claims for what would later become the Yreka copper mine, which operated intermittently until the 1970s. But the colony's cor-respondence with the authorities took on a forlorn, testy tone.

"We are now afraid to advise anybody to come and get free land," Bergh complained to Baker in January 1897, "as long as the possib-ilities are that the Government will charge for it. There are people here now who would not have come if they had thought they would have to pay for the land.... As pioneers we have to endure many kinds of hardships, as you surely know, therefore we think it would be nothing but right to let us have the land free, the same as the rest of the colonies in the Province." Bergh argued that Quatsino, with twenty families or single adults and a total population of forty-three, was close enough to the required size that the deadline should be extended or eliminated. Baker remained unmoved.

The June 30 date passed, however, with nothing appearing in the official record to suggest that the immigration leases were cancelled or that the arrangement with Baker was no longer in effect. Archival cor-respondence from 1897 and 1898 is, as usual, mainly about roads. The colonists were now requesting that a wagon route linking their Quatsino properties take precedence over the Hardy Bay road. They were also demanding that an eccentric British newcomer named Lord Henry Varney—"The Queen's Messenger," according to his calling card—be replaced as road supervisor, as he was "utterly incapable."

Colonel Baker and his colleagues, despite the support of all three registered Quatsino voters, managed to lose the 1898 provincial elec-tion, and a reform-minded government under Charles Semlin came to power. One of its first acts was to demand a review of official expenditures on the mid-coast Scandinavian colonies. Quatsino, it turned out, had cost the taxpayers $2,206 for surveying and road-work. By comparison, $27,645 had been spent on Bella Coola. The size of the colonies was exaggerated in the report; Quatsino's popula-tion was listed at 125 and Bella Coola at 250. Premier Semlin and his ministers decided not to grant any more immigration leases.

In March 1899, Bergh wrote to the new administration, as he had to the previous one, asking for more time and promising that thirty households would soon materialize. In June, he received a terse, devastating letter from the deputy commissioner of lands and works informing him that "all future applications for land must be made under the conditions provided by the Land Act." From that point on, potential Quatsino homesteaders would either have to pre-empt land or buy it directly at five dollars an acre. Pre-emption was cheaper: properties had to be occupied and improved for five years before title would be granted, but the cost was only a dollar an acre.

At the end of July, the settlers were relieved to hear that official attitudes towards Quatsino had softened. They were told that, even though their numbers were deficient, those who fulfilled the lease conditions would be granted free land after the obligatory five-year waiting period. This was doubly indulgent of the government, as many colonists failed to prove that they had the $300 in cash required by the agreement. Even so, only six names appear in the files as eventual recipients of free Crown grants. Many of those who had signed the original indenture forms must have moved on and been replaced by individuals willing to pay for their land. A number of pre-emptions were registered at Quatsino around this period.

Its days as an immigration loophole were now definitely over, but Quatsino continued on, isolated yet stable. Its population has varied over the years but usually stood between 50 and 150. Like other old coastal communities in B.C. that you can't reach by car, Quatsino developed a distinct personality: strong, self-reliant, content. In 1995, 130 people celebrated the village centennial with a reunion. For a few rare souls, the edge of the world turned out to be an ideal place to live.

The band of Lutherans temporarily camped at the mouth of the Bella Coola River in November 1894 had also reached what they felt to be the edge of the world. It was not turning out to be an ideal place to live. They had put up their tents on a flat stretch of ground that was part of the Nuxalk reservation, close to the trading post of John Clayton, the valley's pioneer settler. The weather was so cold and wet and the river so high that almost two weeks would pass before they could move to their land.

In the meantime, small groups of men set off to explore and start surveying. Torliev Viken, a colonist who wrote an account of his early years in Bella Coola, hiked up the valley with three companions. "We followed a trail for approximately ten miles," he wrote, "but it became difficult to proceed since the forest was thick with large trees and impenetrable terrain." The Norwegians were quite amazed at the B.C. landscape.

> *Towards evening we arrived at a small rise in the ground where we erected tents and camped for the night. It was somewhat chilly since the previous day there had been a little snow and we were soaking wet. We gathered wood and decided to sit up through the night, light a camp fire and tell stories. Whereupon Carl Elg shot a partridge. We cooked this on the fire and ate it for supper. The night passed and, when we had breakfast and were to proceed, a large grizzly galloped out of the woods*

Poling small boats against the strong current of the Bella Coola River was the easiest way for the Norwegian pioneers to get to their homesteads. (Ivar Fougner; BCARS G-00981)

towards us. We had only shotguns and it was impossible to
engage such a champion, but when he was only a few steps away
he turned and again vanished into the woods.

In the morning, having reached the river again, two of the
exhausted explorers decided to build a log raft and float down to the
tent town. Viken and his partner struggled back on foot to discover
that their two friends had not yet arrived. "We were afraid they were
lost accidentally in the river," he wrote. "The water was running rapidly and with a few timber or log jams it presented dangerous sailing."
The missing pair showed up two hours later, however, having capsized
and lost their craft. Fortunately, they had managed to get out of the
water and find the trail, "so they escaped spending the night in the forest following their cold bath."

Finally, the rain abated and the Nuxalk boatmen were able to pole
the Norwegians and their belongings up the river in canoes. The tents
were set up once more in two separate locations, and the colonists
began cutting down trees and building log cabins—activities that
would continue most of the winter. After the river froze in late
December, much energy was also expended packing supplies over the
vestigial trails from Clayton's store at the mouth of the river. Before
the end of the year, under primitive conditions, the colony's first child
was born.

A number of early Scandinavian pioneers—from Cape Scott and
Sointula as well as from Bella Coola—have been interviewed for oral
history projects, and their reminiscences make a fascinating addition to
the written record. The Provincial Archives of B.C. has published selec-
tions from taped recordings under the title *Dreams of Freedom*. Ted
Levelton, for instance, who arrived at Bella Coola in 1895 as a five-year-
old, never lost his sense of astonishment at the colonists' tenacity:

> *My personal opinion is, they either wore dark glasses or couldn't*
> *see at all, because frankly, I would never have come here when*
> *I think of what the country was like when we arrived*
> *here.... There was lots of fish, there was lots of game, there was*
> *wild fruit and there was good land and lots of timber.... but for*
> *a man to move in here with just his bare hands, into a wild coun-*
> *try, no transportation whatever except a boat every two months*
> *in those days, and that was uncertain...*

You could raise good crops when you got the land cleared but, boy, it was all back-breaking work. The ground was grubbed with a grubhoe. There were no horses or ploughs, and the patches were too small anyway for a horse even to turn around on. You'd grub out a little spot for a garden, and another little patch for potatoes, and that was it for the first few years. It was the women and the children that did most of this.

Milo Fougner, son of Ivar Fougner, the colony's school teacher, recalled that transportation was the settlers' biggest problem:

My dad says in one place in his diary: "I got up at five this morning and walked to the waterfront and back," which would be twenty-four miles round trip over a rough trail that they had hacked out. He doesn't mention the fact that on his way back he packed all of the things that he needed possibly for the next two or three weeks. They packed cookstoves on their backs; they packed everything that you need in your home, and that's the only way they could pack it—there were no horses—other than the river itself for canoes.

In January 1895, the colonists held their first public meeting. Most of them were "very well satisfied," Reverend Saugstad reported to Colonel Baker, but felt that surveyor Leech was working too slowly. Requests were made for a wagon road and a post office, and the government agreed to spend $3,000 that year on trail and bridge construction. Fifty-three more people, mostly the families of the first group, arrived in May, and another forty-five to fifty would come in November. As the weather improved, the growing colony was able to feed itself without too much difficulty, according to Torliev Viken:

All through the summer everyone was busy with road and bridge building and clearing small garden plots by the houses to seed some potatoes and vegetables, which grew very well when using ashes from the burned trees as fertilizer....A small river ran through my land and sometimes I could put my pots on the stove before going out in the river to catch the fish. Up in the mountains were wild goats, and down in the forest were lots of deer.

In August, Hagen Christensen opened a general store partway up the valley. This establishment became the hub of the community, and the area around the store was known as Kristiania and, later on, as Hagensborg. The colony as a whole was referred to as Nye Norge, or New Norway. The first wedding took place at Kristiania in late October, and a few days later the settlers celebrated their first anniversary in Bella Coola with speeches, choral singing and a fine meal. Trader Clayton was able to drive a two-wheeled pony cart to the feast, as a passable roadway and several "large and costly" bridges had been constructed.

Not everyone liked the land. Some were so horrified by their first impressions of Bella Coola that they didn't even examine the properties they had drawn lots for. At least thirteen people, including a family of eight, waited a month and then hurried away on the next boat. Others left later. "It is a class of men we do not care about," Saugstad declared to Baker, "and shall not regret their departure. As far as I know they have not done a day's work since they came." The vast majority of settlers, though, decided to tough things out, even if the future looked uncertain.

Some who left Bella Coola ended up at Quatsino. Ole Aakre, who had been with Saugstad and the others on the *Princess Louise,* was in Quatsino early in 1895; his was one of the twenty-three names on the letter appointing Christian Nordstrom to negotiate with Baker for an immigration lease. Aakre joined the Klondike gold rush in 1897 and earned good money transporting miners' supplies over the Chilkoot Pass. He returned to Quatsino, settled down and built a store and a row of rental cabins that became known as Aakreville.

There were rumours at the turn of the century that Quatsino might become a great centre of industry. The Quatsino Power and Pulp Company was given an enormous timber lease in the region. Hundreds of mining claims were frantically staked. Land speculators proclaimed that "Quatsino City" had been "recommended by eminent Railway Engineers as a Railway Terminal for Trans-Pacific Trade." It all came to nothing. A pulp mill was eventually built—but at Port Alice, twenty-five kilometres away. Quatsino remained as it had been all along: small and rural and quiet.

Bella Coola was also touted as a major rail terminus, an honour that would eventually go to Prince Rupert. The young colony blossomed anyway. It had over two hundred members by the end of the century. Two schools were erected, the larger one doubling as a community centre and church. A sizeable congregation met there every Sunday. A youth club was formed, a small library and land office opened, and a dock and sawmill were built. Groups of men regularly journeyed south to work at the great Rivers Inlet commercial fishery. Valley gardens produced cabbages, carrots, rutabagas, turnips, potatoes, onions, parsnips and hay; in time, a wide range of fruits would also be harvested.

Bella Coola had suffered a serious blow in March 1897, when Reverend Saugstad died after a short and sudden illness. He had been the Norwegians' unquestioned leader, both in spiritual and secular matters. He was an idealist, according to Milo Fougner, and he had wanted to establish a community of "almost morally perfect people, in an ideal situation away from temptation." The colony might have developed quite differently had Saugstad directed its course for a longer period of time.

A certain cohesiveness and sense of purpose were lost with his death. A new leader was elected, and a new clergyman soon arrived. The colony flourished as never before, and remained tightly knit and

Social calls were an important form of pioneer entertainment; in this archival image, visitors converge on Ivar Fougner's cabin. (Ivar Fougner; BCARS G-00976)

highly co-operative. But its utopian goals gradually faded away. Instead, Bella Coola grew affluent, as all the hard work paid off. In time, even the influence of Lutheranism declined. Today, Hagensborg's Augsburg church, built in 1900 as the focal point of a deeply spiritual community, is nondenominational. Cultural ties are mainly preserved through the activities of a local Sons of Norway chapter.

In the 1900s, Bella Coola continued to grow and prosper, its size allowing it to become fairly self-sufficient. For Quatsino, on the other hand, survival was a constant struggle. Homesteaders gave up and left the tiny village in a steady trickle, but a roughly equal flow of new-comers somehow arrived to replace them. The collapse of the Cape Scott colony around 1907 resulted in an infusion of fresh blood, as several of its members—including Carl Christensen, who had led the Danish settlement through its final days—moved to Quatsino. Christensen taught school at his new home, as he had at his old one. A valuable accumulation of Cape Scott records and photographs was lost when his house burned down in 1912.

House fires and storms at sea were Quatsino's main worries. The village relied on the ocean, not only for transport but also for liveli-hood; many residents worked as fishermen. Bella Coola had different concerns, some of which involved the river that ran the length of the valley and was prone to devastating floods. One deluge, in 1924, dam-aged the Bella Coola townsite so seriously that it had to be moved to the south bank of the river from its original location north of the Nuxalk reserve. Major bridges that served the old townsite and pro-vided access to a side valley where a number of colonists had settled were washed out on several occasions.

In 1953, Highway 20, connecting Bella Coola to Williams Lake, was completed, and the valley was changed forever. Before the road, the community had basically been a larger version of Quatsino, a vil-lage "up the coast," totally dependent on the water for access. After the road, Bella Coola was plugged into the rest of world, even if the Hill— a set of notorious switchbacks that snakes up to the Chilcotin plateau—still keeps out large recreational vehicles. Quatsino, mean-while, remains without a land link to the wider world, which is per-fectly fine with its residents. Quatsino is a world of its own.

"Remember," the water-taxi pilot tells me at Coal Harbour, "if you get caught in a whirlpool, turn into it and it'll spit you right out." How reassuring, I think. Paddling through Quatsino Narrows for the first time, alone, is fraught with enough uncertainty. Timing is all-important. The current in the two-kilometre-long narrows can reach nine knots on the tide's full flood, which could make for a too-exciting ride.

There's always the water-taxi, of course. But I want to reach Quatsino more or less the same way the early colonists had—not by wooden dugout, exactly, but in my fibreglass kayak. The village spent much of its history as a regular port of call for such Canadian Pacific steamships as the *Tees, Queen City* and *Princess Maquinna* on their west Vancouver Island runs from Victoria to Cape Scott. If residents needed to dash over to Coal Harbour or take the trail to Hardy Bay, however, it meant pointing some small craft—a rowboat, most likely—into the jaws of a watery slingshot.

The narrows shoots you through in a jiffy if you catch the tide right, and my passage is anticlimactic. Another hour's paddling brings me past the abandoned Quattishe Indian reserve and across the mouth of Hecate Cove to Quatsino itself. I set up camp at Al Whittaker's Quatsino Lodge, one of two places that visitors can stay. Thomas Nogar had once erected his store and post office here. A family of deer crop the lodge's thick lawns with the aplomb of hired gardeners.

Quatsino's tidy households are spread out on either side of a dirt road that snakes along the shoreline from the Quattishe reserve at one end of town to the old cemetery at the other. It can be a long walk from place to place, which is why bizarre, rusted-out, unlicensed vehicles are often encountered snorting their way down the community's main and only street. As I stand talking to Whittaker, a peculiar grinding noise penetrates my consciousness and gradually gets louder. "That'll be Gwen," says my host, who can identify all forms of local transport long before they heave into view. Sure enough, within minutes an ancient truck appears.

Gwen Hansen, unofficial village archivist and author of *The Quatsino Chronicle,* a local history, has kindly consented to give me a tour. As we bump along, I gaze at neatly groomed, shingle-clad old homes with magnificent flower and vegetable gardens. Rhododendrons, especially, are blooming everywhere. Hansen points out the sights: St. Olaf's Church, built in 1898 as the first school; the Customs House, base for a regional customs official until 1974; the current school, which dates from 1933. We narrowly miss a group of peacocks at the entrance to Aakreville, and pass the driveway to Eagle Manor Retreat, constructed in 1917 as the Quatsino Hotel and now a guesthouse. Local landmarks such as Bergh Cove and Leeson Point remind me of long-gone pioneers.

After the tour I walk back to camp, stopping to commune with a few more old-timers at the village's two atmospheric cemeteries. On the way, I meet Nora Johnson, who rules the tiny post office, set up in front of her house on a wheeled truck chassis so it can be moved if necessary. The postmistress came to Quatsino in 1941 as a school-teacher and married Carl Johnson, who had arrived twenty-four years earlier with his Swedish parents. She recalls how community life was easier and livelier in the forties, with lots of boat traffic, two stores, monthly dances, and bridge and ladies' clubs. "But we keep surviving," she says, "much to our surprise. Nobody bothers you too much here, and you don't bother them."

Over the next day or so, I talk to a raft of residents, some recent, some who have lived at Quatsino most of their lives. Annie Howich, for instance, Quatsino's oldest inhabitant at ninety-seven, arrived as a teenager with her family in 1918. Her son Jack, seventy-three, who bought his first fishing boat at sixteen, shows me where a bear climbed up on his deck the day before and ate a box of apples. "When I do get to the city," he tells me, "I can't wait to get out. Here I've got everything. Except apples, that is. Darned bear." Later, as I walk along the road, a crashing in the bushes makes me think of Howich's bear. It is only Elliot Andersen, a grade-nine mountain-biker who commutes to Port Hardy for school but loves Quatsino well enough to want to keep on living there after graduation.

Doris Wold was working as a nurse at Port Alice in 1947 when she met her husband-to-be, Torliev, whose parents came to Quatsino in 1929. "I thought it had a heavenly quality," she recalls. "I would call Quatsino 'old-world.' Anytime I came back here after being away, it seemed like going back in history. You could believe you were in the nineteenth century. It's unique. But the things that make it unique, like the limited access, also make it hard to live here. Not everyone could. We get very tired of packing our groceries and going everywhere by boat. Men—and women, too, now—get so they can fix everything: houses, machinery, plumbing. We still have to fall back on the old ways. If we ever got a road in, I'm afraid the uniqueness would go."

B.C.'s two Norwegian colonies somehow got their destinies confused. Bella Coola, which started out as an experiment in human virtue and social morality—an idealistic dream in a remote bit of wilderness—ended up vibrant, worldly and well connected. By the 1930s, according to Clifford Kopas, who wrote extensively about the valley, assimilation was complete. Even though people still spoke Norwegian and maintained Norwegian customs, Kopas concluded that, for all its self-sufficiency, the settlement was "not a New Norway. It is Canadian in every aspiration."

Quatsino, on the other hand, began life with a scramble and dreamed of industrial wealth and fame, only to become a detached, otherworldly paradise where a handful of independent souls still practise a way of life that has passed from the rest of the province. "People here value their privacy, but they're always around to help one another when it matters," says Gwen Hansen, as I muse about the character of her community. "I don't think utopian is an inaccurate description of Quatsino." In fact, it may be more utopian in spirit today than it was a century ago.

Isolated Quatsino on Vancouver Island, with its old homes and splendid gardens, is a timeless world unto itself. (Andrew Scott)

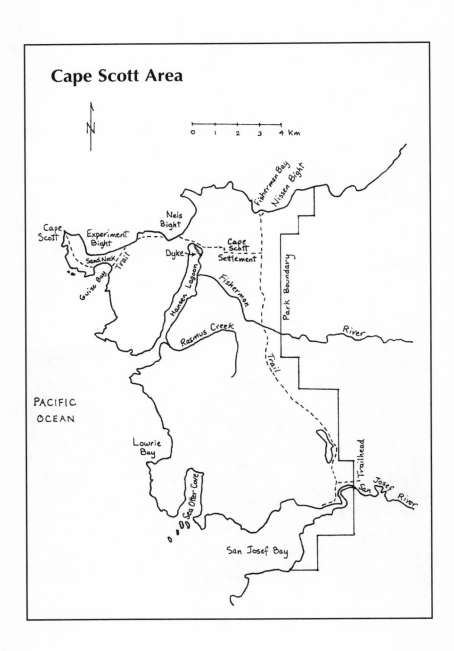

Cape Scott Area

0 1 2 3 4 Km

Fisherman Bay

Nissen Bight

Nels Bight

Cape Scott

Experiment Bight

Sand Neck

Guise Bay

Trail

Dyke

Hansen Lagoon

Cape Scott Settlement

Fisherman

Park Boundary

Rasmus Creek

River

Trail

PACIFIC OCEAN

Lowrie Bay

Sea Otter Cove

Trailhead

San

San Josef River

San Josef Bay

MEADOW AT THE END
OF THE WORLD
Cape Scott and its Danish Settlers

Dare you with me this long voyage take?
Have you the will and courage to sustain?
If so we can now this land possess,
Slowly we will here an Eden make . . .
—from "The Cape Scott Song"

As we trudge over the rough, muddy trail to the northwestern tip of Vancouver Island, the first white settlers to come this way are often in our thoughts. My twenty-kilogram pack—a mere fraction of what they sometimes carried—has me bent double, struggling to avoid a face-first fall into the gumbo. I regard my soaked boots with concern. Will their contents survive the Cape Scott experience or collapse along the way, sprained by some devious root, leaving me to the mercies of weather and wildlife?

The route we are following—twenty-four kilometres from the San Josef Bay trailhead to Cape Scott lighthouse; seventeen kilometres to Nels Bight and the beach where we hope to camp—has been in existence for over ninety years. There are many signs of past travellers: decaying logs laid sideways, corduroy-style; ancient rotting boards and boughs that once helped homesteaders over the swamps; strands of telegraph wire rusting away in the underbrush.

With the nineteenth century nearly at an end, a group of intrepid, hard-working Danes colonized Cape Scott in one of British Columbia's earliest settlement attempts. The members of this co-operative community were in search of more economic and social freedom than they had been able to find in the United States, where most of them had spent several years after emigrating from Denmark. Although its numbers never exceeded one hundred, the colony endured for about ten years, farming a patch of meadow that the colonists extended and protected with a sizeable dyke.

Now, the colony site and the notorious path that leads to it lie entirely within Cape Scott Provincial Park. Some trail sections are in fine condition, complete with steps and long passages of raised boardwalk. Each year, work crews repair the worst of winter's damage and add new bits of walkway if the budget permits. The park staff's efforts seem almost futile, though, against the fertile power of the all-enveloping Quatsino rainforest, whose tendrils and shoots fill every nook and cranny with green life.

Red and yellow cedar, lodgepole pine, hemlock, fir and spruce, much of it old-growth, cover this northern end of Vancouver Island. The forest understorey is choked with salal, salmonberry, huckleberry and ferns. Lakes and lagoons are stopping places for migrating waterfowl, while deer, elk, black bear, cougars and wolves roam the uplands and creek valleys. The area gets little snow, but rainfall is heavy—between four and five metres a year. Cape Scott is famous for violent storms, which can occur in any season, and for fogs so thick you can almost scoop them up and drink them out of a cup. Extended periods of sunshine are rare, even in summer.

When my trekking companion and I finally stumble out of the forest onto Nels Bight's glorious sands, we feel like singing and dancing with relief. But, of course, we have no energy left. A sign greets us there. "Welcome, weary wanderers," it says. "You have hiked the settlers' highway and tasted the exhaustion of a forgotten mode of transportation. Remove your backpack and relish in your reward." For us, that means a few days exploring the park's headlands and wide, driftwood-laden beaches. We watch sea lions frolic in the huge waves breaking off Cape Scott lighthouse. A friendly park ranger gives us a lesson on local plantlife, pointing out red goosefoot, beach carrot, fool's huckleberry and maidenhair ferns with delicate, shiny black stems. Great flocks of killdeer and dunlin forage on the sand, while crows patrol the bordering forest and bald eagles and osprey hover overhead.

But it also means communing with the remnants of the pioneer settlement. The Danes found little reward for their efforts, despite the splendid surroundings. By 1907, the colony had failed. Provincial officials had promised that if enough people were in place, an all-important road link would be built to allow Cape Scott dairy produce to reach southern markets. The Danes kept their end of the deal, but British Columbia reneged on its expensive commitment. The settlers found that relying solely on boat transport was too dangerous and difficult. Isolation, climate, topography and bureaucracy did them in, but remnants of their valiant attempt can be found scattered over the area. These fast-disappearing ruins—dykes and ditches, fences built to hold back sand dunes, dilapidated buildings, rotting machinery, gravestones and skeletal ships—add a powerful touch of nostalgia to what is already a place of great beauty.

A long, narrow, very shallow inlet nearly separates the westernmost part of Cape Scott from the rest of Vancouver Island. Its entrance was once known as Goose Bay or Goose Harbour, and at its head lies a broad expanse of tidal flats much loved by birds. Back from the shoreline, where decaying vegetation has, over the centuries, raised the ground above tide's reach, swampy meadows have formed. Lush layers of coarse grass grow there in the rich, aromatic mud.

The meadows have a pastoral feel rare in B.C., where mountain and forest dominate the landscape. They provide an oasis in the wilderness. In winter, thousands of waterfowl break their annual migration here; in summer, early-morning visitors might spy deer cautiously browsing or a black bear ambling to the lagoon's dank shore in search of a meal. Today, parts of the meadows are relatively firm underfoot, having once been dyked and drained. Walking across them is a delight. Rows of old fence posts, one crowned with a heritage coffee pot, divide the land into fields, giving it a semblance of order. A century ago, streams rich in salmon ran through these open flats. Trying to cross them would have been slow, laborious work. Still, it's easy to see how this place might have attracted early visitors.

One such visitor was Rasmus Hansen, deckhand on a Seattle fishing boat and an immigrant from Denmark. His small schooner, the *Floyborg,* was anchored in Goose Bay some time in 1894 after fishing for halibut off Cape Scott, and Hansen went ashore to hunt ducks at the head of the lagoon. (Both bay and lagoon now bear his name.) When he laid his eyes on the rich meadowlands, though, his thoughts turned from wildfowl to dairy cattle.

Information about Hansen is sparse. In Denmark he'd apparently been a high-school physical-education teacher. However, he and his fellow Danish immigrants must have been talking for some time about the possibility of an ethnic colony in B.C. He almost certainly knew that in 1894 Norwegian colonies were being started at Hagensborg and Quatsino—the latter only fifty kilometres from Cape Scott as the crow flies.

Hansen may have been aware of favourable reports that government surveyors had written about the north end of Vancouver Island for the crown lands department. In 1893, H. M. Burwell described the area as rich in potential for fishing, mining, logging and agriculture. The head of Hansen Lagoon, he noted, might be dyked to create fields for dairy farming. Federal geologist George M. Dawson—who went on to direct the Geological Survey of Canada and give his name to Dawson City—had been the first to survey the region, in 1885. He also considered the possibility of building a dyke to reclaim land, suggesting that it "would not be a very difficult operation."

Hansen put word of Cape Scott out on the Danish grapevine. Some 172,000 of his compatriots had left their homeland for the New World between 1870 and 1900, part of the great wave of European emigration that marked the last half of the nineteenth century. Danish emigration peaked between 1890 and 1892, when over 10,000, mostly able-bodied young men, set sail annually. Denmark's changing social and economic conditions made the risky journey increasingly attractive.

As a result of an 1864 war with Prussia, Denmark had lost the three affluent, mostly German-speaking duchies of Lauenburg, Holstein and Slesvig—forty percent of its kingdom. The Danish people, shocked and demoralized by the war, faced another threat when large-scale imports of grain to Europe from North America and Russia caused grain prices to decline sharply in the mid-1870s. Poor and predominantly rural, Denmark relied heavily on grain-growing for survival. Farm workers were hard hit. They headed for the cities in large numbers, which did little to help their situation. But the same improvements in transportation that had allowed grain to cross the Atlantic also permitted European emigrants, many Danes among them, to cross in the other direction.

Thousands of Scandinavians settled on America's midwest plains, from Wisconsin to Nebraska and North and South Dakota, where they worked in factories and mines and at logging and farming. They brought with them a number of innovative survival techniques, born of necessity back in their homelands as a response to deteriorating national economies. These new ideas, based on co-operative principles, stood the immigrants in good stead in their new home. Economic uncertainty was a fact of life there also. Periods of prosperity alternated with regular intervals of depression.

In Denmark, for instance, the collapse of the grain market had prompted the country's farmers to diversify into cattle-breeding and dairying. The newly invented centrifugal cream separator was key to the production of high-quality butter, but most farmers couldn't afford one. They banded together and formed small co-operative dairies to take advantage of the new technology. These associations were successful (by 1890 there were nearly seven hundred in Denmark), and the co-op idea spread to other agricultural endeavours, such as poultry farms and slaughterhouses, and eventually to retail businesses and factories. The movement freed many workers from dependence on large landowners and contributed to their economic welfare and self-reliance.

A complementary Danish movement in education was taking place at about the same time. A series of rural "folk" schools was established, influenced by principles laid out by one of the country's great men, the educator and visionary Nikolaj Grundtvig. Grundtvig's teachings deliberately combined an unprejudiced, broad-minded Christianity with the heroic virtues embodied in Norse mythology. Schools based on his ideas offered courses in history and poetry as well as practical subjects, such as agriculture. They helped break down rural conservatism. Between them, the folk school and co-operative campaigns contributed to Denmark's survival and prosperity, but they were unable to prevent the young and the poor from seeking a better life overseas.

Many immigrants to North America had been influenced by these new notions of co-operation and self-sufficiency. They hungered to put them into practice. A small, short-lived Danish socialist colony had been established in Kansas in 1877. More ambitiously, several hundred Danes had turned part of New Brunswick into a promising dairy district called New Denmark. Rasmus Hansen was firmly of the belief that Cape Scott could be another such place. He persuaded three other Danes—Y. Christian Jensen, Peter Thomsen and Nels Nelson, of Enumclaw, Washington—to visit the Cape Scott meadows in 1895. They shared his enthusiasm.

Hansen and his associates wrote a number of articles about the proposed colony for Danish weekly newspapers in Iowa and Nebraska. Plenty of Danes in the midwest had become disenchanted with the relentless climate and the unpredictable, boom-bust economy. They were aware that the west coast would be more favourable for dairy farming, their preferred livelihood. A number of them responded with interest to Hansen's ideas. The positive feedback prompted him to make a formal approach to the B.C. government.

He based his request on intelligence from the *Official Handbook of Information Relating to the Dominion Government of Canada*. This emigration primer was published for years as part of a vigorous attempt by Canada to solicit European—especially British—settlers. The 1897 edition, for instance, published a list of "persons wanted in Canada." "Tenant farmers, agriculturists, persons with capital" and "young men desiring agricultural experience" were sought. "Shop assistants, clerks, draughtsmen, telegraphists," and "inmates of workhouses" were "not encouraged."

Immigrants to British Columbia could, at that time, each pre-empt a quarter-section of land (a section equalled 640 acres, or 260 hectares; thirty-six sections made up a township) in certain designated areas. By living on and improving their land for five years, they would eventually receive a Crown grant and the right to buy the property at a rate of one dollar per acre. Hanson and his group were more interested in the immigration leases or indentures that the B.C. government authorized in the 1890s. These agreements permitted groups of thirty or more settlers to receive their land for free after the obligatory five-year period.

Hansen's first letter to Colonel James Baker, B.C.'s provincial secretary and minister of mines, education and immigration, was dated May 6, 1896. "We, the undersigned intending settlers," it began, "who have been at Cape Scott looking for land... promise to form a colony of at least seventy-five settlers." The "undersigned settlers"—Hansen,

Jensen, Thomsen and Nelson—made their promise subject to three conditions: that the government build two schools, a dyke at the head of Hansen Lagoon and, most importantly, a road connecting Fisherman's Cove (now called Fisherman Bay) to Sea Otter Cove, with branches to Goose Harbour (now Hansen Bay) and along the San Josef River. The letter proposed that land be leased to the colony bit by bit over four years as the number of settlers increased, and that the road be built incrementally on this basis also.

The letter went on to describe the settlers' goals:

> *The colony will develop the resources of the country, especially farming and fishing. The farming will be what generally is termed "mixed farming." The fishing will be principally deep sea fishing, halibut and cod.*
>
> *We consider the fishing industry as the part that must carry the colony through the first years until the farm can be able to produce and pay. It is with this in view that we intend to start at Fisherman's Cove, which gives shelter for small fishing crafts and is near the fishing banks.*
>
> *We consider the marshy land in township 43 to form the backbone of the colony and, therefore, it is we ask the Government to build the dyke for to protect the land, because we have learned by experience and investigation that to start a colony in heavy timbered land, even with the best of soil, is almost an impossibility.*
>
> *We are well aware of the necessity of co-operation for the small farmer and intend, from the start, to have a small steamer or steam schooner of our own to carry colonists, their goods and provisions into the country, and fish and farm products of the country to the market.*

Baker, who also championed the colonies of Bella Coola and Quatsino, gave a positive reply. The requested lands would be set aside. Hansen and his colleagues immediately held meetings in Seattle and Tacoma with other prospective settlers. A set of rules was devised, outlining how prospective members might view and select land. One important requirement for those wanting to join the venture was the payment of fifty dollars, to "be used for means of communication, a co-operative store, and other enterprises for the growth and improvement of the colony." A "provisional company" was formed and a board of directors elected, with Hansen president.

In another letter, the group asked that the meadow be divided into small lots so that each colonist, provided he agree to help build the dyke, would receive both a piece of meadow and a wooded acreage. Again, Baker replied in the affirmative. If the stipulated first group of thirty settlers was in place by May 1, 1898, he promised that each one would be granted ten acres of meadow and an additional eighty acres in the forest beyond. The way was now clear for the Danes to head to Cape Scott and commence living their dream. That fall, Hansen and Nels Nelson were landed by the small coastal steamer *Willapa* at Fisherman's Cove, where they built a house from driftwood, and a skiff. Hansen returned to Seattle to organize the main colonization attempt, scheduled for next spring. Nelson spent the winter alone at Cape Scott, to see what that would be like.

Nelson survived his sojourn and sent word that the main group should set off. And they did, on March 19, 1897. Eight or ten women and children went north on the *Willapa,* accompanied by Ernest Cleveland, the government surveyor, and his assistant, who were to plot out the land. Six men travelled up the west coast of Vancouver Island on the *Floyborg,* which Hansen had purchased as the colony's supply ship. A storm caught them, breaking their rudder and anchor line and beaching them, with heavy damage, in Hansen Lagoon. No one was hurt. On this ominous, forlorn note, the little group began a new life in the wilds of British Columbia.

They were not the first to dwell at Cape Scott, of course. The area's original inhabitants—the Tlatlasikwala, Nakumgilisala and Yutlinuk—were part of a large linguistic group or nation known today as the Kwakwaka'wakw (formerly called the Kwakiutl). Their proximity to the sailing routes of the early explorers and the new-found commerce in sea-otter pelts cost them dearly. The European visitors passed on such deadly diseases as smallpox and tuberculosis, which decimated the tribal populations. The Yutlinuk, who occupied several islands west of Cape Scott, had completely died out by the early 1800s.

The fur traders, especially James Hanna and James Strange, who explored the area separately in 1786, named many of the region's landforms. Cape Scott itself—plus the islands to the west and the channel between them—were named after David Scott, a Bombay merchant and the financial backer of Strange's expedition. Guise Bay and Experiment Bight, on either side of a three-hundred-metre-wide neck of sand that leads to the westernmost headland, where the lighthouse and actual cape are located, are named after Strange's crew members and vessels. So is Lowrie Bay, just to the south.

A few place names, such as San Josef Bay and San Josef River, commemorate the region's early Spanish explorers. Many other geographical names—such as Nels and Nissen bights, Frederiksen and Christensen points, Hansen Lagoon and Rasmus Creek—date from the early twentieth century and owe their origins to the Danish settlers.

Anthropologist Franz Boas, after his encounter with the Bella Coola band that toured Germany in 1885, made several expeditions to British Columbia in the 1890s and early 1900s. In northern Vancouver Island, he recorded aboriginal place names and published early descriptions of the region's native culture. Park signs have incorporated some of his research, introducing visitors to a world of myth and danger. The sand isthmus between Guise Bay and Experiment Bight, for instance, is believed to be the birthplace of Kanakelak the transformer—a pre-eminent Kwakwaka'wakw deity who created the animals and gave men and women their present forms. Rather than paddle round Cape Scott, where conflicting tides and currents have created one of B.C.'s most dreaded marine graveyards, native boatmen often preferred to haul their heavy dugout canoes across Kanakelak's dune home.

On the northeast coast of the cape promontory was Kwane, the legendary home of the Koskimo, another branch of the Kwakwaka'wakw nation. (Several myths suggest that Cape Scott was a very ancient habitation site.) North of the sand neck, on the western side of the headland, a series of rocky sea stacks received the name of another supernatural being, one often given to dangerous places: Nomas, or sea monster. Nearby, in a tiny cove, was Ouchton, or "those of the unprotected bay." This former Nakumgilisala village site is one of two aboriginal reserves within park boundaries.

Visiting native people told the first Danish settlers that Ouchton's inhabitants had been exterminated, probably around the year 1830, by an enemy raid. The remote village, they said, had never been repopulated. In fact, the entire Cape Scott area was abandoned in the mid-1850s, when the depleted Nakumgilisala and Tlatlasikwala tribes amalgamated and moved to Hope Island, about forty kilometres to the northeast. There they stayed, their numbers steadily declining, until 1954, when thirty-two remaining individuals decided to move to Quatsino Sound and join the Koskimo. Today, they are known collectively as the Nahwitty.

Apart from occasional visitors, the Danes were on their own in the colony they had named Danevike, or Danish Cove. Their nearest neighbours were many kilometres distant. Not that there was much time for socializing, in any case. That first summer, especially, the settlers rushed to prepare themselves for the worst effects of the coming winter. At the end of July, surveyor Ernest Cleveland provided a mostly positive accounting of his four-month stay at Cape Scott. His report, which resides in B.C.'s Provincial Archives, along with many other documents pertaining to the budding colony, gives an excellent overview of the conditions that the colonists faced.

Cleveland's first order of business—to survey and divide up the meadow lands and decide where and how the dyke should be built— proved to be the colony's next disappointment. "The area of meadow land," he wrote, "was found upon completion of a traverse to be much less than was anticipated, consequently the number of ten-acre blocks into which it might be divided would not be sufficient to grant one to each member of the colony." The grass lands, which only flooded at extremely high tides, covered a mere 50 hectares. The tidal lands, however, which flooded twice a day, covered 210 hectares. "The colonists," Cleveland continued, "were therefore given the option of a block of meadow and eighty acres nearby, or a quarter section just outside the section subdivided into eighties."

The young surveyor, who later in life would plan and administer Vancouver's water-supply system and build the Cleveland Dam on the Capilano River, examined three possible sites for a dyke across Hansen Lagoon. He determined that it would be too expensive for the colonists to try to drain all the tidal flats. A more modest dyke of about seven hundred metres, "crossing the lagoon a short distance above the mouth of the main river—thus avoiding a considerable volume of fresh water," would serve to reclaim an area of about eighty hectares.

Cleveland's report went on to describe the resources of the region. The fine spruce stands, he felt, could supply the colony with valuable construction lumber. He pointed out "the numerous small rounded hills, all of which are covered with timber." He was enthusiastic about the area's agricultural future. "Vegetables and small fruits" should do well, he noted, and "dairy farming and stock raising" had definite potential. He also described the rich offshore halibut banks and the great salmon runs at Rivers Inlet to the northeast.

"Many new settlers from various parts of the United States—principally California and Minnesota—are expected during the autumn," he commented, "having already signified their intention of joining the colony. The coming winter will afford ample opportunity for the settlers to get in good working order." Cleveland had a high opinion of the colony's members, but he was strangely ambivalent about their future chances. "It may be said with certainty," he wrote, "that if our northern coast can be successfully colonized, the Danish colony at Cape Scott will furnish the proof, as no better class of men for the undertaking could be found. They are, without exception, hardy, industrious and intelligent, and well deserve success."

The surveyor's report sounded one other whisper of caution. The harbour that the colonists expected to use—Sea Otter Cove, fourteen kilometres southwest of Fisherman's Cove—was deemed "inferior and difficult to enter—being quite impossible for steamers at low water." Fisherman's Cove was so exposed to northerly winds that even the construction of a wharf was not practicable, but it had to suffice as the settlers' port of call. That summer, the Danish colonists were able to arrange with the Canadian Pacific Navigation Company for steamships to begin stopping there on a monthly basis.

For about ten years, CPN vessels—usually the *Willapa*, the *Queen City* or the *Tees*—made frequent appearances in the bay. The lack of a pier or float made loading and unloading difficult; Fisherman's Cove, in fact, turned out to be the colony's Achilles' heel. Everything had to be brought to shore by dinghy. Cattle could be persuaded to swim from the steamship to the land, but no form of inducement could persuade them to go in the other direction, which made the prospect of selling stock somewhat theoretical.

For easier landings, old hulls were sunk as breakwaters, but they soon washed ashore; their remnants, including the great solid-timber knees of a nineteenth-century windjammer, can still be seen on the beach. In foul weather, the closest that steamships could get to the colony was Shushartie Bay, thirty-two kilometres east. The uncertainty caused by this situation, and by the fact that the settlers' own schooner, the *Floyborg,* was out of commission, was "made painfully real," wrote Cleveland, "by the failure of the transportation company to forward supplies at the time expected, thereby leaving us very short of provisions for about three weeks."

From Fisherman Bay, where Nels Nelson established a co-operative store and, in 1899, a post office, a path still runs about three kilometres through the forest to the meadows. Near its intersection with the trail back to the San Josef parking lot, a side track leads to a peaceful clearing where the house of the colony's teacher, Carl Christensen, once stood. The settlers referred to Christensen as "professor"—partly because he was older than most of them, partly because he had graduated from the University of Copenhagen. He had known Rasmus Hansen in Chicago, and he arrived at Cape Scott in 1899.

Christensen's mossy homesite, bordered with decades-old holly and rhododendron bushes, has a haunting beauty. At the back of the clearing stands a tall granite gravestone. "WILLIAM adopted son of C. B. CHRISTENSEN," reads the inscription. "Died Oct. 17, 1906. Aged 12 years, 9 mo's. The Sun went down while it was yet day." William was one of three orphans the teacher adopted, and one day he cut his foot. The minor wound became seriously infected; the nearest hospital was at Alert Bay, 110 storm-tossed kilometres away, and the boy's life could not be saved. Passing hikers have left shells and leaves and wooden net floats around the base of the marker. About seventy-five metres away, on the far side of the trail, an overgrown cemetery holds a number of crumbling wooden crosses. One in particular, with the name "Baby Hansen" spelt out in nails, offers another poignant reminder of the hardships and sorrows that beset the colonists.

A kilometre or so to the west, at the edge of the grassy tidal flats, many of the original settlers built simple homes that have long since disappeared. Most of their diaries and letters, which might have offered documentary evidence of their day-to-day lives, have likewise failed to survive. But thanks to numerous taped interviews with the colonists' children (mostly recorded in 1982 by Gordon Fish for the Provincial Archives of B.C.), a recounting of those early days can yet be heard.

Petra Amsden, who arrived at Cape Scott with her parents in

1899, recalled that the family first stayed in a two-room log house near the lagoon:

> *One room held our furniture that we'd brought up and the other room we had to sleep and cook. And the following year, our house was built. It was built with the help of settlers. Father built so much and the others got together and the women did the cooking and it was what you call a bee—a housing bee.*
>
> *My father wanted a farm. He wanted to carve a sort of country estate out of the forest. He started to carve out a farm and till the soil in a densely forested district. The soil was very good but all the trees had to be removed. He had a crosscut saw, a double-bit axe, a stump puller—a small one—and steel cable, I suppose it was, and a gun. He had about four or five guns of different types. That was about all his tools. And his knowledge of cultivating the soil. And he was a very good husbandman.*

Eventually, the family acquired a steer to do their heavy pulling, and a horse and a mule, as well. They had no wheeled carts, but built small sleds using red cedar shoots as sleigh runners in order to drag their supplies home from the store. When they were finally able to plant the fields, they grew timothy hay as animal feed. The hay grew well, but drying it was difficult because of Cape Scott's abundant rainfall.

> *We always had a garden—strawberries, raspberries and red currants, white currants, black currants—and father planted apple trees. But large fruit trees were not satisfactory. It was my job to pick one quart of berries every day, and that was terrible because I was afraid of the forest and I soon picked every bush that was near the house.... There were blue huckleberries and red huckleberries, and we could get cranberries in the marshes.*
>
> *Father shot deer and geese and ducks. We had pintails, canvasbacks, butterballs and mallards....Also there were wild grouse in the woods, and they were good too. We had to live on what father could shoot, otherwise we had our hens and our cattle and so on, and we killed a pig every year. We never ran short of supplies, not really. They ran short of tobacco once, the men did. You never forget that; oh, that was terrible.*

For the children, the Cape Scott colony must have seemed like an endless holiday. For the adults, though, life was hard—an equally endless round of cutting firewood, tending gardens and domestic animals, hunting and fishing for food, and walking from one part of the settlement to another, usually carrying heavy loads. This constant itinerary was only relieved by occasional meetings at the parsonage and the infrequent excitement of boat day. But, as Amsden recollected, the daily routine was not without its satisfactions:

> *I remember that we would have rainstorms that lasted two weeks. That sounds very depressing but to people who are making their own comforts, there's something reassuring hearing the rain pattering on the roof when you're cozy and warm indoors with a cup of coffee and a very nice wild goose or wild duck for dinner.*
>
> *Some of the most pleasant days were harvest days in the fields when mother would bring down coffee and cakes for father and we would sit in a haystack and there was the odour of the wild hay drying, the sunshine, a light breeze, and the crowing, caw, caw, caw, of the crows.*

Housebuilding was a regular activity in the early years; construction materials were laboriously whip-sawn or split from cedar logs. The first inhabitants of the area had split cedar for their longhouses in much the same fashion. Johanne Harestad, interviewed about her mother and father, Mary and Carl Rasmussen, who came to the colony in 1897 from Wisconsin, recalled that her steam-engineer father had managed to get a small, dismantled sawmill to Cape Scott. He and his partner, Theo Fredericksen, dragged and floated the parts to a convenient site, then reassembled them.

Lumber from this mill was used to construct sluice gates for the dyke; a halibut dory, which the sea soon destroyed; and the parsonage, whose resident cleric departed in 1899 when it became apparent that the colony could not pay him. Without the mill, the community's treasured freight and passenger vessel, the nine-metre *Cape Scott,* could not have been built. The boat served along the coast from 1901 until 1910, when it sank and its crew of two perished. Rasmussen was hoping, said Harestad, "to saw lumber for homes for the settlers, but eventually went broke because the people needed lumber but they had no money to pay him."

Community improvement schemes were undertaken on a co-operative basis, and the settlers were not paid for their work. The dyke, naturally, was the first big job they tackled. By laboriously haul-ing thousands of wheelbarrows of dirt and rock, the colonists were able to complete their Herculean task by 1899. The great barrier was, as Ernest Cleveland had recommended, seven hundred metres in length, with a set of four-metre-high floodgates partway along. According to Lester Peterson, who grew up in the area and whose *Cape Scott Story* is an essential source of information about the colony and the lives of its members, the community held a night-long celebration after finishing the dyke. But when they went to examine their handi-work in the morning, it was gone. A southeast gale had come up while they were merry-making and torn it apart.

A second dyke was built further up the lagoon, constructed at an angle to the prevailing wind direction in order to reduce the effect of the tide. The new rampart was not completed until 1905 and is still visible today. Petra Amsden's father, Bertold Bekker, described the project in a 1919 newspaper article for Victoria's *Daily Colonist*. "The dyke is 1,100 feet long," he wrote, "bottom width twenty feet, three

A driftwood fence kept the dunes from invading Theo Fred-ericksen's hay field at the Sand Neck between Guise Bay and Experiment Bight. (BCARS B-01529)

feet on top, and seven feet high. There is a sluice with four gates and a box sluice. The material is taken on the spot. A ditch fourteen feet wide and three feet deep was dug on either side, the dirt thrown and wheeled up thus forming the dyke. The turf was carefully cut in square pieces and piled, forming a protective coat over the interior. Afterwards it was fenced on both sides and on top was made a gravel path."

While the farmlands were being drained and improved, fishing was a vital form of livelihood for the colony. The very first summer they arrived, fourteen settlers travelled up the coast to Rivers Inlet. The canneries there used to rent gillnets and skiffs to individual fishermen. Steam tugs would tow a line of skiffs out to the fishing grounds. Later, they'd return to collect the fish in scows. Working at night so that the coarse mesh would be invisible to the salmon, the men set and hauled in their nets by hand.

The canneries wanted sockeye. Pink salmon brought such low prices that the Cape Scott fishermen would take barrels and salt along with them to preserve the disregarded fish. When they returned home, they would smoke the pinks for winter use. Between 1897 and 1901, salmon fishing was generally poor, but for most of the rest of the decade, strong sockeye runs meant a steady source of income for the Danish settlement. Other colonists earned money by trapping the plentiful marten and mink for their furs. They also hired on at logging operations on the east coast of Vancouver Island, often rowing as far as two hundred kilometres just to find jobs.

The colony's dream was to practise dairy farming. N. P. Jensen, one of the original members and an experienced butter-maker, brought in milk-condensing machinery and set it up near the dyke. He passed on his butter-making skills to his daughter, who had married Theo Fredericksen. While some colonists farmed the tidal meadows, the Jensens and Fredericksens reclaimed the sand neck, setting up drift-wood fences and planting clover to stabilize the dunes. The settlers were good at raising cattle and processing dairy products. They even managed to transport modest shipments to many coastal camps and communities. But sending larger quantities of perishable foodstuffs to urban markets by boat was neither economical nor practical. Without a road, commercial agriculture was doomed.

In this brief description of the daily lives of the Cape Scott settlers, the colony may not seem much different from any other rural B.C.

community of the period. In what sense was the Danish settlement utopian? Many descendants of the original colonists, indeed, would probably rail against the use of the word. "It was going to be no paradise, no utopia," reflected author Lester Peterson in another archival interview. "People came out then with the knowledge that they were going to work."

> There was going to be a certain degree of freedom and a certain degree of local autonomy. I think it was much the same as many others—Hansen probably dreamed of a little bit more freedom from working on a halibut boat, in the same way as my father later on dreamed of a little more freedom to get out of an iron mine. So it was not with the thought that you'd avoid work, but with the thought that you might have a little of your own freedom. And it was possible to form a colony which could be very much like the modern municipality, in which you'd have your own local laws in a framework of federal and provincial laws.

But several significant factors did distinguish Cape Scott from typical rural settlement attempts in B.C. The Danish colonists were not a collection of disparate individuals. They were a cohesive group, one that shared a common heritage and spoke an uncommon language. Their goal was freedom: freedom to own their own land, freedom to live according to their own customs. They sought to achieve their goals through personal and economic co-operation, based on a set of rules and philosophical principles that they themselves drew up. And they deliberately chose a remote wilderness location, not to hide away from the world but as a practical method of furthering their ideal of cultural independence.

"Those who came to Cape Scott," remarked Petra Amsden, "had an idea of having a little Denmark away from home. And in the main, they were very nice people. Dreamers? Idealists? No, only my father and maybe Mr. Christensen." But the colonists could not maintain a realistic, workable link with the rest of the world. "They had gone right up to Cape Scott and isolated themselves," said Amsden. This isolation was their downfall.

British Columbia's Sessional Papers recorded a population of fifty for Cape Scott in 1898 and ninety in 1899. A public expenditure of

$4,443.22 was acknowledged for survey and road costs. Several founding families left early on, due partly to the fact that the colony could not support its Lutheran clergyman, Reverend Jens Nyland. A life without spiritual comfort and leadership was not for them. But glowing articles about Cape Scott in U.S. Danish-language publications ensured a steady trickle of new arrivals. And even the vacated parsonage had its uses: as a meeting hall and a school.

In 1899, less than three years after their arrival, the colonists were informed by B.C.'s deputy land commissioner, W. S. Gore, that no further leases of land would be let at Cape Scott (the Norwegians at Quatsino were written a similar letter on the same day). No reasons were given for this change of plans. Colony secretary Martin Jensen wrote back in dismay. "As we are not aware of not having fulfilled our part of the contract," he replied, "this decision came very unexpected." But Premier J. H. Turner, who had replaced Premier Davie, had lost the 1898 election, and the colony had lost its patron, James Baker. The next government had a different attitude towards immigration. B.C. still needed newcomers, but elected officials were becoming much more selective about whom they would let in.

Throughout the 1870s and 1880s, Canadian immigration policy was primarily designed to attract large numbers of able-bodied settlers. In theory, all nationalities and races were tolerated. Beneath the surface, though, an unwritten but clearly understood pecking order existed: British settlers were preferred (Canada was a British colony, after all), then northern and western Europeans, then other Europeans, then the rest of the world. As immigration from the United States and—most conspicuously—from China, began to increase, fears about British ethnic sovereignty grew. Giving big chunks of B.C. land to non-English-speaking colonies was becoming a less acceptable prospect to many people.

Even groups such as the Danes and Norwegians, with their relatively benign heritage, were seen as a threat. Ironically, Cape Scott's colonists had put a high priority on learning English and on teaching it to their children. Several educated members could already speak English well. Archival documents written by colonists exhibit a facility with the language that many of B.C.'s British immigrants would have been hard-pressed to match.

The xenophobic Charles Semlin administration, which took over from J. H. Turner, viewed the Scandinavian colonists as pampered foreigners with access to free land. Wishing to end their special status, it stopped granting immigration leases and also passed the controversial Alien Exclusion Act. This legislation, aimed at preventing the Chinese from owning gold claims, managed to inflame public opinion against all forms of foreign ownership. The turn of the century was a lively time in B.C. politics. Between 1898 and 1900, four different governments rose and fell, creating chaos in the civil service and a total neglect of public affairs. It was easy for agreements such as the one with the Cape Scott group to be overlooked or disregarded.

According to that agreement, roads were to be built connecting the colony to the San Josef valley and the wider world if fifty settlers had arrived by 1898, sixty-five by 1899 and seventy-five by 1900. By the government's own count, the settlers were in place, and a few kilometres of road were duly constructed from Fisherman's Cove. By refusing to grant further leases, B.C. could, in Lester Peterson's felicitous phrase, "hope to avoid" fulfilling the rest of its costly obligations. The Semlin government did not feel it had to honour its predecessor's agreements. Instead of more roads, a trail was built—the same one that determined hikers must follow today. Too rough and marshy even for packhorses, it must have been a bone-grinding, soul-wearying method of getting supplies in when boats failed to reach the colony.

The colonists' agreement with B.C. stipulated that, after five years, settlers who occupied and improved their homesites would receive a Crown grant and free title to their land. Thus, March 1902 shaped up as a major anniversary for those founding families still at Cape Scott. But no Crown grants were forthcoming. Fearing that they might never own land, some members moved away and pre-empted land in the San Josef valley. Market access for agricultural produce would prove easier from there, they believed. The rest of the colonists, discouraged but not embittered, remained at the cape under the leadership of Professor Christensen.

Despite the transportation problems, and the consequent economic stagnation, the diminished group struggled on until 1907. Two critical events then sounded the colony's death knell. One was the cessation of steamer service. The coastal navigation companies felt they could no longer justify the effort and expense of stopping at Fisherman's Cove. From 1907 on, only Shushartie Bay to the east and

Quatsino to the south would be regular ports of call. And in July of that year, for the first time, the B.C. government allowed individual settlers to pre-empt land across the entire northern tip of Vancouver Island.

This was the final blow. Now anyone could come and homestead within the very boundaries first planned for the colony. And the Danes themselves were precluded, as a group, from leasing any more property. The Cape Scott settlement had no choice but to disband. Christensen orchestrated the departure of most colonists to San Josef and Holberg, fifteen kilometres further east; other people just gradually packed up and went away. The Rasmussens headed to Sea Otter Cove. Christensen himself ended up teaching school in Quatsino. Some colonists left the area altogether. Only the Jensens and the Fredericksens remained at the cape, stubbornly farming the land they had laboured so long to wrestle from the dunes and the tides.

From the old Christensen homesite, the firm, broad trail running due west to the meadows passes through an enchanting landscape of dwarf pines and cedars interspersed with micro-gardens of low-lying bunch-berry, ferns and moss. About a kilometre down this pleasant pathway, visitors come across a cluster of tumbledown buildings and a scat-

The Fall Fair was a major annual event at the remote community of Cape Scott. About two hundred people attended the 1914 celebration. (BCARS A-09988)

tering of implements: buckets and saucepans, saw blades, stove parts and bed frames, an old ploughshare. Side trails lead to a collapsing toolshed, a clearing where a large farmhouse stood for many years and, eventually, to a small Caterpillar tractor, Cape Scott's first motorized vehicle, wedged permanently between two tree trunks.

These ruins, which include the remains of an older meeting hall, were once the focal point for a second flourishing of the Cape Scott settlement. Between 1909 and 1913, dozens of hopeful homesteaders moved to the cape. Unsurprisingly, they were mostly British, but Italians, Swiss, Poles, Belgians, Swedes and Norwegians also arrived. While Cape Scott lost its Danish flavour, a boundless mood of co-operation continued to prevail. "There was a tremendous community spirit," remembered Lester Peterson in an interview. "Even if there were language difficulties, they were always overcome in the building of community halls and the holding of dances and fairs and parties and Christmas parties and so on. And as long as that could possibly be maintained, it was."

Sadly, that spirit could not be maintained. The same litany of complications that had plagued the early colonists also afflicted this next wave of settlers. Transportation by boat was unpredictable and unsafe. The government, despite repeated entreaties, adamantly refused to build proper road connections (though it did install telegraph service and funded some road work between San Josef and Holberg). For the second time, economic survival proved well-nigh impossible.

Provincial records show that sixty people lived at Cape Scott in 1909 and as many as two hundred by 1913, when the population reached its peak. In the San Josef valley, where just about every quarter-section available for pre-emption was taken up, the numbers reached nearly five hundred. Altogether, about one thousand people occupied Vancouver Island's northwestern tip in 1913. But by 1917, when conscription was instituted for World War I, the region was virtually deserted once again.

In the San Josef and Sea Otter Cove areas, a Danish atmosphere was temporarily re-created. Former colonists were early home-steaders there, running the general store, the post offices and the local boat service. The *Cape Scott* and, later, the *Cape Scott II* connected Quatsino Sound villages such as Holberg, on its long, protected arm, to the settled coves and bays around the northern coast. Now this small logging centre, named after famous eighteenth-century Danish historian and dramatist Baron Ludwig Holberg, is the only village of consequence in the entire district.

The Cape Scott saga was not completely over, though. In the meadows, the grasses regained their tangled freedom. In lonely clearings, where human voices once rang out, the rainforest crowded in. Cougars could once more make tracks across the sand neck without fear of falling into the Fredericksen children's homemade trap. The last few homesteaders were driven half-mad by the promised, absent road; at the archives, a fat file of angry letters gathered dust. But the wild tip of Vancouver Island, jutting far out into the Pacific Ocean, still had strategic value. And with the arrival of World War II, the Canadian military decided that it was time to take advantage of Cape Scott's key location.

Today, just east of the sand neck, several decaying cabins and the vestiges of a plank road testify to a no-longer-very-secret radar station. In 1942, when the site was under construction, radar was a new technology; the installation was strictly off-limits to the area's few visitors.

A modern-day hiker to Cape Scott Provincial Park examines a few of the metal artifacts that still litter the main settlement area beside the trail to Hansen Lagoon. (Andrew Scott)

After the war the post was abandoned, but northern Vancouver Island was not forgotten. In the early 1950s, three unusual towers bearing great white spheres were erected atop 624-metre-high Mount Brandes, just west of Holberg. At the foot of adjacent Mount Hansen, an airforce base sprang up—RCAF Station Holberg, later known simply as San Josef. The mysterious balls were revealed to be part of the Pinetree Line, a Cold War radar network designed to warn North America of potential U.S.S.R. bomber attacks. The station became obsolete almost as soon as it was built, and was closed in 1991.

Nowadays, the large, manned lighthouse station, built in 1960 on the very tip of the Cape Scott promontory, forms a more contemporary bastion of defence—against wind and water instead of communism. In 1971, as a B.C. centennial project, Holberg base personnel began an arduous task: reopening the historic settlers' trail from Holberg to Cape Scott. In 1973, B.C. dedicated a fifteen-thousand-hectare swath of rugged coast and upland as Cape Scott Provincial Park. Two decades later, almost a thousand hikers a year struggle over the trail to experience the cape's perennial fog, walk the lighthouse station's slick wooden walkways and dramatic suspension bridge, and laugh at the signpost with the arrow pointing to Peking.

While harmful to the Danish settlers, the Semlin government's perfidy and the stubborn intransigence of succeeding provincial administrations have left the rest of us a fine legacy. A road would have changed everything. For now Cape Scott will remain as it is: an exclamation mark in B.C.'s maritime wilderness, a point that rewards many times over the effort of getting there. The preservation of this beautiful, remote refuge, site of so much pioneer energy, seems appropriate. At Cape Scott, one can commune with nature—and also with the high ideals, commitment and integrity of those who lived here long ago.

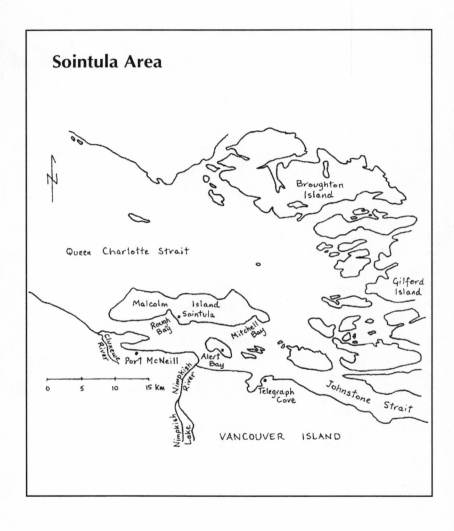

Sointula Area

Broughton Island

Queen Charlotte Strait

Gilford Island

Malcolm Island
Sointula
Rough Bay
Mitchell Bay

Cluxewe River

Port McNeill

Alert Bay

Johnstone Strait

Nimpkish River

Telegraph Cove

0   5   10   15 km

Nimpkish Lake

VANCOUVER ISLAND

HARMONY ISLAND
The Finnish Colony of Sointula

*Come here to live with us in freedom, where all
are equal in the harmony of shared thoughts, and all find
satisfaction and pleasure in the protection of the weak.*
—Matti Kurikka, *Aika,* 1901

A young woman comes up as I stand with my wife beside our car, waiting to board the little ferry that connects the industrial Vancouver Island town of Port McNeill with Malcolm and Cormorant islands.

"You must be the writer," she says.

"How did you know that?" I stammer, taken by surprise.

"Well, it's not tourist season, and you two are obviously not from around here," she replies. "People know that some guy is coming to do an article on us and take photographs."

I'm astounded. The cliché is true: in a small place, everyone does know everyone else's business. I'd made a few phone calls the previous week, arranging to meet people and setting up interviews for a magazine assignment. Word had gone around.

In my confusion, I ask a dumb question: "How do you feel about having a journalist here?"

The woman looks away for a moment, her gaze resting on the dark waters of Broughton Strait, then she turns back and meets my eye.

"We don't mind," she says. She shrugs her shoulders and smiles. "I guess we're used to it."

I am the latest in a long line of writers to visit Sointula, an unlikely settlement founded in 1901 on remote Malcolm Island by a group of hardy, idealistic Finnish immigrants. A little research will uncover historical studies in academic quarterlies and a long article in the popular journal *Raincoast Chronicles*. In 1958, the same year Sointulan Aili Anderson published a hometown account, prolific Vancouver author George Woodcock contributed an essay on Malcolm Island to a B.C. centennial anthology. In 1995, the most complete version of all— *Sointula: Island Utopia*—appeared, written by former resident Paula Wild, who conducted dozens of interviews and had many documents translated from Finnish.

Of all the attempts in British Columbia to form a utopian or ideal community, Sointula may be the best known. Perhaps this is because the gossipy reputation it earned earlier in the century as a colony of fierce and possibly pagan freethinkers still lingers. Perhaps it's because, unlike most other utopian efforts, Sointula is intact, its ethnic heritage still evident in its residents' surnames and their backyard saunas. The colony may have failed, but the individuals and their descendants stayed on.

Today, Sointula, which means "place of harmony" in Finnish, is a bright, modern fishing port. In contrast to the gloomy towns on the northeastern shore of nearby Vancouver Island, its oceanfront setting faces west, smack into the setting sun. The air is fresh and rich, with a tang of seaweed. Neat white cottages are set on a rectangular street grid, and the pebble beach is lined with weathered boat sheds, net lofts and small fishing craft in varying states of repair.

The forested bulk of Malcolm Island protects the village from the bitter prevailing winds that slice out of Knight Inlet to the east, where Mount Waddington, B.C.'s highest mountain south of the Alaska border, reigns. From the north side of the island, you can see seventeen-hundred-metre Mount Stephens on the mainland; to the south, Vancouver Island's Karmutzen Range surges to fifteen hundred metres. Despite its idyllic site, enough westerlies soak Sointula to ensure that Rough Bay, the body of water it faces, is appropriately named. Rough or calm, seven times a day, the twenty-seven-vehicle ferry *Quadra Queen II* makes the twenty-five-minute crossing to Port McNeill.

No other place in British Columbia is remotely like this Finnish settlement by the sea. Sointula's inhabitants have managed, through many changes, to keep spinning a thread of continuity with the old days; strong roots—both Finnish and utopian—connect the village with its unusual past. There is a genuine pride of place here, persistent but not showy, and it's easy to find residents who speak with respect and wonder of the village founders and their brave ideas. Sointula's peaceful appearance and unusual history are beginning to attract a few tourists, allowing several bed and breakfast operations to flourish. But Sointula has yet to become a household name, and that's the way most residents would like to keep it.

About one thousand people claim Sointula as home; another five hundred or so are scattered elsewhere on Malcolm Island, most of them in the hamlets of Kaleva and Mitchell Bay. There is no hard data on the percentage of the population that can still claim Finnish ancestry, but half a dozen knowledgeable people I ask each guess that the figure would be fifty percent or more. A flip through the telephone book reveals a slew of Finnish names—Aro, Harju, Pakkalen, Rihtamo, Siider, Tarkanen, Tynjala, Vuorela—but does not tell the whole story, as other descendants of the original settlers have married non-Finns or anglicized their surnames. Fourth- and fifth-generation Finns abound in the village, though second-generation residents such

The afternoon sun catches the heritage boatsheds that line the pebble beaches of Rough Bay and are still used by members of Malcolm Island's active fishing industry. (Shiane Scott)

as Tauno Salo—or Ray, as he was known to most people, having adopted a North American nickname—were rare indeed.

Salo, who died not long after our interview, lived with his wife Ruth in a tidy beachfront cottage. He is one of the people I'd phoned and arranged to interview. We sit at the dining-room table, bathed in late-September afternoon sunshine, while he tells me a little about his life on the coast as a logger, lighthouse-keeper, pilot and outdoorsman. Although his body is bent from a recent hip operation, and his face furrowed like that of an aged elf, Salo's voice is strong and clear, his stories studded with dates and names and vivid details now decades old. He was born in Sointula in 1912, and he seems to me to embody the spirit of a small community that has thrived against many odds for nearly a century.

Salo gazes out the window intently, as if the past is as bright as the prospect. "Oh, I had several close calls," he remembers. "I shouldn't be alive to talk about them." Like the time he was out on the float of his '46 Luscombe, stalled in the middle of nowhere, trying to crank the propeller from behind. The seaplane somehow started up full throttle and began to take off, slamming the door closed in the process. Desperate but determined, Salo managed to climb back along the float, force open the door and cut the engine just before he became airborne.

From our dining-room seats, we can see all the way up Broughton Strait to a point on Vancouver Island called Cluxewi, where Salo's parents homesteaded ninety-five years ago, before they came to Sointula in 1903, less than two years after it was founded. Arriving just after the colony's birth pangs, they were pioneers in every sense of the word. But to glimpse the true origins of Sointula's story we need to go back in time even earlier, and head further south, down the coast to Nanaimo.

In the late 1800s, the great coal mines around Nanaimo were always in need of labourers. Even though the underground work was dangerous and wages were low, a constant stream of hard-up immigrants poured into the area, driven by economic desperation. B.C.'s forest industry was still in its infancy at this time, and the mines were one of the few places on the south coast where regular employment could be found. Among the migrant workmen was a group of Finns.

The Finns had played a minor but significant role in the great nineteenth-century Scandinavian exodus to the New World. Like their

Norwegian, Swedish, Danish and Icelandic compatriots, they were mainly rural peasants and artisans. Their language, however, set them apart: Finnish is unlike any other modern European tongue except Estonian. In North America, the Finns were not numerous enough to try to settle in large, co-operative groups (only 85,000 had emigrated by 1900, compared to 172,000 Danes, 367,000 Norwegians and 635,000 Swedes). In any case, most had left Finland late in the emigration sweepstakes; the best homestead lands had already been staked out by the time they arrived.

The immigrants brought with them a strong sense of ethnic identity. Despite the fact that Finland was a "grand duchy" of Russia for most of the nineteenth century, Finnish nationalism had grown strong. After wresting its new domain from Sweden in 1809 after 250 years of sporadic warfare, Russia had granted Finland substantial autonomy, and Finnish gradually supplanted Swedish as the territory's language.

Finnish national pride was boosted by the 1835 publication of the *Kalevala,* a twelve-thousand-line epic folk poem composed by small-town doctor and scholar Elias Lonnrot. Named after a mythical land of heroes and created from hundreds of runes or song-poems that Lonnrot had painstakingly gathered, the *Kalevala* gained great fame. It prompted a patriotic movement similar to the one in Denmark that had been fostered by Nikolaj Grundtvig's folk schools and inspired by Norse legends.

Patriotism, alas, could not feed the Finns. Agricultural modernization and the widespread development of forestry arrived too late for a burgeoning number of farm workers. Unemployment and a severe famine struck the country in the 1860s, and the first emigrants began to find their way across the Atlantic. In the 1890s and 1900s, as Russia's policy towards Finland changed and hardened, eventually culminating in press censorship and mandatory conscription, this initial trickle broadened into a stream.

In North America, most Finns were forced to take poorly paid labouring jobs, often as miners or loggers. Hundreds of Finnish immigrants who came to Canada in the early 1880s ended up working on the Canadian Pacific railroad. But by 1886, the rails had been laid, the jobs disappeared and many workers drifted to B.C.'s shores and the grim reality of James Dunsmuir's mines. Dunsmuir, a politician as well as a coal magnate and the province's premier from 1900 to 1902, was an enormously powerful individual who exerted absolute control over the lives of his employees.

Working underground was a kind of hell. During the early 1900s, one miner was killed for every forty thousand tonnes of coal produced in B.C. As he descended each day into the bowels of the earth, each man must have wondered if he would see the light again. And if he did, he had other problems. His housing was inadequate. He was expected to move, and to buy a housing plot from the company, each time a new mine was opened. Drinking and fighting were the only entertainments available. Alcohol consumption was actually encouraged by mine owners, in the belief that it would prevent the miners from organizing. Beer was delivered to the camps, and workers could charge purchases against their pay. Any attempts to improve conditions or raise wages were ruthlessly suppressed.

British Columbia's Finnish miners spent a lot of time together; perhaps their linguistic isolation stimulated a certain solidarity. Desperate to improve their lot, one group living at Wellington, near Nanaimo, formed a temperance society called Lännen Rusko ("western glow") in 1890. The following year, another society, Allotar ("water nymph"), was organized. The societies aimed to provide for ill and injured miners, discourage alcohol use and unite the Finnish community. Allotar, in particular, was very successful and soon had a meeting hall, reading room and library. It even supported a brass band.

Many Finns were literate men who received publications from home and discussed the social issues of the day. They were aware of major changes occurring back in Finland. During the 1890s, Russia gradually increased its control of the duchy, annulling Finnish laws, forcing some departments to use the Russian language and overseeing others, such as the post office, directly from St. Petersburg. At the same time, a network of popular, effective Finnish labour organizations had rapidly formed, as well as an underground independence movement. The progressive strides being taken in their homeland must have made the dismal working conditions of B.C.'s Finnish miners seem even worse by comparison.

The Nanaimo temperance societies represented a cultural breakthrough for the Finns, enabling them to gain a few basic creature comforts and some self-respect through co-operative effort. But their dissatisfaction with work also grew, and they yearned to leave the coal mines.

Influenced by news from home, they talked about how they might establish an independent socialist community. A group of miners became committed to this idea and began to cast around for a leader who could turn their dreams into reality.

For North America's immigrants, the 1890s were an era of hope and high expectations. A breath of change was in the air: dreams *could* turn into reality. The idealistic theories of European social and political thinkers were popular and widely known. The concept of private property had been vehemently decried as obsolete by anarchist Pierre Joseph Proudhon; Karl Marx and Friedrich Engels had called for their working-class revolt.

The Finns at Nanaimo were aware of the ideas of Charles Fourier, a French social theorist who had suggested that small, co-operative agricultural communities called phalansteries, where work and profit were shared equally, would be the wave of the future. One had already been attempted at Brook Farm in the eastern United States and attracted such well-known New Englanders as Hawthorne, Emerson and Thoreau. Other well-publicized socialist experiments—Etienne Cabet's Icaria, Robert Owen's New Harmony, and Oneida, founded by John Humphrey Noyes—had also sprung up in this region.

The belief that a deliberate reorganization of society could give rise to human fulfillment and social harmony fired many newcomers to Canada. Today's sufferings, they considered, might well lead to a brighter tomorrow. Given the great empty expanses of the Canadian west, they were eager to test their theories and plant the seeds of a new order. Even as the Finns were discussing their future, other Scandinavian immigrants were already hard at work at Hagensborg, Quatsino and Cape Scott.

In their deliberations, the Finns had been impressed with the writings of Matti Kurikka, an eloquent playwright and former editor of the influential Helsinki labour daily *Työmies,* founded in 1895. Apprehensive about Russia's intentions, Kurikka had left Finland in 1899 to found a model socialist society in Australia. His brand of socialism owed more to the New Testament and to the budding doctrines of the theosophical movement than it did to Marx: he believed that love, justice, personal freedom and harmony with nature could create a new world. Although deeply committed to the working-class movement, he eschewed violence. His Christian idealism, however, did not prevent him from adopting a fervidly anti-clerical attitude. He wished to live, he wrote, "away from priests who have defiled the high morals of Christianity, away from churches that destroy peace, away from all the evils of the outside world."

Australia did not turn out to be that place. The colony never got off the ground. Three of its members who moved from Australia to British Columbia brought news of Kurikka's difficulties to the Nanaimo socialists, who promptly invited him to lead a new settlement on the B.C. coast. Kurikka agreed. Funds were raised for his passage, and in August 1900 he came ashore at Nanaimo and assumed the presidency of the hastily formed Kalevan Kansan Colonization Company. Matti Kurikka was divorced from his wife and about thirty-seven years old at the time of his arrival. A tall, handsome man with thick dark hair, stylish beard, flashing eyes and abundant charisma, he made a strong impression on the local Finnish community.

Over the next fifteen months, Kurikka and his supporters drummed up support for the colony and dickered with B.C. over a land grant. Kalevan Kansan members were expected to purchase a $200 share in the company to help raise operating capital. Many Finns, of course, did not have this kind of money and either made a $50 down payment or guaranteed to pay for shares with their labour. In Victoria, Kurikka examined maps of Crown land and determined that Malcolm Island might make a good settlement spot.

Without even visiting the site, Kurikka approached the government about settling Malcolm Island, only to find that it was part of a huge timber lease recently awarded, under giveaway terms, to a pulp company. The Finns arranged to log the island for the company under contract and continued to lobby for a land grant. The Semlin administration, which had cancelled further land grants to the Scandinavians at Cape Scott and Quatsino, was no longer in office; the government headed by coal baron Dunsmuir appeared to be better disposed towards the idea of immigrant colonies. The Finns were "industrious, frugal and easily contented people," according to the Victoria *Daily Colonist*. Fears about land ownership by non-English-speaking immigrants were still strong, but there was sympathy for the Finnish bid.

An old press that had belonged to the defunct *Nanaimo Review* was purchased, and Kurikka began to produce a weekly Finnish newspaper called *Aika* ("time"). *Aika* publicized the colonists' plans and helped attract prospective members. It soon had subscribers in Finland, Australia and the U.S. as well as Canada. "The only road to a better life," wrote Kurikka in an early issue, "lies in co-operation, love and generosity." British Columbia's Finns, he believed, "would show the way to freedom for the working class." Not all B.C. Finns were thrilled with the colonists and their leader, however. Some were devout Lutherans; stung by Kurikka's attacks on organized religion, they viewed him as dangerous and evil.

Kurikka was a passionate, impetuous man. Perhaps realizing that he needed a calm, dependable lieutenant to counterbalance his energies, he arranged for his friend and former co-worker Austin Mäkelä to be brought over from Finland. Kurikka clearly believed that once the colony got rolling, the Finnish population would show up on its doorstep *en masse*. "To have a home is the Utopia of a Finlander," he declared. "Once this model is seen, people can no longer continue their former lives, but will hasten to join us."

Finally, on November 29, 1901, the province granted Malcolm Island to the group on condition that they find 350 settlers to build homes, improve the land to the tune of $2.50 per acre, construct their own roads, wharf and public buildings, become British subjects and educate their children in English. If these terms were met, legal title to the island would be conferred after seven years and an additional, similar grant of land would be made.

To Kurikka and his followers, Malcolm Island must have seemed custom-made for their purposes. About twenty-four kilometres long and four kilometres wide, with an area of more than eleven thousand hectares, it was large enough for future growth and flat enough for agriculture. There was game, timber, good fishing, ample water (Sointula's artesian-well water is still delicious today), a decent harbour—and isolation. Located three hundred kilometres northwest of Vancouver, the colony would be far removed from the distractions and conventions of civilization, yet reasonably close to shipping routes.

The first five colonists—one of whom had to be sent immediately to Nanaimo after suffering an accidental shotgun blast to his arm—arrived at the island in mid-December. As they started to clear land and build cabins, they soon found the abandoned settlement attempts of earlier visitors. In 1895, an English cleric named Joseph Spencer had tried to found a commune at Rough Bay under the auspices of the Christian Temperance Commonwealth Society. His followers barged in a sawmill and steam plant, but the venture only lasted a few months. A Danish hermit named Elliman had survived on the island until the summer of 1901.

The Finnish settlers also saw signs that Kwakw<u>a</u>ka'wakw families had camped on Malcolm Island: shell middens, cedars stripped of their bark, axe heads and other tools, petroglyphs. In summer, small bands canoed there to gather seaweed and fish for halibut and salmon. There was little need to raise a permanent village, as the rich Nimpkish River salmon runs on nearby Vancouver Island furnished aboriginal people with nearly all the food they needed. In 1890, a native group from Fort Rupert had been refused a land grant on the island by the government.

Many Finns arrived at Malcolm Island in the spring of 1902, and another large group showed up to celebrate the summer solstice in June. By that time, the colony had 127 adult members, mostly living in tents. It was decided to locate the village on Rough Bay and name it Sointula instead of Kodiksi (or "home place"), an alternative sugges-tion. A board of directors was elected, with Kurikka as president, Mäkelä as secretary and Oswald Beckman, the colony's doctor, as vice-president and manager. Labour issues were debated and rules set out: eight-hour shifts would be assigned by elected organizers; men and women would be treated equally.

From the outset, Sointula was dedicated to the ideals of equality and co-operation. Everyone pitched in. Everyone ate communally. Although Kurikka was the undisputed leader, decisions were only taken after full and often lengthy discussion. Self-sufficiency was the immediate aim: the Finns hunted, began to raise stock, made shoes and clothes, started a smithy and foundry and a brickworks, gathered salal berries and processed dogfish oil for lamps. Over the summer and fall of 1902, several communal structures were erected, including a large three-storey building with twenty-eight sleeping rooms and a meeting hall, irreverently named Melula, or "noisy."

The colony's principles appealed especially to the women. "At that time women had no property rights," said Kaisa Riksman, who arrived in Sointula as a young mother in June 1902. "They had no rights what-soever in wages, so this was one thing that was applied here."

Interviewed by Imbert Orchard for an oral history project that would eventually result in the book *Dreams of Freedom*, she described the colonists' unattainable vision:

> *They were going to share everything. Everyone would be working for the common good. No one owned anything separately and individually. They planned to farm and log, and all the proceeds would be divided equally.*
>
> *I think the main idea was to have a free society. Especially, they emphasized that women should have equal rights with men.... The women had a dollar a day wages, as the men did, and they had a right to speak at meetings, and they had a right to vote. And they had to work. Everyone had to work.*
>
> *The company was to look after all the children—all the expenses, clothing, food and schooling. No one would be charged extra for children. The idea was that later on the children would be the workers and they would look after the elders.*

Despite its fellowship and apparent advantages, the colony soon ran into difficulties. The newcomers were not really suited to the work at hand. Until sufficient land had been prepared for farming, they proposed to cover their expenses by harvesting and selling the two commodities abundantly close at hand—fish and timber. They needed

A postcard of Sointula's main street, dated about 1912, shows the colony's cows taking full advantage of their relative freedom. The building at the far left is the old schoolhouse. (Author's collection)

fishermen and loggers, therefore, but only miners, writers, farmers and craftsmen were available. What they lacked in experience, though, the colonists made up for in determination. Slow progress was made clearing land, and a small sawmill was constructed.

A more serious problem was money. Kurikka was desperate to attract settlers with funds, but those without money were never turned away. At one point, he had been willing to strike a deal with James Dunsmuir whereby colonists would be hired for the coal mines at less than the going rate, with part of their pay diverted directly to Kalevan Kansan. The company's board of directors soon aborted that plan. Ironically, the fledgling socialist utopia received its supplies by virtue of credit extended by Vancouver merchants. "We were always in the same predicament," recalled Mäkelä in an interview years later. "Purchases had to be made first, and payments dragged ever further and further behind." The colony's indebtedness mounted rapidly, soon exceeding $60,000.

Agricultural progress was painfully slow. Even after two years, the only crop grown was potatoes. Most provisions, including hay for the few cows still alive after a winter without shelter, had to be imported. By November 1902, two hundred people were living on Malcolm Island. The comings and goings of hundreds of other visitors attracted by *Aika*'s misleading optimism—some, as predicted by Kurikka, arriving directly from Finland—put a heavy stress on the inadequate stock of food and housing. Then, on January 29, 1903, tragedy struck.

Just after 8:00 p.m., while fifty-three colonists were crowded into Melula's third-floor meeting hall and eighty-four more, mostly women and children, were in the sleeping rooms, someone noticed a burning smell. As people rushed downstairs, they encountered thick smoke. Within minutes, the draughty, wooden building was an inferno and a desperate scene ensued. Adults threw children from windows, then jumped themselves, their hair and clothes ablaze.

"I jumped out of bed and looked around to see what I would take," remembered Kaisa Riksman, "and then realized that I could only take the children. So I took one under each arm and I went out." Some of her neighbours were not so lucky; eleven people died in the holocaust—eight children and three adults. The colony also lost most of its supplies and papers. A large oven, used for baking and heating, had probably ignited a wooden hot-air flue to cause the disaster.

Many settlers grew disheartened and bitter after this setback, some even accusing Kurikka of deliberately setting the fire. Angry words became frequent in the place of harmony. Kurikka's personality did not help. He was dynamic but arrogant. His opinions, although articulate, were fanatically held. He was incapable of soothing his flock's pains, and disillusioned members began to protest and criticise his leadership.

The colonists pulled themselves together and struggled on. Melula was replaced with several smaller buildings. The sawmill, which everyone agreed was the most likely source of much-needed revenue, was expanded, and a tug was acquired. Men and equipment were barged to Knight and Kingcome inlets on the mainland to cut wild grass for livestock. A press was set up, and the publication of *Aika* resumed. In the evenings, some colonists held classes and discussions, while others read plays, sang in a choir or played in a band. By the spring of 1903, the community's population was 238.

Even though Malcolm Island's fame spread, especially among Finns (a California commune named itself after Sointula), the cracks in the colony were growing wider. One appeared over the institution

The cultural life of Sointula was not neglected. In this 1903 photo, bandmaster Voitt Peippo sits in front of his numerous fellow musicians. (University of British Columbia, Special Collections)

of marriage. Kurikka believed that marriage was a form of slavery and enforced morality; he held that women should be encouraged to bear children out of wedlock and raise them communally. Not surprisingly, his ideas were too advanced for the colony's married couples. In the minds of many outsiders, Sointula developed a reputation as a godless and unbridled place of free love and heathenism. They were mistaken, however; Kurikka's ideas were never put into practice.

In 1904, Kurikka made a successful bid to build two large wooden bridges over the Seymour and Capilano rivers in North Vancouver for the sum of three thousand dollars. After four months of logging, milling, barging and building, a dreadful fact became evident: the bid had been grotesquely low. It didn't even cover the cost of tools and equipment needed for the job. Such anger and demoralization followed this debacle that, in October 1904, Kurikka was forced to resign as leader and leave Sointula. At least half the colonists went with him.

At Webster's Corners, sixty kilometres east of Vancouver, Kurikka started a new utopian settlement in January 1905, called Sammon Takojat, which refers to a legend from the *Kalevala*. Sammon Takojat was a bachelor commune; its members lived together in one large cabin and eventually bought a farm. They cut shingle bolts for a contract Kurikka obtained, and also fished. But while Kurikka was away on a lecture and fund-raising tour, the bachelors decided that celibate life was no longer for them. They also sent a letter to their leader suggesting that he not bother to return.

Kurikka went to Finland, where his old socialist colleagues soon tired of him. He remarried, did some writing and editing, and pursued his interests in mysticism and astrology. In 1908, he and his new family emigrated to the U.S., where he lived modestly in Connecticut, raising chickens and writing for Finnish-American newspapers. He died in 1915. The colony at Webster's Corners lasted for seven years then disbanded, and the land was divided among the surviving members, who gave the district a Finnish flavour for many generations.

Those who remained on Malcolm Island elected Mäkelä as their leader and tried to keep the colony alive, but their efforts were doomed. Kaisa Riksman recalled the final collapse in the spring of 1905:

> *There were two sawmills and all these homes, and they had two boats—large boats—and all this was mortgaged. And finally,*

when they got a good load of lumber which they sent to Vancouver, the mortgage company took this load which was supposed to be sold to bring in enough money for them to live on until they were able to make more lumber.

But since this load was taken away from them, there was just no money. Everyone had to go out on their own, that's all there was to it. They couldn't go on as a community any more, or as they had before. They were bankrupt.

The mortgage company would have sold all this equipment back to them for $10,000, but they didn't have enough business heads, or people knowledgeable in business ways. They were disheartened too, by that time, some of them.

The Kalevan Kansan Colonization Company was dissolved in May 1905. About one hundred people, including Tauno Salo's parents, bought individual lots and stayed on Malcolm Island to homestead.

"People were more independent after the colony broke up," recalls Salo, as we sit in his sunny dining room, "but they were still very cooperative. The hall was constructed with volunteer work. The graveyard was done co-operatively. And there's the co-op store yet." Today, the big, cream-coloured Sointula Co-operative Store opposite the ferry dock is the heart of the community. The bustling co-op and the aging Finnish Organization Hall—site of thousands of meetings, dances, performances and weddings—dominate the village landscape.

In Philip Au's office at the back of the co-op hangs a series of black-and-white photographs showing the store's evolution from its humble, one-room beginnings to its present 350-member magnificence. Au manages the credit union as well as the co-op, and at the time of my visit, he and his family are Sointula's only Chinese Canadians. After twenty-eight years on the island, they are as much a part of the community as any non-Finn could expect—but still newcomers.

As Au points out, the store, founded in 1909, lays claim to being the longest continuously operating co-operative in Canada, and its two warehouselike floors stock just about everything anyone could possibly need to eke a living from the coastal wilderness. Legal alcohol, however, only arrived recently. Like many communities on the coast, Sointula has had a love/hate relationship with the demon booze.

The annual co-op meeting was never better attended than in 1985, when it was proposed, successfully, to add a liquor outlet.

Independence and co-operation are the twin poles of life on Malcolm Island. Both are necessary for survival, as every fisherman knows, and despite the recent chaos in the industry, fishing is still how Sointula makes its living today. The fleet, snug in its fine, artificial harbour, numbers several dozen gillnetters and trollers and a few big seiners; it goes after herring in spring and halibut whenever it can. The big fall salmon season is halfway through on my last visit. Business is good. Everyone is out: the husband-and-wife teams, the female skippers, a man and his dog. Along the shore, businesses are sorting and carrying off the silver torrent, and people in pickups are racing around with nets and supplies.

Sointula's fishermen got their start renting skiffs from the Rivers Inlet canneries, 120 kilometres to the north, for the short summer season. Commercial fishing suited the Finns, and they began to build their own boats. A row of boatyards soon lined Rough Bay. A Malcolm Islander, Laurie Jarvis (formerly Jarvelainen), built and patented the first gillnet drum, a design that revolutionized the industry. In the 1920s, Finns played an important role in the coast's first fishing unions and co-ops. The United Fishermen of B.C. and the B.C. Fishermen's Co-operative Association were both based at Sointula.

Indeed, the village became famous up and down the coast for its left-wing politics. Sointulans were very active in the Socialist Party of Canada. The Finnish Organization of Canada, to which nearly everyone on Malcolm Island belonged, became affiliated with the Communist Party of Canada; at one point virtually all adult Sointulans were card-carrying Communists. Despite Sointula's union heritage, many fishing boat owners have recently gone independent or joined separate gillnetters' and trollers' associations. A long strike in 1989 created friction and bitterness among the various groups, sometimes pitting father against son and brother against brother.

In the early days, about the only other employment available besides fishing was with one of the coastal logging outfits. Arvo Tynjala recalled some of his forestry experiences in *Dreams of Freedom*:

> *We used to go from Sointula with rowboats all the way down to Seymour Narrows on this side and into the different inlets and*

islands, sometimes hundreds of miles looking for jobs.

*They were hard years and there weren't too many jobs open.
In many cases they would prefer the men that came from town,
because they had no boat to row away in if they got into trouble.
We were kind of independent you know.*

*The conditions in those days were awful as far as living quar-
ters go. The loggers carried their own blankets and bedclothes,
and there was nothing in the bunkhouses but the mattresses and
bedbugs. There were plenty of them!*

Traditionally, many Malcolm Island men left the island to work,
while the women laboured at home. "You learned how to be handy,
both men and women, and how to do a variety of things—or you did-
n't survive," explains Gloria Williams, a third-generation Finn whose
husband's original family name was Honkala. Women provided much
of the energy for the volunteer groups that kept the social fabric woven
with cultural activities. They also provided services for the sick and the
aged. Willie Olney, a senior newcomer with thirty-two years' residen-
cy, established the little museum in the old schoolhouse, which also
shelters a library, preschool and thrift store. Many Finns have worked
hard to keep Sointula's heritage alive, and the links with the past have
given the village an ageless quality. "Time is not important here," says
Williams, "but the tides and the weather are."

Sointula's young adults are concerned that they will be the last
generation with a deep connection to that past. Gloria Williams'
daughters, who understand some Finnish but cannot speak it, are in
their thirties now, with young families of their own. They were raised
in a community with recognizable Finnish traditions, but their children are growing up in a much more diverse, global culture. "I'm still
interested in the history," says Audrey Williams, Gloria's younger
daughter, "but I worry that the interest is eventually going to die out
with my daughter's generation."

Perhaps the village needs more parties. Sointula may have been
isolated, but that did not mean its inhabitants were unable to entertain
themselves. Accounts of village history are full of stories of dances and
performances. May Day was a major celebration. "We had no car to
run around the streets with," remembered old-timer Ole Anderson in
an archival interview. "There were no streets. So we just had to make

our own fun. I don't think there was a night in the week that there wasn't something doing at that hall. There was athletic practice or song practice or show rehearsals; you name it. There was a show there just about every Saturday."

As well as trying to stay true to its past, Malcolm Island has also tried to welcome newcomers eager to take up island life. For most of this century, Sointula remained a vibrant but solitary ethnic enclave where Finnish was the official language. That segregation came to an end in the late 1960s and early 1970s, when a wave of young idealists from urban Canada and war resisters from the United States showed up.

Some old-timers would have you think that "the hippies" got off the ferry just yesterday instead of over twenty-five years ago, but the newcomers have earned a cautious respect. They brought useful skills and enthusiasms, and their outlook on life was curiously similar to that of the islanders: socialistic, self-sufficient, independent. Many came for the same reasons as the original Finns. They also brought with them, unintentionally, the end of an era. No longer could residents take short-cuts home over just anyone's property. The old ways had changed forever.

Sointula's perch at the edge of civilization may be a boon for fishers and loggers, but it also attracts those keen to record the beauty of wild nature. Malcolm Island artist Robert Field, for instance, who once held a major Vancouver Art Gallery exhibition under the name of R. Fish, has a passion for Pisces. He paints fish, makes prints of fish, sculpts fish—all of them marvels of detail and expression. When I talk to painter Stewart Marshall, he tells me about the four-month kayak trip to Bella Bella and back to Sointula he has just completed, one of his shorter ventures. The fifty-three-year-old Montreal native, who now lives in the Queen Charlottes, was based for years on Malcolm Island. A well-known solo sailor and paddler, he explores the B.C. coast in gleaming wooden kayaks he builds himself, camping, living off the land and crafting watercolour landscapes that sell worldwide.

With such an infusion of outsiders, Sointula has become a community made up of smaller communities: Finns and non-Finns, old-timers and new arrivals, socialists and capitalists, environmentalists and loggers, fishers and shoreworkers, union members and non-members. Political debate thrives. Today's inhabitants no longer have the hammer and sickle carved on their tombstones, as did a few early colonists. Instead, a variety of viewpoints prevails. As in the old days, however, everyone's business is discussed at length. Informal groups can be found pro and con a wide range of topics: tourism, for instance, or incorporation as a village.

The community has a settlement plan that stresses slow growth, rural values and cottage industries. Rezoning and subdivisions have to be approved by a Malcolm Island Advisory Planning Commission. But you only have to compare the clean air of Broughton Strait to the permanent haze of the Strait of Georgia to the southeast to guess what's in store. Island building lots are selling steadily. Tourism figures are up; bed and breakfast resorts and fishing lodges are following along behind. B.C.'s population will inevitably expand northwards, and Malcolm Island, as a very pleasant spot on a hard-to-get-at shoreline, is already receiving its fair share of attention.

But for now, anyway, Sointula is still on the frontier. There is no community of comparable size north of here until Bella Bella, two hundred kilometres up the coast. And with their backs turned firmly on the cities, it's to the north that Sointula's residents look for their future. The fishers and loggers, especially, know the network of inlets and passages that forms the central B.C. coast. Tauno Salo, for one, hunted seal and cougar for bounty here during the Depression. He fished Rivers Inlet in the glory years, when up to fifteen hundred skiffs at a time would be setting gillnets by hand for the huge sockeye salmon runs. He towed his logging float camp up the channels and flew his floatplane over the sounds.

Despite the inevitable setbacks, the waters and forests of this isolated piece of British Columbia coastline continue to provide a good living for those who remain here. "If I had to live my life over again," Tauno Salo once told me, "I'd do exactly the same things as this time." But would the place still be the same? The Sointula of Salo's memory has earned a legendary niche in the culture and history of the B.C. coast. Yet despite its vitality and its deep roots, this Finnish fishing village of strong-willed socialists and utopian pioneers is slowly fading, like an aging photograph from another era.

The Boundary and West Kootenay Areas

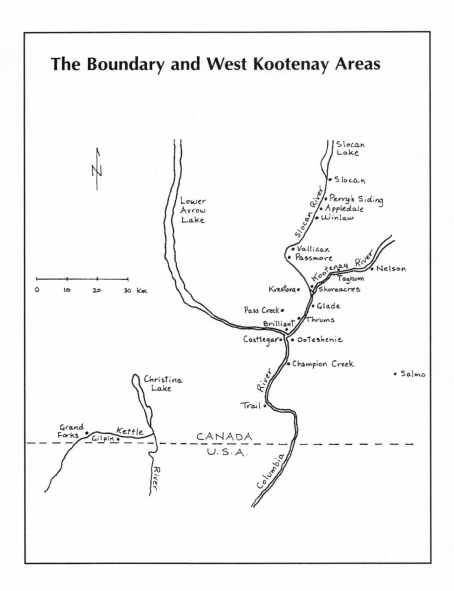

ALL THINGS STRIVE
FOR PERFECTION
The Story of the Doukhobors

*Our mortal body is not man; man is spirit
in the flesh with celestial divine intelligence.*
—from Doukhobor psalm,
"Our Heavenly Father"

On a distant hillside, the midsummer sun has turned the grass to gold. We can see the weathered vestiges of a brave experiment: a two-storey building, sturdy and square with a wide verandah and exterior facings of brick. Once it had served as the heart of a village collective, home to fifty people or more, part of a bold attempt at communal living. Such buildings—in pairs or alone—used to be a common sight through British Columbia's West Kootenays. Only a handful have survived. None fulfills its former function. But this house, high above the irrigated fields and orchards of West Grand Forks, has been saved as a museum. It tells the troubled story of an extraordinary group of Canadians: the Doukhobors.

The Mountainview Doukhobor Museum is the private initiative of Peter Gritchen, a Doukhobor performer of Russian folk music with five albums to his credit. "I figured at least one original village should be preserved," he explains, directing me around the ground floor, now walled into rooms and full of artifacts. In its heyday, this level would have consisted of just two simple spaces: a meeting area and a huge cooking and eating zone with benches at long tables and a great brick oven in the kitchen. Upstairs: four identical bedrooms on either side of a central hallway, eight in all, with curtains for doors. Home, sweet home.

Steamrooms for bathing and laundry, guesthouses, more bedrooms, barns, workshops and storage sheds originally surrounded the big houses. Each village occupied about forty hectares, most of which it farmed in field, root or orchard crops, including about a quarter-hectare kitchen garden. The Doukhobors, besides being pacifists who recognized no other authority than God, were ardent vegetarians. After years of persecution in Russia, nearly 7,500 members of the religious sect came to Canada in 1899 and spent a decade farming the Saskatchewan prairie. To secure final title to their land grants, they were required to sign an oath of allegiance to the Crown. Most refused, claiming the only allegiance possible for them was to God. Between 1908 and 1912, about 5,000 Doukhobors moved to B.C., planting orchards, growing crops and working together. They soon became self-sufficient.

Down the hill from Gritchen's museum, close to the old Doukhobor cemetery, I find the last remaining example of the sect's many communal economic enterprises: a 1915 flour mill, complete with miniature elevator. The original grinding stones sit out front, replaced with more up-to-date electric-powered machinery. Once a month, Wallace Dergousoff still fires up the small rolling and hammer mills and turns out enough Pride of the Valley flour, bran and "shorts" (sold as animal feed) to keep local health-food and specialty stores happy.

Dergousoff is not a miller by vocation. "It's just a machine," he says. "The question is how to get the best results." The mill has become a hobby, really—an anachronism. A plan is afoot to turn it into a modest heritage site and tourist attraction. But in the old days, it had been a busy place, centre of a small complex that included sheds for drying fruit and pressing flax, hemp and poppy seeds for their oil. And though the mill may be a curiosity, there is nothing substandard about the flour. Dergousoff proudly holds some of the additive-free wholewheat out in his hand. "You make pancakes from that," he jokes, "and they'll stay until noon."

The Doukhobors established other communal industries after arriving in B.C.: brickyards, sawmills and a very successful jam factory.

From a regional storehouse, each village drew the few supplies it couldn't manufacture or grow. Individuals rarely handled money. Villagers wore linen clothing made from flax grown in their own fields, irrigated with elaborate pipe and reservoir systems. Wary of government and the written word, they kept their faith alive by singing and passing down a body of Russian psalms and hymns that summed up their beliefs—a sort of living Bible.

Today, about thirty thousand Doukhobors are scattered across western Canada. A handful more live in California and Oregon. Most belong either to the formal Doukhobor organization—the Union of Spiritual Communities of Christ (USCC)—or are Independents, who respect and often follow the Doukhobor faith but have removed themselves to one degree or another from the USCC. Community Doukhobors make their homes throughout the Kootenays, with centres at the cities of Grand Forks, where the USCC headquarters is located, and Castlegar. The Sons of Freedom, a breakaway organization that renamed itself the Christian Community and Brotherhood

Mountainview Doukhobor Museum, a former village commune located in West Grand Forks, is one of the few original structures still standing from the sect's early days in British Columbia. (Andrew Scott)

of Reformed Doukhobors, claim a few hundred adherents, most of whom reside in the West Kootenay hamlets of Krestova and Gilpin.

For over fifty years, the Freedomites resisted what they perceived to be the materialism of the age. Guerilla tactics such as bombings, arson and public nudity punctuated the faction's sporadic but deeply felt campaign, scandalizing British Columbians, many of whom have unfairly tended to identify all Doukhobors with the splinter group. Community and Independent Doukhobors, however, are quick to point out that the Sons of Freedom represent a tiny minority of the sect's overall population. Newspaper editors still find it hard to resist using images of burning schools and naked protesters with any article on the Doukhobors. But the Freedomites are now an aging generation, and incidents are rare—though not unknown. (A Grand Forks resident heard a commotion and went outside recently to find his porch on fire and an elderly woman disrobing in his yard. Intending to torch the new home of USCC chairman John J. Verigin, she had mistaken her target.)

The Community Doukhobors are also aging, and their numbers are shrinking. They no longer live communally. Their leaders may have borne the name of Verigin for over a century, but today their grandchildren rarely speak Russian—a serious matter for a people whose spiritual integrity relies on the oral transmission of culture. Young Doukhobors are marrying outside the faith and becoming part of the Canadian melting pot. Middle-aged Doukhobors also resemble their non-Doukhobor neighbours, with regular houses and regular jobs. But their history—a strange, sad tale of prejudice, persecution, forced migration and exile—is anything but regular. And their future as a spiritual association, cultivating their own customs and beliefs, is in jeopardy.

A true tour of Doukhobor territory would have to take in large parts of Russia and its surrounding republics, where forty thousand more Doukhobors still survive. Because the sect sprang up among illiterate peasants in the Ukraine 350 years ago, no records or accounts exist of its early activities and little is known about its origins. Europe had been a hotbed of sectarian revolt throughout the Middle Ages, and many well-established groups had similar beliefs to the Doukhobors.

The first traces of Doukhobor lineage become discernible in the seventeenth century with a wandering preacher named Danilo Filippov. According to George Woodcock and Ivan Avakumovic, whose 1968 *The Doukhobors* remains the best book on the subject, Filippov rejected the Bible and church liturgy and taught that the truth was to be found instead in the holy spirit, which dwelt within each person—and especially within Danilo Filippov. Early Doukhobor teachers were probably followers of Filippov, and the first historical Doukhobor leader, Silvan Kolesnikov, who died in 1775, was certainly influenced by his ideas.

Kolesnikov encouraged the Doukhobors to maintain a low profile and practise their beliefs in private to avoid persecution. His successor, Ilarion Pobirokhin, was much less conciliatory, openly denouncing the ceremonies of the Russian Orthodox Church. Establishing his headquarters in Russia, in the village of Goreloye southeast of Moscow near Tambov, he set up a form of religious communism under his own authoritarian leadership and greatly expanded the sect's oral literature of hymns and psalms. His belligerent stance also attracted the government's notice. After announcing to the citizens of Tambov, for instance, that he had come to judge the world, Pobirokhin was judged instead and found worthy of exile to Siberia.

As converts to the Doukhobor cause grew in number, ecclesiastical authorities began to pay closer attention to the upstart group. An Orthodox archbishop, in fact, gave the dissidents their name in 1785. *Dukhobortsi* meant "spirit wrestlers." The word was intended to disparage the sect by identifying it as a band of heretics who fought against the holy spirit. But its members embraced the term. They were indeed fighters, they claimed, but only for God and Christianity, and against evil.

The Orthodox church saw them as a threat, which is not surprising, as the Doukhobors' creed seems designed to infuriate established powers. From their core belief—that God exists within each human being—it followed that there was no actual need for the church or the priesthood. Services, sacraments, festivals, symbols such as the cross—all were superfluous. Even the Bible was yesterday's wisdom, fixed in amber, obsolete. If people wanted to find the ultimate source of inspiration, they should look into their own hearts. The human conscience encompassed both heaven and hell.

Such schismatic doctrines led to heretical practices. The

Doukhobors did away with baptism and communion. They buried their dead with little ritual. They considered marriage a free union between consenting adults. They repudiated the right of the state to dictate their activities, particularly regarding conscription, the education of children, the swearing of oaths of allegiance and the registration of births, deaths and marriages. Pacifism, the strongest and longest lasting of their traditions, was an absolute necessity, given the fact that all humans harbour the divine spark.

In their spare meeting places, the Doukhobors displayed three simple ceremonial objects: a jug of water, a shaker of salt and a loaf of bread. Thus were life's basic elements symbolized. A deep bow, which acknowledged the holy spirit within each of their brethren—and has intriguing parallels with the Buddhist namaste or wâi—was one of their few rituals. At a Doukhobor prayer meeting, or molenie, the faith was affirmed through singing and chanting. At the subsequent community meeting, or sobranie, village affairs were decided by consensus, often after lengthy discussion.

The Doukhobors considered the human conscience to be of fundamental importance, but also valued dreams, prophecies and spontaneous acts, believing them to be divinely inspired. Music was of great significance, but in vocal, choral form only. The corpus of Doukhobor psalms and hymns, referred to as The Living Book, consisted mainly of anonymous folk compositions. Various leaders added to and changed the chants over the centuries, retaining the Christian substance but altering the form to reflect evolving circumstances. They often obscured words and ideas deliberately in order to protect the faith from prying, possibly hostile observers.

The Russian government found the Doukhobors' more aggressive attempts to reform and chastise the official church extremely annoying. The 1790s became a hard decade for the sect, marked by mass trials, cruel punishments, exile and dispersion. But in 1801, when the relatively enlightened Alexander I became tsar, their prospects began to improve. They were granted tracts of fertile land in a frontier zone near the Black and Azov seas, a region known as Milky Waters. Here, the authorities reasoned, even spirit wrestlers could cause no trouble.

With their communal ways, voluntary simplicity and appetite for work, the Doukhobors thrived at Milky Waters. Their motto, "toil and peaceful life," had finally come true. But on the deaths of Alexander and their latest leader, Savelii Kapustin, their fortunes changed. The new tsar, Nicholas I, opposed leniency for dissident groups. Kapustin's son and grandson, who succeeded him as the next two Doukhobor leaders, turned out to be degenerate drunkards. And what had once been the frontier was now attracting Russian settlers, followers of the Orthodox church.

In 1841, Nicholas gave the Doukhobors an ultimatum: join the church or move to a new frontier region beyond the Caucasus Mountains. Almost to the last individual, they moved. And though the climate and terrain at their journey's end were inhospitable, a stalwart way of life allowed them, once again, to prosper. Their next leader, Peter Kalmykov, Kapustin's great-grandson, was reasonably competent, and the next tsar, Alexander II, famously liberal. Even though Kalmykov died early and childless in 1864, he designated his young wife, Luker'ia Kalmykova, as his successor.

The sect's emphasis on leadership has often confused outsiders. Despite rejecting all forms of human authority, Doukhobors have, since the 1700s, followed a hereditary chief, whom they revered as a living Christ. The divine spark that lit each human soul apparently produced more illumination in some than in others. The one who shone most brightly came to be regarded as a prophet—and a prophet's powers were believed to pass to his or her descendants. This style of leadership has changed in the modern era. The current head of the USCC, for instance, goes by the title of "honorary chairman" and plays a more ceremonial, administrative role.

Luker'ia Kalmykova led the Doukhobors through a golden era of twenty-two peaceful years. Her flock's numbers grew, new villages were established on better land in neighbouring districts, and many villagers became quite affluent. Kalmykova co-operated with Russia's rulers, even to the extent of supplying wagon teams and drivers for the war effort against Turkey. The Doukhobors were rewarded with money and additional fertile lands. In Russia, however, stability was a fleeting concept. After the assassination of Alexander II in 1881, the repressive Alexander III took his place. Within months of Kalmykova's death in 1887, military conscription was announced and an internal struggle began over who would be the next prophet.

Kalmykova had, in 1882, taken into her household and trained as her successor a young man named Peter Vasil'evich Verigin, who could

trace his lineage back to Savelii Kapustin. But she never formally nom-
inated him as her heir, and upon her death, her brother attempted to
take over as leader. He was unsuccessful, but his supporters, who
comprised about thirty percent of the sect's members, broke away and
formed their own organization: the Small Party. Verigin headed the
Large Party. In a dispute over property, Small Party members collab-
orated with government authorities and accused Verigin of posing as
a false tsar. He was arrested and exiled to Siberia, and the schism
between the two parties became deep and bitter.

Peter Verigin, however, would go on to become the Doukhobors'
most celebrated leader. The long period he spent in Siberia, where he
came into contact with many articulate dissidents, completed the education begun by Kalmykova. Trusted couriers carried his instructions
to his people, and over the years those instructions became increasingly radical, directing the Doukhobors to return to their ancient traditions of Christian communism and to give up alcohol, tobacco, meat
and, at least temporarily, sex.

He gave his party a proper name—the Christian Community of
Universal Brotherhood (CCUB)—and a credo of "common thoughts."
The community must "honour and love God as the source of all
being." It should "respect the merit and worth of mankind" and
"regard all that is, lovingly and with delight." God was to be understood as "the power of love." For "material food," sect members were
to subsist on "air, water, fruits and vegetables." Violence and the taking of life were condemned without exception. Verigin's vision had an
ideal, utopian quality. "The world is based upon going forward," he
declared. "All things strive for perfection, and through this process
seek to rejoin their source, as seeds yield ripe fruit." He concluded that
"the life of mankind is communal," and put forth one moral law:
"Whatever I do not want for myself, that I should not wish for others."

The new doctrines were soon put to the test. In 1894, Alexander
III was succeeded by the equally repressive Nicholas II, who immediately demanded an oath of allegiance from all his subjects. Verigin
refused and insisted that his followers refuse also. In addition, he com-
manded them to reject military service, to which many Doukhobors
had passively submitted (with strict instructions from home to shoot
over their opponents' heads if worst came to worst). Finally, he sent
the directive that would push official tempers past the boiling point:

All Things Strive for Perfection ✦ 121

on June 29, 1895, all weapons were to be ceremonially burnt in an act
that would demonstrate the Doukhobors' fresh resolve and unwilling-
ness to compromise.

Verigin's commands were carried out, and a wave of persecution—worse than any they had known before—deluged his long-
suffering supporters. Those who refused military service received bar-
baric punishments, while the Caucasus settlers were beaten and forced
into nearby penal settlements, where hundreds died from malnutri-
tion and disease. Influential Russian author Leo Tolstoy publicized the
plight of the Doukhobors in Europe and North America, and the
Quakers took up their cause in England. Reluctantly, the Russian government agreed to allow the sect to emigrate. With Tolstoy and the
Quakers helping raise the necessary funds, over eleven hundred
Doukhobors sailed to Cyprus in 1898.

In the meantime, Canada had emerged as a better possible home.
Russian anarchist-philosopher Peter Kropotkin had travelled across the
Canadian prairies in 1897 and written about the Mennonites, another
dissident sect, many of whom had been admitted to Canada in the
1870s and become successful farmers. With the help of Kropotkin,
Toronto university professor James Mavor and others, negotiations
were conducted with immigration authorities and Doukhobor representatives toured potential settlement sites. An agreement was eventually reached that saw 7,500 refugees—including the Cyprus contin-
gent, who were miserable on their hot, parched island—cross the
Atlantic in 1899 and travel by train to east-central Saskatchewan.

Confused and leaderless, the Doukhobors spent their first two
years in Canada barely surviving. Settling gingerly onto the reserves,
they farmed the virgin prairie by hand, raising potatoes and grain.
Women and men took the place of animals, harnessing themselves to
ploughs and carts. Even children laboured. In 1902, Peter Verigin was
allowed to join his people, and he moved among them like a born
statesman, solving problems and healing conflicts. The communal,
pacifist habits of the Doukhobors were at odds with the Canadian way
of life, which celebrated individualism and competition. But Verigin
found workable compromises with those who were hostile towards
the new immigrants. His adoring followers began to refer to their
robust, handsome leader, with his fine moustache and regal manner,
as Peter the Lordly. In its turf-roofed villages, the sect thrived yet again.

Peter the Lordly proved as good a business manager as he was a diplomat and spiritual director. He sent most men to work outside the villages, on road and rail projects, and invested their income, plus money from bank loans, in agricultural machinery. Productivity sky-rocketed. The Doukhobors soon began to enjoy a standard of health and prosperity they had never known before. But a slow process of social fragmentation also set in. Some individuals wished to live sep-arately and pursue more materialistic goals; others disagreed with modernization and affluence and sought to return to a stricter ascet-icism. And so the first *edinolichniki* (Independents) and *svobodniki* (zealots or Sons of Freedom) came on the scene.

Canadian politicians, though, turned out to be the sect's greatest threat. Verigin had persuaded his followers to register for land indiv-idually, but they farmed collec-tively and did not necessarily live on and improve each regis-tered plot—as the law required regular homesteaders to do before title would be granted. Interior minister Clifford Sifton had assured them that this would be acceptable. But a growing clamour for homestead lots— and the sect's unpopularity— caused the government to change its tune.

A new interior minister, Frank Oliver, announced that unimproved Doukhobor lands would be confiscated and sold. In addition, title would be subject to naturalization, which involved an oath of alle-giance to the Crown. Had the sect challenged Oliver, the courts would probably have disallowed the government's

Peter V. Verigin, affectionately known as Peter the Lordly, arrived from Russian exile in 1902 to lead his people in their new Canadian home. (University of British Columbia, Special Collections)

actions. Instead, the Doukhobors began to look around for other places to live. After all, migration was in their blood; they expected officials to lie and promises to be broken. As human vultures gathered to buy cheap Doukhobor property, Verigin considered moves to the U.S. and back to Russia. In 1908, however, he travelled to eastern British Columbia and purchased 1,100 hectares of land on the edge of Grand Forks and 1,150 hectares southwest of Nelson.

Above the Kootenay River, facing south and west over the Castlegar valley, is a rocky vantage point with an unusual feature: a monolithic white slab of painted concrete. Surrounded by manicured gardens and many species of beautiful trees, this raised platform is the tomb of the Verigins. It speaks with quiet strength about the experiences of the Doukhobors in B.C.

Its first words are literal ones, awkwardly translated from the original Russian and etched into the stone bluff right behind the memorial:

> *Here flowed once in Doukhobor tears*
> *a coffin with body of a leader strong, mighty*
> *with mournful prayer of spiritual wrestlers.*
> *Into the bowels of earth grievously lowered,*
> *his spirit—arise for memory everlasting*
> *in many loving hearts.*

The gravesite reflects the internal conflicts of the Doukhobor people. It is bounded by a chain-link fence topped with barbed wire, like a prison. Great padlocks secure its gates, and visitors must appreciate the beckoning gazebo and close-trimmed lawns from afar. The monument—and the original stone-cut tomb that preceded it—was a favourite target for Sons of Freedom bomb attacks. Both were badly damaged on several occasions.

The Verigin tomb is also an emblem of lost dreams. It was designed to overlook the heart of the Doukhobor empire, which was at the height of its communitarian glory in 1924 when Peter the Lordly died. In those days, almost all the arable countryside one could see from the grave was owned by Doukhobors and had been worked and brought to a peak of fruitfulness by them. But that empire has now disappeared.

Due south, on a great shelf of land beside the Columbia River, below its confluence with the Kootenay, was Ooteshenie, or "valley of consolation"—the most populous Doukhobor district in B.C. Twenty-four pairs of the ubiquitous community houses once sheltered several thousand individuals there, but only a shadow remains today. This shadow is the Doukhobor Historical Village in Castlegar, reconstructed from bricks and other materials salvaged from the buildings of the former commune. Ooteshenie itself is mostly covered by the runways and hangars of Castlegar Airport.

At the historical village, one can catch a glimmer of what life in a community house might have been like. Unlike the Mountainview Museum at Grand Forks, with its good-natured clutter and decaying authenticity, the Castlegar village is a neat and efficient facsimile, run by a nonprofit society. In one building, the commune experience has been re-created, with a brick oven, tables and benches, and the over-sized kitchen utensils needed when preparing meals for fifty. Women from two families would have cooked for a week, then taken charge of a week's laundry, then had two weeks off.

Young families or pairs of older boys or girls usually occupied the upstairs bedrooms in a community house, sometimes with an older single woman as a kind of dormitory supervisor. As families expanded, they migrated to rooms in an outdoor annex. They would congregate daily in the frugal downstairs meeting room, where bread, salt and water would be set out on a table.

The symbols of life have been set out also in the replica building. From the wall, a translated psalm from The Living Book exhorts visitors to "be devout" and "avoid drunkenness as you would Hades." The psalm offers timeless advice: "Do not believe everything you hear. Do not desire all you see....Hold thriftiness in esteem....If someone has hurt you, make peace with him....To the enquirer, give an answer; to the ignorant, give advice; to the sorrowing, give comfort. Do not envy anyone. Wish well to all."

In the other, identical community house, a theatre or performance space has been built, where videos can be watched and music appreciated. A vast gallery of fascinating photographs covers the walls. Outside, a bronze statue of Leo Tolstoy, the Doukhobors' protector, gazes benevolently at the garden and outbuildings, which include a barnful of farm machines and horse-drawn conveyances. At the Spinning Wheel Eatery across the way, tourists can round off their cultural adventure by sampling Doukhobor food: delicious borsch (vegetable soup), galooptsi (cabbage rolls), voreniki (dumplings), phyrahi (savory tarts) and nalesniki (sweet crêpes).

A kilometre or so northwest, near the grounds of Selkirk College, the waters of the Kootenay River have almost turned a flat stretch of meadow and cottonwoods into an island. This was Peter Verigin's favourite spot for holding mass outdoor sobranies, at which a panoramic group photograph was usually taken, like those on the museum walls. To see these pictures today—where hundreds of women in head scarves and long dresses stand beside hundreds of men in collarless shirts and pants with suspenders—is to be transported to the Russian frontier. At first, the figures may seem as irrelevant to B.C. history as a delegation of Zulus posing in the rainforest.

But they are not irrelevant. The men and women in the photos put their mark on the countryside with unprecedented vigour and dedication. Just below the Verigin gravesite, the Doukhobors threw a fine suspension bridge—still standing, though no longer used—across the Kootenay River in 1913. It connected Ooteshenie with Brilliant, the sect's former spiritual and industrial hub, now a Castlegar suburb. Brilliant was home to the Kootenay Columbia Preserving Works, where the well-regarded K.C. brand of jams and jellies was manufactured. It also boasted a grain elevator, sawmill, flour mill, boarding house, community store and railway station, plus Verigin's office and residence—all surrounded by twelve more community houses and many hectares of orchards. Today, a large, modern USCC community centre maintains the Doukhobor presence.

In the valleys around Castlegar were sixty more community houses. Along the Slocan River, Doukhobors dwelt at Winlaw, Passmore, Perry's Siding, Vallican and Appledale. Settlements flourished beside the Kootenay and Columbia rivers, at Glade, Shoreacres, Thrums, Taghum and Champion Creek. Naturally, the communes had Russian names, too: Kirpichnoe ("place of bricks"), Persekovoe ("peachland"), Lugovoe ("meadow") and Prekrasnoe ("beautiful valley"). Collectives could be found as far away as Salmo and Creston. Doukhobors still live in these places, though their homes and way of life no longer stand out as distinct and unusual.

North of Castlegar, on a dry upland plateau, is Krestova, "land of the cross," a community that became notorious from the 1930s onwards as the headquarters of the breakaway Sons of Freedom. The landscape here was once littered with the charred remains of wooden shacks, burnt in protest of government policies. Today there is no sign of this violent past; modest homes and gigantic gardens are all that greet the eye. But in a remote corner of Krestova—at New Settlement, a piece of land purchased as a home for a group of long-imprisoned Freedomites released in the 1970s—the communitarian spirit has survived longer than anywhere else in the Doukhobor world.

Even New Settlement is split by differing outlooks. Half of the sixty families that live there are traditionalists, the last of a dying breed, who refuse to own property or pay property taxes and scorn education, television and material possessions. The other half are modernists, willing to pay taxes and send their children to school. The divisions in the community came to a head in the late 1980s, when power and telephone lines arrived over the objections of the conservative faction.

As late as 1994, more than twenty-five traditionalists were jailed for preventing school buses and road crews from entering New Settlement. In February 1996, a "land stewardship" agreement was finally negotiated with the traditional, "community" Freedomites. Thirty individual lot titles were erased, and a society was set up to hold the land in trust. The former title holders agreed to pay fees for government services equivalent to the property taxes levied on their neighbours. The land cannot be subdivided, sold, mined or logged under the new agreement, and is once again held collectively. In this last communal corner of the Doukhobor kingdom, a remnant group still hangs onto its utopian ideals, defying earthly powers to follow, without compromise, what it deeply feels to be the one true path.

The search for a place to live has been a determining force in Doukhobor culture almost since its inception. Questions concerning the status of land have been the sect's main, if reluctant, preoccupation. Can land legitimately be owned? If so, who will own it? If not, how can it be occupied? What relationship will prevail between those who live on Doukhobor land and those who live in the world beyond? From 1909 to about 1912, these questions and others drove Peter Verigin and nearly five thousand of his followers from Saskatchewan to B.C.

Not all Doukhobors in Canada made the move. At least one thousand Independents remained on the Prairies, acceding to the government's demands by living on the plots of land they had registered for and taking the oath of allegiance. Some Community Doukhobors stayed on a large tract that Peter the Lordly, perhaps anticipating problems with the government reserves, had bought near Yorkton, Saskatchewan. He had established his first headquarters there, in a village named Verigin. Today, about eight thousand Doukhobors live in Alberta, Saskatchewan and Manitoba.

In B.C., the sect was determined to avoid any repetition of the problems that had forced its members to leave the Prairies. All land was registered in Verigin's name, and a will was drawn up bequeathing the properties to the Christian Community of Universal Brotherhood when Verigin died. Prominent CCUB members were designated as trustees. Early purchases were financed ingeniously: title deeds were placed in escrow, while the paycheques of six hundred Doukhobor day labourers were deposited to the seller's credit every two weeks until the land was paid off. Other properties were bought through a combination of mortgages and contract work.

Buying and owning real estate were not consistent with Doukhobor beliefs. "We do not want to own the land," sect members repeatedly told federal officials during their prairie sojourn. "All we want is to be permitted to make a living thereon." But ironically, ownership solved their problem with the hated oath of allegiance, which only had to be sworn to receive a government grant and did not apply to private transactions.

The community gobbled up as much land as it could afford, including 900 hectares at Pass Creek and 450 at Slocan Junction. By 1910, it owned 4,000 hectares in B.C.—by 1912, 6,000 hectares. Verigin bought more prairie property, too, at Kylemore and Kelvington in Saskatchewan, Benito in Manitoba and Cowley and Lundbreck in Alberta. By 1924, the year of his death, the CCUB held almost three hundred square kilometres, over thirty percent of it in B.C. This was less than a quarter of the original reserve set aside for the Doukhobors when they arrived in Canada, but it was better land.

After first establishing a new headquarters at Brilliant, Peter the Lordly began to pursue one of his pet projects: the large-scale farming of fruits and vegetables. "Tender fruits," he believed, were "the natural food of mankind." By eating foods raised with "an abundance of solar heat," Verigin thought that mankind could improve in energy and wisdom. Fruits and vegetables certainly improved Doukhobor self-sufficiency. They could be manufactured into jams and jellies, exchanged with the prairie colonies for grain, and sold—along with grain, lumber and bricks—to the wider world. Sect members also started to produce serious quantities of honey.

All revenues went into paying off loans and purchasing more land. The internal Doukhobor economy was virtually cash-free. Warehouses were constructed to receive surpluses and dispense necessary supplies. Trade between individuals was not permitted. Community life was austere; such luxuries as bicycles, jewellery and musical instruments were forbidden. Despite these severities, there were few defections. Where would renegades go? They spoke no English. They didn't understand Canadian customs. They were from another century and another world.

The Doukhobors' unique B.C. villages were based on a design by Verigin himself. In many ways, the sect's social and economic structures, including the operation of its large community houses, were similar to those of the original Utopia described by Sir Thomas More in 1516. More's imaginary country differed in other major respects, though. In Utopia, education was of vital importance and made available to all men and women. The right to freedom of belief was upheld, and religious differences were tolerated.

Most sect members were content in British Columbia. Oral histories collected from elderly Doukhobors in the 1970s by Marjorie Malloff and Peter Ogloff, and published as part of the B.C. Provincial Archives' Sound Heritage series under the title *Toil and Peaceful Life,* reveal a deep sense of satisfaction and fulfillment, even in the midst of hardship. "We lived in such poverty, but we were happy," Nastya Semenoff reflected. "We ate," recalled Vasya Chernoff. "There was enough of everything. There was so much gaiety."

Doukhobor life centred around the kitchen. Polya Kanigan remembered what it was like to be in charge of preparing the food:

> We women, we cooked by twos.... We had a lot of work to do.
> There were three long tables of men. For lunch we had cooked
> cereal or borsch and fruit drink. We didn't have tea. And in the
> evening we made soup and dried-fruit pudding. We made
> yogurt.... The food was good but, of course, we didn't have tarts

or pancakes. Mostly soup. I liked it here so much. The air, the clover, was so fragrant.

Anuta Popoff recollected mealtime from the diners' point of view:

There was a big kitchen and as we came from work and approached it, we'd start singing a hymn of some sort. As we came up to the kitchen we were greeted. We finish singing the hymn, then exchange greetings. The cooks invite us: "Please be invited to the table for dinner." We go into the kitchen and sit down. Those who can sing, a group, all sit in one row. By the time the cook sets out the bowls of borsch, we'll sing a hymn or sometimes we'll sing two, depending on how the cook finishes. She asks that we may now say grace. And so we say grace at the table....Such was the custom.

While all seemed harmonious in the villages, it didn't take long for conflict to arise with neighbours and officials. Newspapers inflamed anti-Doukhobor sentiment by accusing the sect of refusing to support local businesses. And, although oaths of allegiance had been avoided, bureaucrats were soon pestering Verigin on three other requirements: education, registration and taxation. A growing number of children had actually been attending classes when, in 1912, four Doukhobor men were arrested and imprisoned for neglecting to register a death. In what was to become a familiar pattern of response in the West Kootenays, all Doukhobor children were immediately withdrawn from school. At a mass sobranie, sect members agreed to refuse to comply with government directives.

Premier Richard McBride appointed a commission of enquiry under a Conservative newspaper editor named William Blakemore. Blakemore turned out to be sympathetic to the Doukhobors. In his report, he outlined their objections to the education system—that it taught militarism, caused young people to drift away from the faith and was impractical for farm workers—and made sensible recommendations for settling the dispute. But one bizarre statement undid all his useful work: he suggested that the exemption from military service—a key aspect of the agreement that had originally brought the group to Canada from Russia—should be dropped.

Naturally, the Doukhobors regarded Blakemore and his report with horror. Once again, they began to look around for a new country of residence. Things did not cool off until 1915, a full year into World War I, when it became clear that the federal government would honour the sect's non-combatant status. Verigin sent many children back to school, and peace reigned until the early 1920s. The war, however, prompted a deep split between the CCUB and the Independents, whom Verigin attacked, claiming without success that they had lost their right to military exemption. And local resentments were increased by the sect's pacifist stance. A group of returning veterans even went so far as to make an abortive attempt to take over Doukhobor properties in 1919.

The events of the early 1900s revealed a central characteristic of Doukhobor culture: whenever outside social pressures on the group became intense, fringe elements grew active. The sect was a fragile organism; if you squeezed its main body too tightly, the extremities got twisted out of shape. The Sons of Freedom, who at first served as the community's conscience, criticising worldly trends, started to feel obliged to take direct action. They struck out at examples—both real and symbolic—of materialism, assimilation and anti-Christian authority, eventually attacking CCUB and Anglo-Canadian facilities, as well as their own homes and institutions.

From the end of World War I to the mid-1920s, many changes took place within the CCUB. The association was incorporated as a business, and a small clique of literate managers arose. Economic activity expanded rapidly. By 1924, the Christian Community of Universal Brotherhood Ltd. had assets of $6.4 million and debts of $1.1 million. But as any farmer knows, taking on debt to expand agriculture is risky. A series of crop failures in the early 1920s resulted in new austerities being imposed on the community. The membership became restless; discontent increased. And among the Freedomites, activists graduated from civil disobedience to violence.

The origins of the next wave of defiance are not clear, but children were again withdrawn from the schools. The authorities reacted by fining parents and seizing property when fines weren't paid. The first school was burnt in 1923; over the next two years eight more were destroyed. Then, in October 1924, a disaster: a railway coach headed from Brilliant to Grand Forks was obliterated by a bomb, killing nine people, including Peter the Lordly.

A police investigation resulted in no arrests, though there were

plenty of suspects. Verigin, if indeed he was the target, had many ene-
mies, both Doukhobor and non-Doukhobor. His assassination marked
a turning point in the sect's fortunes. Its next leader—Verigin's son
from an early marriage, which had been dissolved when Kalmykova
began training her young protégé—quite lacked the Lordly foresight
and management skills.

This was Peter Petrovich Verigin—also known as Peter Chistiakov,
or the Purger or Cleanser, after his self-proclaimed intention to "divide
lies from truth, and light from darkness." In Russia, he had been head
of a large group of Doukhobors who had been permitted to settle in
the Don region of southern Russia, near Rostov. His duties there prevented his appearance in Canada until October 1927. Asked upon
arrival if he would comply with B.C.'s education laws, he responded,
"Yes, we will take everything of value that Canada has to offer, but we
will not give up our Doukhobor souls."

Instead, he took everything of value that his Canadian followers
had to offer, revealing in the process a personality both brutal and

*The 1924 funeral of Peter the Lordly, who was murdered in a
still-unsolved train bombing, was attended by thousands of Doukhobors from all over western Canada. (Boundary Museum)*

decadent. Stocky and tall like his father, and with a similar signature moustache, Chistiakov did manage a considerable reduction of the CCUB's enormous debt with his effective, energetic fund-raising. He also used his followers' money to indulge earthly passions for alcohol and gambling. Under his command, Doukhobor society became more decentralized. Each village—or "family," as it was now known—assumed greater control over its own economic affairs and paid an assessment to a Supreme Council.

The Purger's attempts to unite the various Doukhobor factions were so contradictory that they were doomed to failure. He encouraged the Sons of Freedom, called them his "ringing bells" and urged them to maintain a vigilant eye on sect purity. Yet he also tried to induce Independents to join a new, all-inclusive Society of Named Doukhobors by lifting objections to registration and compulsory education.

After a brief lull, extremist activity flared up again. The Sons of Freedom had discovered, somewhat to their surprise, that nakedness—intended as a symbolic gesture of voluntary poverty and simplicity—had unbelievable shock value. Beginning in Nelson in 1929, nude marches became a regular feature of their protests. The federal government responded by prescribing a mandatory three-year prison term for the hideous crime of public nakedness. By today's permissive standards, such a punishment seems tyrannical, but the 1930s were a prudish time.

The law was soon enforced. In 1932, a series of mass nude parades resulted in the arrest and conviction of six hundred Freedomite men and women. A special penal colony—deserted Piers Island, just north of Sidney between the Saanich Peninsula and Saltspring Island—was created to contain the nude menace. The prisoners' children, some of whom would grow up to form the nucleus of the next generation of extremists, were sent to industrial schools designed for delinquents, and to orphanages.

In the meantime, Chistiakov's behaviour grew progressively stranger. In 1931, he was jailed for perjury over a land-purchase dispute with a prairie Doukhobor. Federal officials thought they could rid Canada of this Russian nuisance by secretly pardoning and deporting him, but the scheme was foiled. Verigin's recklessness continued. He engaged in much vengeful litigation, was fined for drunkenness and visited jail twice more (for assault and harassment). As a result of negative publicity, Doukhobors left the CCUB in droves; many joined the Sons of Freedom, whom Peter the Purger now denounced, as the "ringing bells" were playing unpleasant tunes.

Remaining Community members, faced with raging fanatics on one side and a mad leader on the other, also had to cope with a deteriorating Depression-era economy. It was too much. By 1937, the CCUB was bankrupt. For a debt of about $1 million (subsequently reduced to $350,000), they had given mortgages on assets worth $6 million. The prime creditors, Sun Life and National Trust, won foreclosure proceedings and, in 1939, blithely prepared to issue eviction notices to about five thousand people. The B.C. government finally stepped in, paid off the debts and acquired the community's lands. To prevent hardship and social disorder, individuals were allowed to remain on their properties and pay a nominal rent. But the CCUB's communitarian ways and commercial prowess had been destroyed forever. Its main structures were dismantled and sold, or incinerated

Peter P. Verigin, also called "The Purger," (with hand on boy's shoulder) is shown presiding over an outdoor sobranie, or prayer meeting, after coming to B.C. in 1927. (University of British Columbia, Special Collections)

by Freedomites. Twenty-three years would pass before the Doukhobors were able to buy back their lands.

The Christian Community of Universal Brotherhood Ltd. was finished, but the community, of course, was not. In 1938, out of its predecessor's literal ashes, a new organization arose, which still exists: the Union of Spiritual Communities of Christ (USCC). A year later, after supervising his sect's dubious transformation, Chistiakov died of cancer and was buried in his father's tomb. His son, another Peter P. Verigin—more commonly known as Peter Iastrebov or the Hawk—was elected leader. But the whereabouts of the Hawk were unknown; he was presumed to be languishing in some Russian gulag. Chistiakov's grandson, eighteen-year-old John J. Verigin—who, with his grandmother, had escaped Russia in 1928 to join the Purger in Canada—assumed a caretaker role as secretary of the new USCC. It was not until 1960, when Iastrebov's death was indisputably proven, that John J. Verigin took over full leadership of the USCC, a position he holds today.

After World War II, during which the Doukhobors' pacifist beliefs were again respected, the Sons of Freedom raised the stakes in their long, sensational dalliance with terrorism. The faction had grown; it may have had as many as 2,500 members at its peak in the 1950s. While most Freedomites protested with marches, nudity and the occasional symbolic cleansing by fire of their own homes, a more sinister and desperate core of incendiarists and bombers had formed. This small group was not interested in symbolic targets; they went after schools, USCC homes and centres, railroads and power lines. Their aim was to instill fear in mainstream Doukhobors and the Canadian public, and they succeeded.

Neither a 1947 commission of enquiry by judge Harry Sullivan nor the 1950 Doukhobor Research Committee headed by University of British Columbia professor Dr. Harry Hawthorn had much success in pacifying the angry zealots. Persuasion was replaced with force. From 1953 to 1959, B.C. officials shamefully redefined the meaning of compulsory education by seizing 170 truant Freedomite children, constraining them to attend school during the day and incarcerating them at night in an unused New Denver tuberculosis sanatorium. In the early 1960s, many convicted arsonists were imprisoned in a special fireproof facility at Agassiz in the Fraser Valley. Over six hundred sympathizers, led by "Big Fanny" Florence Storgeoff, marched from the Kootenays to the coast and set up camp outside this prison for nine years.

But in the 1970s and 1980s, the Doukhobors finally dropped from the front pages of the newspapers. Violent protests declined. The last major communal experiment—at the tiny Freedomite community of Hilliers on Vancouver Island, led by Michael "The Archangel" Verigin—had been abandoned by the late 1950s. The B.C. government breathed a sigh of relief. The threat of the unknown had been averted. A few minor concessions, such as a special procedure for recording marriages, had been granted the Doukhobors. Otherwise, they had finally been made to live like everyone else—on their own little plots of land, with their children at school and their births and deaths neatly registered. Many sect members, though, are still fighting a rearguard action against assimilation and the threatened loss of their religion and language. And many are still working towards a utopian ideal of toil and peaceful life through involvement in international efforts for disarmament and world peace.

We wait in the parking lot behind the Grand Forks USCC centre, watching people greet one another and make their way up the steps to

Peter P. Verigin, while not as popular and effective a leader as his father, Peter the Lordly, nevertheless attracted a great number of followers to his 1939 funeral procession. (BCARS C-07803)

the entrance. It is the first Sunday in August, Declaration Day, an important ceremony on the Doukhobor calendar. I had phoned the USCC office and asked if my friend Katherine and I could attend. Visitors were welcome, I was told. Somebody would be assigned to look after us and help explain the proceedings, which would mostly be in Russian.

A car pulls up and a friendly gentleman beckons us to come in. We have been camping for the past week, and I feel awkward in my crumpled, casual clothes. Everyone else seems to be dressed in their Sunday best. But nobody even glances at what we are wearing. Kind, curious faces surround us and usher us into the huge, bare hall. We pause at the threshold to make the traditional bow.

"*Slava bohu,*" say our escorts upon entering the room. Glory to God.

"*Kristos vas kres,*" is the response from those inside. Christ is risen.

The men stand on the left; the women, all wearing platki, or head shawls, gather on the right. Bread, salt and water have been placed on a central table. A few minutes past 10:00 a.m., the voices of the congregation rise in the first of a series of hymns. Fred Horkoff, whom we had met earlier, whispers pertinent facts in my ear as the chanting progresses.

Horkoff had been present when we visited the old Fructova school, now a cultural heritage centre, a few days before. He had given me a tour of the Russian-language library and shown me some of the artifacts that had been donated, including a cat-shaped cutting board that Horkoff himself had made there as a child in the 1930s. The school, built in 1929, is one of the few older Doukhobor institutional buildings to have survived—despite several Freedomite arson attacks.

Its graceful verandah and arched windows had once looked out over an enterprising scene. Horkoff identified where the steampowered brickyard had stood—and the sawmill, the cannery, offices, apiaries, water flumes, grapevines and orchards of cherry, apricot, peach, apple and pear. All were long gone, replaced today by green fields and rural homes. When the Doukhobors bought back their foreclosed lands in the 1960s, they had wanted to settle on the valley's higher slopes and farm the lowlands collectively. But the government insisted that the land be separated into small lots. The official intent,

Horkoff explained, was clearly to discourage any collective activity, and to further divide and subdue the sect.

I had heard a note of sadness in his voice, and I hear the same note as I listen to the chanting on Declaration Day. The Doukhobors love to sing, and their choirs and choral recordings are famous. The rich, sonorous voices, so deep with feeling, transcend the language barrier and hint at the universal and the divine. Between hymns, a couple come to the front of the hall and reaffirm, first in Russian and then in English, the lengthy declaration of faith that delegates to the second convention of Named Doukhobors had proclaimed exactly sixty-two years ago at Verigin, Saskatchewan.

"We, the Union of Spiritual Communities of Christ," they thunder, "having acknowledged and submitted ourselves to the law and authority of God, by this have liberated ourselves from the guardianship and power established by men, because we cannot serve two masters and...cannot be slaves of men....Members of the Union of Spiritual Communities of Christ have never recognized and do not recognize any political party....They have never given nor will they ever give their votes during elections, thereby, are free from any responsibility before God or man for the acts of any government established of men."

After a round of ritual handshaking and cheek-kissing, interspersed with exchanges of deep bows between the men and the women, the assembly breaks for a picnic lunch. Outside the centre, blankets are spread on the grass. Sandwiches, potato salads, ripe tomatoes, homemade pickles, juices and all kinds of wonderful desserts pour from hefty hampers. The afternoon festivities consist of more singing, but in a relaxed, informal atmosphere. Benches are put out so that people can sit, and large choirs from Grand Forks and Castlegar perform.

Declaration Day seems to be a devout, vibrant success, but I find myself worrying about the Doukhobors and their future. There are, for instance, a mere half-dozen younger people at the ceremony; the average age of the participants is probably well over sixty. On this important occasion, about one hundred individuals have turned out—a far cry from the thousands that attended the mass sobranies of the 1920s and 1930s. And apart from a family of Doukhobors from Russia—where old connections have been rebuilt over the past decade—we are the only visitors. I feel as if I am observing the end of an era.

I speak to Eli Popoff, a noted Doukhobor historian and author, about my fears. "We find it very difficult to try and live as the rest of the country lives and keep our young people with us," he tells me. Many Doukhobors yearn to live communally again on large shared properties, something virtually impossible now in B.C. due to high land prices. "We would even consider moving," Popoff declares, "so we can live as a community."

The introduction of Russian into the school curriculum at Grand Forks and Castlegar has enabled young people to at least read and sing the hymns. "But it really doesn't help them get the meaning of what they're singing," says Popoff. "You still have to explain in English what they are singing about in Russian. To translate the psalms and hymns into English is very hard to do. I have tried. Unless you were born and raised a Doukhobor for six or seven generations, it is so hard to get the proper meaning of what is originally in the Russian. There are some phrases that just don't translate." Popoff says he cannot imagine his culture surviving in English.

Folklorist Mark Mealing, a professor at Castlegar's Selkirk College who specializes in Doukhobor studies, believes that growing numbers of young Doukhobors want to hold onto their culture. They are grappling, he maintains, with the question of how to translate their traditions into a modern context. "It won't be a restoration of the practices of the past, of communal life as it was in the 1910s, '20s and early '30s, but whatever adaptation is possible that will allow them to retain a Doukhobor identity."

Mealing points to the fifth of Peter V. Verigin's "common thoughts," the one that develops the seemingly utopian notion that "the world is based upon going forward" and claims that "all things strive for perfection...and seek to rejoin their source." But these sentiments are not really utopian, says Mealing, because "the idea there is that you don't stay in one place. You look to a perfect society eventually but you don't expect it right away....it's something you continuously progress toward. And that is a very healthy point of view for a society that sees itself as necessarily opposed to the establishment."

No matter how their future unfolds, the Doukhobors will remain an important part of the Kootenay landscape. Visitors can easily while away a few fascinating days learning about their history and culture at museums and other heritage sites. But the best way to breathe in Doukhobor lore may simply be to explore the glorious mountain countryside. Take the tiny cable ferry to the community of Glade, once known as Plodarodnoe, or "fertile land." Meander through the Slocan Valley investigating the dozens of sideroads with Russian names ending in "off." Or drive by the last brick community houses of West Grand Forks. Renovated but still recognizable, they symbolize the Doukhobors themselves—a courageous people struggling to preserve their idealism in a cynical, imperfect world.

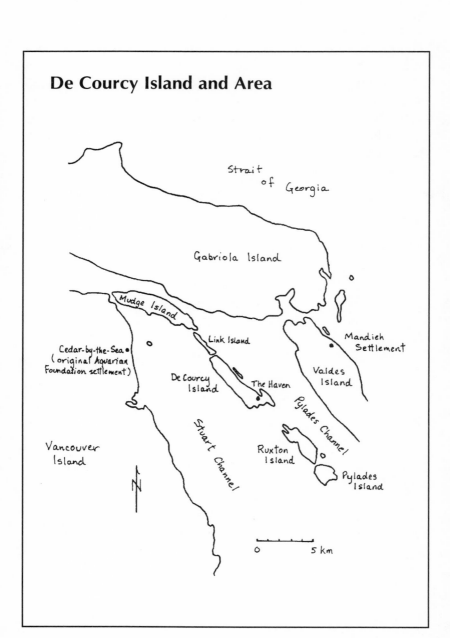

De Courcy Island and Area

Strait of Georgia

Gabriola Island

Mudge Island

Link Island

Cedar-by-the-Sea •
(original Aquarian
Foundation settlement)

De Courcy
Island

The Haven

Mandieh
Settlement

Valdes
Island

Pylades Channel

Vancouver
Island

Stuart Channel

Ruxton
Island

Pylades
Island

N

0   5 km

6

THE APOSTLE OF DARKNESS
Brother XII and the Aquarian Foundation

*Labour in this Vineyard, and thou shalt eat
of its fruit. Build thou the City of Refuge; it shall
hide thee in the Day of Adversity.*
—Edward Arthur Wilson, note to
Aquarian Foundation members

The elderly woman minding her grandchildren on the beach is a sociable soul, and she stops for a chat as we prepare to unpack the kayaks. Katherine and I have just returned from a paddling expedition to the smaller northern Gulf Islands. For three balmy days, we've been camping at an idyllic marine park on De Courcy Island and leisurely exploring the other islands in the De Courcy group: Link, Ruxton, Whaleboat and Pylades. The old boat ramp and pebble shoreline at Cedar-by-the-Sea—a pretty spot on the inland coast of Vancouver Island, just twelve kilometres southeast of Nanaimo—make it a perfect launch and take-out site for our small craft.

As we bask in the warm September sunshine, the talk soon turns to Edward Arthur Wilson, the tiny community's founder and most famous former inhabitant. Our new acquaintance volunteers the fact that her daughter-in-law lives in a house that had once been part of Wilson's Aquarian Foundation. After more conversation, she reveals the location of several other buildings that had belonged to Wilson and his followers over sixty years ago.

"That shack," she says, pointing to a tiny cabin perched on a bit of high ground overlooking the beach, "was his meditation hut. Oh, yes. This whole village is caught right up in the story of Brother XII."

And no wonder. The story of Brother XII, born Edward Arthur Wilson, is a strange and mesmerizing one. A sailor turned religious leader and seer, Wilson attracted hundreds of followers to British Columbia between 1927 and 1933 to join his Aquarian Foundation. Several communities were formed, at Cedar-by-the-Sea, on De Courcy Island and on Valdes Island further east. At first, Wilson's goal of preparing the way for a new age of spiritual enlightenment seemed honourable enough, and the foundation's activities had a distinct utopian air about them. But things went dreadfully wrong. Brother XII's empire eventually collapsed in a series of sensational lawsuits, amidst allegations of black magic, sexual misconduct, brutality, fraud and theft.

Indeed, Brother XII is on his way to becoming one of B.C.'s most enduring legends. Several books on his life and times offer wildly conflicting accounts of his exploits. Much mystery about the man remains. The questions surrounding Brother XII were magnified by his sudden and complete disappearance at the height of the scandal— and by rumours that he had amassed a fortune in gold that was still buried somewhere nearby. It's not surprising that some residents of Cedar-by-the-Sea would like to put their village on the map with a Brother XII Museum and Visitors Centre.

After loading the car, we drive around the little community, which is set at the edge of a gently rolling, pastoral landscape, and pass some of the homes associated in the past with the Aquarian Foundation. They are modest enough, shingled and wood-sided, but with a sturdy, well-made look. Outside one of them, a middle-aged man is energetically tending his yard. He knows all about Brother XII.

"I've been looking for that guy's gold for over twenty years now," he says, pointing up the street to where a large, immaculately groomed house stands at the top of a low rise. "That's where he lived," he tells us. "And over there," he gestures across the street at another 1920s-style home, "that's where his partner-in-crime lived, the infamous Madame Zee."

In order to take a photograph, I inch down the driveway that the tyrannical Madame Zee may once have used. Suddenly, a barking dog comes flying towards me and an anxious female voice calls out. I explain my business to the voice and wait to be sent on my way. But instead, to my surprise, I'm invited in for a look around. Madame Zee's old home, if indeed she actually lived there, is deceptively large—almost 350 square metres—with a handsome living room and a big fireplace of beach rock. And the size of the house isn't the only thing deceptive about it.

In the centre of the building, our host informs us, is a dead space that the configuration of the rooms does not account for. I cannot help asking if she has broken into this secret room; perhaps Brother XII hid gold there. But no, she says, she doesn't want to do that. A ghost named George occupies the house, opening and slamming doors and turning on lights; he tends to be a bit protective about this hidden space. We are standing in a gloomy bedroom closet as these details are explained, knocking on the thin walls and listening to hollow echoes. Goosebumps are forming on my arms, and I half-expect George to materialize right behind me. A clear sequence of priorities is forming in my mind. Soon, I know, I want to find out all I can about the enigmatic Brother XII. But first, I have to get out of there and satisfy my sudden, overwhelming desire for fresh air and daylight.

Many writers—including Pierre Berton, novelist Howard O'Hagan and British Columbia journalist Bruce McKelvie—have been drawn to the strange story of Edward Arthur Wilson. But facts about his life have proved hard to pin down. Things grew a lot more confusing in 1967, when the first book on the subject, a lurid little paperback called *Canada's False Prophet: The Notorious Brother Twelve,* appeared. The author, Herbert Emmerson Wilson, claimed to be Edward Wilson's brother, but the book was a complete fiction.

Herbert Wilson, ex-convict and former preacher, was as shifty as the subject of his pseudo-biography. Perhaps that was the attraction. He had lived in the Cedar area and heard about the Aquarian Foundation's leader. What he didn't know about "Ed" he simply invented: a Canadian birthplace, a circus background, a career as a spiritual swindler. His lurid exposé, complete with sex scenes and misleading reports about hidden treasure, added fraudulent momentum to the growing Brother XII saga. It also fooled many subsequent writers, who treated some of his fantasies as facts.

The latest and most trustworthy book is *Brother Twelve: The Incredible Story of Canada's False Prophet* by John Oliphant. I have relied on his findings and conclusions throughout my account. Oliphant, who meticulously tracked down and interviewed the descendants of many of the colonists and amassed a unique archive of original source materials, appears to have finally sorted out much of Wilson's story. But with so much deception involved, it is impossible to be certain.

According to Oliphant, Edward Arthur Wilson was born in Birmingham, England, in 1878, the child of Irvingite parents. Irvingites were members of a strange and often persecuted religious sect that believed in the imminent second coming of Christ and put great literal faith in the prophecies of the Book of Revelation. Wilson, who used to give a different account of his early years—one featuring a missionary father and an Indian princess for a mother—had unorthodox origins that clearly influenced his later life.

As a young man, Wilson apprenticed with the navy. He worked for many years on sailing vessels, visiting exotic countries and eventually becoming an experienced and skillful mariner. In New Zealand, aged twenty-four, he married, and five years later brought his wife and two children to British Columbia. He worked in Victoria as a baggage clerk for the Dominion Express Company and, later, as a pilot on coastal steamers. In 1912, he deserted his family, joined the crew of an Orient-bound ship and disappeared.

The mysterious figure does not show up again until 1924, in the south of France. By this time he had another partner, whom Oliphant refers to as Elma Wilson, though whether or not they were actually married is uncertain. As a result of a powerful vision, Wilson believed he had become a conduit for a spirit entity, a member of an other-worldly brotherhood that guided humanity's destiny, called the Great White Lodge. Over the next year or so, in Genoa and elsewhere, Wilson completed several manuscripts he claimed were transmitted by this ethereal Master of Wisdom. Then, still following his master's instructions, he moved to England. Hereafter, as the sole disciple of the lodge's twelfth brother, Wilson referred to himself as Brother XII—or, more precisely, The Brother, XII.

Wilson had long been a seeker of spiritual truth and arcane knowledge. He was especially drawn to theosophy, the philosophical system that had also attracted Matti Kurikka, Sointula's leader, thirty years earlier. The Theosophical Society had been founded in New York in 1875 by Helena Petrova Blavatsky and others, and posited the existence of a universal soul or lifeforce and a spiritual world beyond death. Theosophy, which would have a major impact on the New Age movements of the 1970s and 1980s, had much in common with Buddhist and Hindu doctrines, including a belief in reincarnation. Contact between physical and spiritual realms was possible for highly evolved souls. Theosophy was in its infancy in Kurikka's day, but by the mid-1920s it had evolved in popularity and scope to form a world-wide network of publications and believers.

It was to London's theosophical circle that Brother XII presented himself. In *The Occult Review*, a leading spiritualist periodical, he began publishing the writings he had received from his spirit master. The articles caused a sensation. Their basic import was that before the dawning of the Aquarian Age (a two-thousand-year period of peace and universal brotherhood, set to begin about 1975 and heralded by the shift of the spring equinox from the sign of Pisces to that of Aquarius), several calamitous decades would ensue. Only a chosen few would survive this interlude of war and excess, and on them would fall the burden of preparing for the future.

In *A Message from the Masters of Wisdom,* a booklet published in 1926, Wilson elaborated on the job ahead. True spiritual knowledge was to be preserved at several "centres of safety," which would be established with the help of the Masters of Wisdom. To ease mankind through a troublesome period of transition, various masters would reincarnate as children born to those who lived at the centres and go on to become leaders of the new age. "We have to train these children in just Principles and in true Ideals," Wilson wrote. His personal task was daunting: nothing less than raising a race of new, improved human beings and overseeing the next stage of evolution.

Wilson's vast ambitions were, by all accounts, matched by an equally vast erudition. A short, slender, bearded man with a sallow complexion and a strange mole on his cheek, he also wielded considerable personal charm. He corresponded with Arthur Conan Doyle. He supposedly knew such high-ranking individuals as Neville Chamberlain and Jan Smuts. Many people contacted him about his spiritual project, and as he cultivated his growing coterie, further details about the great work were revealed: the association that led it would be named the Aquarian Foundation, and the first centre of refuge would be located in the innocent wilds of British Columbia. His followers should liquidate their assets and prepare to move there immediately.

Wilson sailed for Montreal in February 1927. He made a cross-Canada speaking tour that drummed up surprising support for the foundation and visited several prominent spiritualists in California who were interested in his plan. At the end of April, he met his followers in Vancouver and sailed to Nanaimo, where they set up house temporarily. He claimed he had never been to B.C. before; the locations for the centres of refuge, he said, were dictated to him by higher powers. The foundation had many members by this time, but only four people besides Wilson and Elma were dedicated enough to drop everything and move to B.C.: astrologer Alfred Barley and his wife Annie, a young man named Frederick Pope and an eccentric ex-army officer, Sidney Sprey-Smith.

From the moment Wilson and his group arrived on Vancouver Island, the Brother XII story gets slightly easier to follow. A number of local individuals—especially Edward Lucas, a Vancouver lawyer who helped Wilson incorporate the fledgling Aquarian Foundation as a society under the province's Societies Act—became involved. And after the first signs of dissent in the colony, newspapers began to feast on the personalities and events associated with the unconventional organization.

Within weeks of arriving at Nanaimo, Wilson learned of some land for sale at Cedar-by-the-Sea. The group inspected and approved the fifty-hectare property, and it was purchased. Most of the down payment came from the colony's newest member, Phillip Fisher, whose father was a wealthy English manufacturer. Over the summer of 1927, a "centre building" was raised, which would also be Wilson's personal residence. It still stands. To raise funds, he sent an urgent, successful appeal to the foundation, which had expanded and now numbered over a thousand subscribers. This was partly due to the appearance of a book, *The Aquarian Foundation: A Movement for the Unification of All Men of Good Will,* in which Joseph Benner of Akron, Ohio, whom Wilson had met on his cross-Canada tour, reprinted some of Wilson's writings and included a membership application form.

In July, the foundation held its first general meeting. Wilson had appointed a board of seven governors to direct the organization's affairs. As president, he could veto their decisions, so he had total control. At Cedar-by-the-Sea, all the governors met for the first time. From California came Will Comfort, a mystic and well-known adventure novelist; Coulson Turnbull, a leading American astrologer; and Baron Maurice von Platen, retired lumberman and German-American philanthropist. Publisher Joseph Benner travelled from Ohio. Wilson, Fisher and Lucas were the remaining governors. The composition of the board reflected Brother XII's prescient belief that most of the interest—and most of the funding—for the Aquarian Foundation would come from the United States.

The fall and winter of 1927 was a busy time. Almost two dozen Aquarians would soon call the colony home; houses were going up everywhere. Wilson's *Foundation Letters and Teachings,* which outlined the core of his philosophy, was prepared for publication, and a monthly periodical, *The Chalice,* inaugurated. Retreating to his personal meditation cabin, known as the House of Mystery—the same building we had seen at Cedar-by-the-Sea, only in a different location—Wilson

Aquarian Foundation members in 1927. The front row, from left to right, includes Elma Wilson, Joseph Benner, Edward Arthur Wilson (Brother XII), Will Levington Comfort and Coulson Turnbull. (Schwarze Photographers; John Oliphant collection)

received the inspiration for an outpouring of articles and letters. In *The Chalice,* he laid out some of his prejudiced, extremist political views.

Brother XII subscribed to the conspiracy theory of politics. He believed that a cabal of Jewish bankers and a clutch of Roman Catholic religious leaders were each working towards the goal of world domination. According to Wilson, these conspiracies had been gaining ground for centuries. War was promoted for profit and to demoralize the masses, who were then turned by a controlled media into sport- and celebrity-addled human fodder, incapable of resistance or original thought. The plotting would culminate the following year with the U.S. presidential election, where Democrat Al Smith, a Catholic, would face Republican Herbert Hoover, whom Brother XII considered a tool of Jewish financial interests.

His ambition was to form a Third Party and endorse Ku Klux Klan spokesman Senator Thomas James Heflin as its candidate for president. Wilson founded a Protestant Protective League as an umbrella organization for various Protestant groups to gather their forces for the great political battle to come. He made two trips east in 1928 to implement his doomed, delusory plans, and on the second of them he met two women—one young, one elderly—who would become critical players in his unfolding drama.

The first was Myrtle Baumgartner, encountered on the long train journey to Chicago. The impressionable, unhappily married Baumgartner was seduced by the bewildering brother, who convinced her that she was a reincarnation of the Egyptian deity Isis, while he was Osiris. Their purpose, he explained, was to conceive a child as a vehicle for a potent spiritual being—a child destined to become a "world-teacher" who would lead mankind into a new age of peace and spiritual progress.

After attending several pre-election political conventions and watching his dreams of power come to nought, Wilson, unfazed, arranged to see his wealthiest supporter in Toronto. Mary Connally, an heiress from North Carolina who had donated generously to the Aquarian Foundation, had asked to meet its leader and learn more about his vital work. She was so impressed with Brother XII that he was able to return to the west coast with a pledge for $23,000. Connally was not the foundation's only major backer. Earlier, another wealthy American, Oliver Hess, had given $20,000.

Wilson also brought back to British Columbia a pregnant Baumgartner, whom he secretly installed on a 160-hectare property the foundation had recently purchased on nearby Valdes Island. This land was referred to as the Mandieh Settlement, named after Osiris's birthplace in the Nile delta. It was designed to be a kind of inner sanctum, "an actual place of refuge," where the child prodigies of the elect would be trained to wield earthly dominion. Only those who had completely abandoned the ways of the world would be permitted to set foot there. Wilson entrusted his secret to a few chosen followers and assigned one couple to look after Isis on Valdes, but the shocking news soon leaked out.

Then, much to the astonished disgust of Elma Wilson and several other Aquarians, Isis was discovered to have been reinstalled in the House of Mystery, where Osiris paid her numerous divine visits. Confronted by several of the foundation's governors, Wilson blithely explained that he and Baumgartner were involved in deep spiritual work that less highly evolved beings could hardly be expected to understand. The governors were not satisfied with this clarification. Criticism of Brother XII's methods mounted, and the first cracks appeared in the colony's façade.

Baumgartner wasn't the only problem. Wilson had already constructed a sailboat for his personal use; now he spent $5,000 on a tug to ferry supplies to Valdes, where he embarked on a building program. He did not consult his fellow governors about these plans, nor about other expenditures of foundation funds. The Aquarians had also noted a new and even more paranoid aspect to the brother's suspicion-prone personality. He was training his followers to fend off the psychic attacks of certain "black adepts," and had become incensed at an article in *The Canadian Theosophist* condemning him as an impostor. His reply in *The Chalice* was so venomous and personal that some foundation members began to wonder about his sanity.

Events came to a head in the fall of 1928. Several governors demanded that Wilson either leave the organization or dissolve it. Others resigned. Then Robert England, the foundation's accountant, absconded with $2,800, and Wilson had him arrested and charged with theft. This excitement was followed by a flurry of charges and counter-charges alleging various misuses of funds, including the Connally donation. Wilson signed up his supporters to replace those governors who had resigned, which gave his faction a majority when decisions were to be made. Disaffected members managed to get an injunction freezing Aquarian bank accounts and suspending all business activities, then petitioned the province to dissolve the foundation. And the newspapers had a field day.

The *Province's* Bruce McKelvie got things rolling at the end of October with a front-page story hinting at "weird occult doctrines" and a "mingling of the sexes...in defiance of recognized marriage laws." McKelvie got so caught up in the case, according to Oliphant in *Brother Twelve,* that he wrote a self-righteous letter to the province's attorney-general, Harry Pooley, urging him to "take some action to preserve decency in our regard for morality." At the same time, he promised his readers "revelations that will startle the public." U.S. newspapers picked up the story, especially in California, and many eyes and ears were soon straining to catch the latest gossip about B.C.'s "free love cult."

Local people were surprised to find such notoriety in their midst. Many of them had mistaken "Aquarian" for "aquarium" and assumed that the friendly, otherwise unremarkable folk out at Cedar-by-the-Sea had something to do with fish research. But they followed the hearings in Nanaimo with keen interest, like everyone else. Despite the arrival of Mary Connally on the coast and her testimony that she had intended Brother XII to have complete freedom to do whatever he wished with her financial contribution, the case was still bound over for the November assizes.

But when the trial finally began, Robert England, out on bail, was nowhere to be found. In fact, this key witness was never seen again. The jury dismissed the charges against both England and Wilson, much to the disappointment, no doubt, of the newspapers. Wilson also succeeded in having the injunction lifted, allowing him access to foundation funds. He celebrated these successes with several open letters to Aquarian members, justifying his actions and ascribing all that had happened to predestination. They were being cleansed by fire, he believed, so that "weak and faulty elements" in the organization could be weeded out and the work brought to a higher level and new pitch of intensity.

Poor Myrtle Baumgartner, meanwhile, had suffered a miscarriage and a nervous breakdown. Eventually, she would have a second miscarriage. Osiris then had little further use for Isis, though he continued to rationalize his relationship with her. She was dispatched to a hotel outside Victoria, where Mary Connally looked after her for a time, then moved to Toronto and was not heard from again.

The public was startled by further revelations at the end of the year, when other charges were heard against Wilson. This time a man named James Lipincott was suing him for unpaid wages earned at the Mandieh Settlement. Ex-governor Coulson Turnbull had made a special trip to Nanaimo in order to testify, but when he attempted to do so he fell to the floor in a fainting fit, as did several spectators. When the judge tried to adjourn the court, he was only able to growl like a dog. The proceedings resumed, but the prosecuting counsel was stricken with a debilitating memory lapse and was unable to continue. The charges were dropped. But Brother XII's reputation was sealed that day; everyone present agreed that he possessed magical powers of a decidedly dark and evil nature.

Along the shoreline of De Courcy Island, wind and waves have carved strange, organic patterns in the sandstone. Arbutus trees and Douglas firs overlook the ocean; a thick layer of salal, ferns and moss carpets the ground at their feet. Territorial kingfishers scold from high branches; cormorants rest on warm rocky ledges; bald eagles and ospreys soar overhead. The southern edge of the island has been scalloped into a series of bays, and we point our kayaks into the largest and most easterly one, where a fine pebble beach beckons.

The beach, and the little peninsula to the north and east of it, are part of one of the province's prettiest marine parks, Pirates Cove, established in 1966. We are the only campers that September day and set up our tent beside a picnic table in a lovely arbutus grove. After a swim and some supper, during which a persistent pair of young raccoons make brazen attacks on our food supply, we watch a large family of river otters enjoy their supper out in the bay, where small fish seem plentiful. As evening falls, a stroll along verdant Brother XII Trail brings us to Pirates Cove itself, a boat anchorage just north of our campsite.

This aquamarine lagoon was the eventual heart of Brother XII's empire. In April 1929, after the tumult of the trials had died down a bit, Wilson brought Mary Connally to Valdes by boat in order to show her the cabins and assembly hall that were being constructed there. Then he cruised his favourite benefactor around the De Courcy Group, which divides the broad channel between Valdes and Cedar-by-the-Sea. They ended up at the paradise of Pirates Cove, known in those days as the Haven, or Gospel Cove. Wilson explained that if the colony could acquire these islands, one of which had a deserted farm with excellent soil, it might become self-sufficient. They would grow their own food, and be free to live as they pleased. Connally fell once again for the smooth sales pitch, went to Nanaimo and purchased De Courcy and Ruxton, the group's largest islands, a total of 275 hectares, for $10,000. She then returned to the U.S.

Steadily but cautiously, Wilson moved ahead with his plans. New arrivals—and there were still plenty of them, as most foundation members had only heard the brother's side of the previous year's scandals—had to sign a waiver declaring that they were volunteers and expected no pay for any labour. Brother XII had come up with a new fund-raising twist: to be one of the truly elect and live on Valdes, now called the Brothers' Centre, candidates not only had to turn their backs on the world, they had to give up the idea of a "personal self." As a test of dedication, all possessions had to be surrendered to the foundation. Food and clothing would be furnished from a common fund. Life would be simple.

About this time, an important newcomer appeared on the scene: Mabel Skottowe. Born in England, raised in Saskatchewan, this manipulative siren had a fascination for the occult. As her mystical name, she had adopted the letter "Z." She arrived with a man named Roger Painter, "the poultry king of Florida." They were in love—until Skottowe met Brother XII. Besides losing his lady friend to Wilson, Painter also handed over almost $100,000 to the cause and was then sent back to Florida. He returned for more punishment, however, bringing with him a young wife.

Madame Zee, meanwhile, quickly made herself indispensable to Wilson, supervising the city of refuge under construction on Valdes while the brother busied himself with his latest acquisition, De Courcy Island. He did not intend to live on Valdes. He had a home built at the Haven and put money into improving De Courcy's old farm. Elma Wilson, having survived the Osiris/Isis debacle, was sent off to assist the Swiss branch of the foundation. She was never permitted to return to the colony, and after hanging around Vancouver for a couple of years, she moved to Scotland.

In the fall of 1929, Brother XII and Madame Zee moved to the new island. Skottowe oversaw the colony and the brother retreated from public life, explaining to his disciples that he now needed to spend most of his time communing with higher realms.

Madame Zee was not a popular taskmaster. Quick-tempered and surly, she was reported to have carried a riding crop with her and used it on the unfortunate colonists, who soon found themselves reduced almost to slaves. Some left. Others, seemingly under Brother XII's baleful psychic influence, remained, working the land like feudal serfs.

As Wilson had transferred most of his activities from Vancouver Island to Valdes and De Courcy, which were virtually uninhabited before his arrival, he was able to stay out of the public eye. The B.C. government still kept tabs on him; the police paid several visits to the colony but could find nothing untoward. The petition to dissolve the Aquarian Foundation was finally granted by the provincial cabinet; home owners at Cedar-by-the-Sea were each given title to their land. The decision did not really threaten Wilson, as the foundation's assets

The children of the Aquarian Foundation members posing at the Cedar-by-the-Sea spring pageant. (John Oliphant collection)

were now negligible. The colony's funds and island properties were directly under his control.

At the end of the year, Wilson and Skottowe made a sudden, surprise trip to England, leaving Alfred Barley in charge of the colony. In London, he arranged for another book, *Unsigned Letters from an Elder Brother,* to be published and spent time on the Devon coast at Brixham, where he bought a nineteen-metre trawler and renamed it the *Lady Royal.* Almost twelve months and many adventures would pass before the couple got back to B.C., having sailed their new vessel halfway round the world. Additional crew members were hired in the Caribbean, but they could not prevent the *Lady Royal* being blown hundreds of kilometres off course after a Pacific storm. She had to be rescued by a passing liner—news that made the Victoria papers.

Upon his return, Brother XII's behaviour became increasingly erratic. He kept his troops subdued and obedient by requiring them to change abodes or move between settlements on very short notice. The colonists believed that Cedar-by-the-Sea was for low-ranking disciples, Valdes was for initiates and De Courcy was for the inner circle. Each move was seen as a promotion or demotion letting people know where they stood in "the work." Ruxton Island, with its rudimentary facilities, was reserved as a prison, a place where nonconformists could reconsider their loyalties. Elderly followers, including Mary Connally, who had returned from the U.S. to dwell at Cedar-by-the-Sea, were forced to live in primitive conditions and perform heavy physical labour. They thought that Wilson's peremptory demands, often delivered through Madame Zee, were a form of spiritual testing.

The contributions of recent arrivals and monthly pledges of other colonists were handed over directly to Edward Wilson. He had all monies converted to gold coin, using a trusted follower and doing business at banks in several Vancouver Island towns. The "buried treasure" portion of the Brother XII legend derives from his practice of storing the coins in Mason jars, which were sealed with wax, then placed in rope-handled wooden boxes. Wilson moved his savings from place to place at night, burying them in different locations around the colony. Each jar held about $10,000; in his book, John Oliphant reports that one colonist claimed to have made forty-three of the wooden containers.

In 1931, Brother XII and Madame Zee officially changed their names to Amiel and Zura de Valdes. Their relationship, however irrational, seemed to be evolving, but nothing had changed for the other members of the colony. By the end of the year, an impressive amount of work had been done on Valdes: an orchard of fruit and nut trees bloomed, a big storage shed was filled with preserves. They had a dairy, greenhouses, a chicken coop and a sawmill. Several hectares were planted with vegetables. A number of cabins had also been built on De Courcy, across the lagoon from Wilson's house.

Various brushes with the law occurred, as disillusioned or raving colonists made their way to the authorities with one bizarre story or another. Nothing serious enough transpired for the police to lay charges. Nevertheless, Brother XII developed a marked paranoia about the outside world. Five earth-and-log forts were constructed around the Haven, designed so that any boat attempting to enter the lagoon would be within shooting range. Rifles were ordered by mail, guards posted, defence bulletins issued and sentry duties outlined. Unsuspecting vessels were warned off. Gunfire was reported.

Before the colony fell into discord, Brother XII's followers were content to till their gardens by hand. Alfred Barley is at the far right, Roger Painter at the far left. (John Oliphant collection)

As Wilson's preoccupation with conspiracies deepened, the colony started to fall apart. Amiel and Zura de Valdes were constantly at each other's throat. The abuse of the long-suffering colonists intensified. Why did they put up with it? Because of fear, John Oliphant suggests in *Brother Twelve,* and because of the psychological control that Wilson achieved with his demoralizing tactics, dividing husband from wife, child from parent, banishing and forgiving, threatening and rewarding. If his followers left, they were destitute in a foreign country, having given everything to the Master of Wisdom.

Finally, the colonists summoned up what will power they still possessed and persuaded Alfred Barley to write a polite but beseeching little letter to Brother XII, describing their "growing sense of dissatisfaction and bewilderment" and asking for a meeting. Outraged at this revolt in the ranks, he responded by shipping small groups off Valdes and De Courcy and depositing them at Cedar-by-the-Sea. By the summer of 1932, Amiel and Zura had the islands to themselves. At the city of refuge, birds called and small animals rustled in the tinder-dry undergrowth. The clear, blue-green waters of the Haven held the *Lady Royal* in a quiet embrace. But the familiar sounds of the settlers had been silenced forever. Edward Arthur Wilson's dream of nurturing a new world order was officially over.

The rest of the Brother XII story seems anticlimactic, though newspaper readers were treated to another helping of spicy scandal. The colonists, thrown together in one location and finally free of their tyrannical lord and his supernatural powers, gathered their wits about them and approached a Nanaimo lawyer. In September, Mary Connally filed a claim against Brother XII and Madame Zee for $42,100 plus $10,000 in personal damages. Wilson and Skottowe had plotted "to deceive, ensnare and delude" her, she charged. She had been fraudulently cheated out of her fortune. Alfred Barley followed suit in November with a claim for over $14,000.

The cases were heard in April 1933. Although they feared psychic retribution, former cult members managed to testify in support of Connally and Barley, describing how they were manipulated and intimidated, and how Valdes was little more than a "slave colony." Roger Painter reported that Wilson had ordered the colonists to assassinate the attorney-general and other officials by the mental process of separating their "etheric" bodies from their physical ones. The judge awarded both claims in full and gave Connally ownership of De Courcy, Ruxton and the Valdes acreage.

The plaintiffs never collected any money from Wilson, of course. He and Skottowe were long gone by the time the cases came to trial. They left a scene of carnage behind them, destroying buildings and leaving a scuttled *Lady Royal* to rot in the Haven, and escaped on the colony's tugboat. In his book, Oliphant tracks the couple to Roberts Creek, near Sechelt on the mainland coast, and later to Victoria. From there they took the tug all the way to Prince Rupert, then boarded a train to Montreal and a ship to England. Wilson died in Switzerland in 1934, seeking help for a heart problem at a Neuchâtel clinic. At least, a death certificate and numerous obituaries assert that he died there. Subsequent sightings of both Wilson and Skottowe have been reported. The fortune in gold, however, was not seen again.

The ex-colonists planned initially to stay at Cedar-by-the-Sea and continue with Wilson's spiritual program. A few held onto their Vancouver Island homes for decades, and Mary Connally lived for a time on De Courcy Island. But the group gradually dispersed. Rumours of buried gold still exert a strong hold over local treasure hunters. The island properties were dug over and torn apart so systematically over the years that little remains of the old buildings except a ramshackle farm structure now used as a storehouse. On De Courcy, Connally's caretaker found a hidden trapdoor in a chicken coop. In the vault below, reportedly, was a scrap of paper with the following inscription: "For fools and traitors—nothing!"

Edward Arthur Wilson was not the first charismatic personality to lead a utopian settlement in British Columbia. William Duncan, Christian Saugstad, Matti Kurikka and Peter Verigin had tried before him, with varying results that rarely reflected the founder's original intentions. And Wilson would not be the last; the year he died, aristocratic, twenty-five-year-old Martin Exeter was busily immersing himself in occult and spiritualistic writings at his family's 100 Mile House ranch, and would soon lead both a sect and a colony (see chapter 7). But the brief career of Brother XII certainly illustrates the dangers involved.

Of all the community leaders portrayed in this book, Wilson seems to have been the most corrupted. Either lust for power and gold changed him from a mystic to a monster, or his entire operation was a confidence trick and a swindle from beginning to end—which seems unlikely, considering the earnestness of much of his behaviour. On the basis of our present understanding, his story must serve as an example of what can happen when utopian efforts become subverted to evil ends. His intentional community turned into a classic dystopia, the archetype of the modern cult. Brother XII himself has entered B.C.'s collective unconsciousness as a dark and eerie figure, a personification of fear. He represents what can happen if people hand over their free will when joining a collective enterprise.

LIVING ON THE LAND
Post-War Alternative Experiments

*The seed we wish to cultivate is the building of a new
society, based on taking from Mother Earth our basic needs
while giving back to her to the best of our ability.*
—Ochiltree Commune, *In Defense of Nature*, no. 1

In the "Country Neighbours" section of *The Smallholder*, the headline read: "A Land Co-op Needs Members." The text announced briefly that eight "households" were each preparing to invest $5,000 in order to "create an intentional community based on co-operative principles of land ownership and development." The task of writing about and promoting this venture had fallen to me, a budding freelance journalist. "We are in need of several more members before we can effectively get started," I admitted. "Our first goal is a group economy founded on organic market gardening but, naturally, we have many other ideas and hopes."

The year was 1976. As potential back-to-the-landers, we had located a piece of property very much to our liking: about forty hectares, "mostly flat with beautiful woods and extensive meadows," on Texada Island in the Strait of Georgia. The price of this land was about what a beat-up, twenty-year-old, one-bedroom condominium would sell for today in Vancouver's least-attractive suburbs. Even so, we couldn't afford to buy it unless we roped in a few like-minded visionaries. But how difficult could that be?

I composed my notice and sent it off to a place I'd never heard of called Argenta, where a tiny magazine was produced that served as a forum for "ideas and information of interest to country people." An identical message appeared in *Catalist,* the monthly newsletter of Vancouver's Fed Up wholesale food co-operative. I remember being very pleased when these quasi-literary efforts appeared. But our co-op dream never took on substance, and our "ideas and hopes" have grown dim in my memory.

I have a faint recollection of standing in the rain with a number of other people, wondering if the wet, bushy terrain all around might suit me as a place to live. The idea of rural homesteading, while intriguing, did not thrill me quite the same way it thrilled many of my friends, especially those who had families—or spouses, at least—to keep them company in the handcrafted homes they were eager to build. Insecurity, not utopian idealism, accounted for my presence on Texada Island that day. I wanted to invest my modest savings in land, so that sometime in the near future—when urban life would surely become too awful to bear—I might have a place to go. Many acquaintances were preparing to leave the city for a blissful existence in nature. I thought I'd better get in on the action, too.

Brother XII and his prescient Aquarians anticipated the social turbulence that would accompany the new astrological era due to dawn in the 1960s and 1970s. But they could not have predicted the weird, wonderful spectrum of initiatives that the back-to-the-land movement would foster. Our attempt at settlement was pale and prudent compared to some. We sought strength in numbers and hoped to maximize our purchasing power. By forming a legal entity—the Salal Rural Housing Co-operative—and agreeing to certain conditions, we believed we could have some control over how our immediate neighbourhood might develop. We weren't interested in living communally or worshipping together. We followed no guru. We each wanted a private piece of paradise in a friendly, united community.

Other groups founding communities in B.C. at roughly the same time, however, had wildly varying political, spiritual, sexual and economic agendas. Dozens of these tribes had become permanent enough by the mid-1970s to join B.C.'s Coalition of Intentional Co-operative Communities—"an amorphous network," according to the coalition's *Open Circle* newsletter, whose members were "somewhere on the same road in creating co-operative settlements." Sadly, the Salal Co-op never became part of the CICC circle; our clan soon disintegrated and moved on to other things. But B.C., with its mild climate, spectacular landscape and reputation for tolerance—and bolstered by numerous young Americans dodging the Vietnam War draft—was at the forefront of renewed interest in alternative lifestyles.

This interest did not spring, fully fledged, from nowhere. There had been local precursors to the New Age movement, starting with Edward Arthur Wilson and the Aquarian Foundation. The Emissaries of Divine Light, whom we will meet later this chapter, also got an early start. Sixty fundamentalist members of the Canadian Young People's Society of Alberta and Saskatchewan were reported by Vancouver's *Daily Province* to be involved in a communal-living experiment at Sooke on southern Vancouver Island in 1932. While it's unlikely the Steadfast Bible Students would have considered themselves spiritual kin to Brother XII and his friends, their goals were not incompatible with those set by the members of our land co-op.

"In the fields and in the community halls of the colony," the newspaper revealed, "it is intended that those tired in body and spirit may find relief from the competitive struggles which commercialism has imposed on mankind. It is hoped, too, that, at the colony, scope will be given for the development of communal and poetic interests." Instead, the students organized themselves as the Star Construction Company and started up a cheese factory. The Star Brethren, as the group was sometimes known, apparently succumbed to the economic woes of the Depression.

A longer-lasting effort at alternative community-making took place twenty years later, when a group of Quakers from California, fed up with what they perceived as the growing dollar-devotion and militarism of U.S. society, decided to drive north to B.C. and start a new life. The community they helped create predated the 1970s commune era by several decades, yet when the time came, it managed to plug itself neatly into the Coalition of Intentional Co-operative Communities. Argenta, in fact, can be seen as a bridge between "the Sixties" and the era preceding it.

If you drive north from Kaslo on a clear evening, along the shores of vast Kootenay Lake, you find yourself in the shadows of the Selkirk Mountains. By following Highway 31 to its conclusion—a journey involving many kilometres of gravel and, eventually, a ferry—you will be led to Revelstoke and the Trans-Canada. In the meantime, on the far side of the lake, the beckoning hills are still lit by the sun; they gleam like gold in the clean air. The eye can pick out streaks of light green, clearings among the dark frosting of conifers. One of these is Argenta.

Decades ago, you could get to Argenta from Lardeau or Kaslo, or even from Nelson, by paddle-wheeled steamships such as the *Moyie*. Now you must drive round the north end of Kootenay Lake, cross the green, frothing Duncan River, pass duck-haven marshes of rush and sedge, and bounce along a little shoreline road. The route passes the former site of Argenta's long-dismantled dock, then curves up onto the benchlands above the lake, where a few-dozen homesteads cluster.

The two original Quaker families—the Stevensons and the Pollards—arrived in B.C. at the end of March 1952. At a stately fifty-kilometre-per-hour average speed, it had taken them two full weeks to drive their scruffy cavalcade of ancient vehicles and brakeless trailers north from California. They spent six more weeks roaming the West Kootenay backroads, "looking for places that might fit our low income potential," John Stevenson explains, when I visit him at his Nelson home. "We were completely ignorant about the value of land." Wherever they went, property prices miraculously rose.

According to Helen Stevenson, a number of "friendly gestures" by people living at Argenta helped make up their minds to give the place a try. One man offered to lease them some property and take sixty dollars off the selling price if they ended up buying it. "He told us we could grow turnips there," says John. In May, they transported everything important—including children, chickens, a library and a large supply of home canning—across the lake on the weekly mail boat. Within a year, they were joined by two more Quaker families from California, the Boyds and the Rushes. There were enough children in Argenta now to reopen the village's one-room school, which helped the Quakers gain acceptance, and Helen was a qualified teacher.

"We did not start Argenta," John emphasizes. Indeed, the newcomers might not have survived without the kindness of the community's original members, who loaned them a cow and offered much useful advice about rural living. A turn-of-the-century mining boom gave Argenta its start, and silver—*argentum* in Latin, *argent* in French—gave the place its name. When the boom was over, a handful of families remained, logging and farming the lakeside benches and sending produce to town on the weekly sternwheeler.

The Argenta Quakers were not the first of their kind to come to B.C. The Religious Society of Friends, as Quakers are officially known, formed chapters, or "monthly meetings," in Victoria in 1908 and Vancouver in 1911. The meetings still continue, and Quakers also gather in Qualicum, Duncan, Vernon, Nelson, Prince George, Kamloops and on Quadra Island. But few monthly meetings have been as active as the one at Argenta.

The Society of Friends was founded in England by George Fox in the 1650s. Fox proclaimed the immanence of God within each individual, and the consequent irrelevance of creeds, churches and priests. Quakers and Doukhobors thus share a similar outlook, and both have been persecuted for their teachings. Although their attitudes differ in many ways, especially concerning the importance of the Bible, the two sects have enjoyed a close relationship, often working together on international peace projects. In the 1890s, English Quakers played a key role in helping the Doukhobors escape Russia; Quakers also served on various commissions formed in B.C. to try to put an end to Freedomite violence.

Its traditions of dissent and belief in universal brotherhood have led the sect into the realms of social reform. Quakers are involved in protecting the rights of prisoners, women, aboriginal people and the poor. They raise funds for all kinds of causes and are active worldwide in the fields of education, emergency relief, environmental preservation and peace-making. The Argenta Friends were also interested in community-making. "We moved from California with a definite intent," says Helen Stevenson. "We wanted to find a place where people could meet together to pursue a common purpose or dream."

In 1954, after the arrival of several more families, an initial economic experiment was attempted. "If we really were a spiritual community," says John, "we thought we should be doing something more than just meeting and talking together." The result was the Delta Co-op, which included some of Argenta's original inhabitants as well as Quakers. Co-op members agreed to pool the earnings from whatever work they could find—farming, logging, teaching and construction—and share the income. Each family ended up with a modest sixty dollars monthly, plus an additional five dollars per child.

But life was rich in other ways. The villagers were finding a new sense of freedom and purpose. Despite the hardships, they were enjoying themselves. Everyone played an instrument, and regular community parties and dances were held—with live music, of course. Argenta became well known for a particular type of celebration: one that started at seven, ended at midnight and welcomed children. For kids, growing up at Argenta was like living in an enchanted forest. They loved everything about it.

The next community project grew out of considering the needs of the children. "About 1957," says Helen, "we wondered what else we could do besides building roads and farming, and realized that more than half the adults associated with the co-op had some kind of teaching experience." The idea of a private high school was born. It took two years to work out the details but, in 1959, the Argenta Friends School opened its doors and would keep them open for the next twenty years.

Argenta's students were far more involved in every aspect of their education than their contemporaries in more traditional schools.

Elmo Wolfe and Bob Boyd hewing timber in the late 1950s for the construction of the Argenta Friends School. (Ruth Boyd/David Gluns)

Although adults were definitely in charge, the students assisted with curriculum planning and the development of school policy. They dealt with discipline problems and even helped decide whether or not new students and staff should be accepted. "We spent a *lot* of time discussing and debating rules," Helen remembers, "but the students also learned a lot about creating a consensus, about decision-making and responsibility."

Enrollment was kept to about twenty-four students, who came to Argenta from all over Canada and the U.S. and lived with local families while attending the school. There were usually between six and eight full-time instructors, with other people, including a number of community members, teaching part-time and acting as house-parents. "We challenged kids to think about values," says John. "I wanted them to experience a sense of community," adds Helen, "and to learn how that sense of community might be built."

The Friends School was a success. Justine Brown's *All Possible Worlds,* an important source for information on B.C.'s hippie communes, describes it as "the avant-garde of the alternative-school movement in British Columbia." Other alternative education institutes would be formed later in Greater Vancouver (Relevant High, Contemporary High, New School, Windsor House), on Saturna Island and elsewhere. Sometimes referred to as "free schools," most charged fees—$1,800 a year, in the case of Argenta—though exceptions were often made for those in financial difficulty. The school thrust Argenta into the New Age limelight, and many freedom-seekers soon found themselves drawn to the sunny side of Kootenay Lake.

Other ventures, such as the Kootenay Co-operative Land Settlement Society, sprang up. This enterprise, with half a dozen families homesteading eighty hectares of land, became a core member of the CICC, linking Argenta to countercultural activities around the province. The society still exists today, and has more than doubled in population. "It's nice to live here," secretary Ryan Dunnett reported in 1979 to *Communities,* a "journal of co-operative living" published in Virginia:

> When a home burned a few years back at the onset of winter the whole community contributed work, materials and energy to have a new one built in a couple of weeks. When someone needs a lot of people power to work on a project for a day or so, as

many as thirty people will show up....What we have is a
responsible community, highly educated both academically and
practically, friendly, loving and nurturing.

The Herbison family came in 1961, from Nelson, well before the
hippie phenomenon got rolling. Hugh Herbison became principal of a
small school fourteen kilometres from Argenta. Neither he nor Agnes
Herbison, his wife, were Quakers at the time. "People at Argenta had
a wonderful commonality of purpose," he reflects. "They pursued an
intentional rural life with the ideals of respecting the environment and
their neighbours and providing the best possible place for their families. The community was cohesive but not exclusive. The Quakers
established a mystique that attracted other people."

Today, the Herbisons live comfortably on sixteen hectares of land
they share with several grown offspring. Like most people in Argenta,
they have a splendid vegetable and flower garden. On the day of my
August visit, a profusion of plants are in bloom: delphiniums, gloriosa
and shasta daisies, day lilies and, of course, Quaker roses. In the
house, where exposed log beams and a fancy stone fireplace reinforce
the rustic atmosphere, upright and baby-grand pianos attest to Agnes's
love of music.

Argenta's cultural facilities, which would be the envy of most small
towns, were an important draw for many new arrivals. The Herbisons,
for instance, found a community orchestra their children could join,
as well as a drama group and classes on such crafts as puppetry and
clay modelling. Music continues to enhance village life, with folk and
square dancing, the Argenta Old Time Band and concerts by visiting
performers. One of the Herbison's children, now living in London,
England, so thrived in this musical environment that she became a
classical soprano. In tribute to her place of origin, she uses the stage
name Nancy Argenta.

The day after interviewing the Herbisons, I have a chance to feel
Argenta's spiritual heartbeat by attending the Sunday meeting at the
Friends' meeting place. Thirteen people of varied ages, including two
who had come from Kaslo, show up at the former teachers' residence
and student boarding house. Quaker meetings are very simple; after
half an hour's hymn singing, with Agnes Herbison at the piano, the
gathering sits in silence for an hour. The stillness is broken only twice:
once when someone follows George Fox's bidding and speaks quietly

on a topic "that they thought savoured of a Divine spring," and once when a bird flies into the room and has to be rescued.

After the meeting, tea is served, business conducted and news of fellow Quakers exchanged. I have a chance to chat with other community members, including Mary Pollard, at eighty-nine the last of the original Quakers to still live in Argenta. (The Stevensons moved to Nelson when John's health began to deteriorate.) I am happy to take up Betty Tillotson's offer to stop by for a bite of lunch, one of several invites I receive to visit people in their homes.

I want to talk to Tillotson not only because she has lived at Argenta for twenty-five years and been involved in most aspects of its growth, but because she is a mainstay of *The Smallholder,* which is still being published—by a volunteer collective, naturally—after all these years. The magazine is printed by the Argenta Friends Press, another local enterprise, which also produces a Quaker periodical and does commercial jobs.

Hugh Elliot, founder of the Argenta Water Power Company, in front of the building where a Pelton wheel provides electricity for the community. (David Gluns/Natural Image Photography)

Tillotson shows me around the property she shares with other families and individuals. After touring the obligatory fantastic garden and a group of Finnish-style log homes, originally built in the 1950s by early settler Elmo Wolfe, I feel as if I have come full circle. My own attempts at joining an ideal community may have been ineffectual, but at least some of the social experiments that started up in those early days are still flowering. They have evolved, of course. For one thing, they never were—and never could have been—"ideal." But they have something that allows them to survive, something Betty Tillotson calls "a spirit of sharing."

"It feels like it's a little harder to find around here than it used to be," she says, "but the basic spirit is still there. Whenever there's an occasion or need for it, then it's still there."

It's time to leave Argenta. On the way back to my Kootenay Lake campsite, I stop at the community centre, finished four years ago after seven years of construction. As it is Sunday, the post office is closed and nobody is around. But the doors of the centre are never locked. Its walls are festooned with bulletins: the minutes of Argenta Community Association meetings, an announcement that the theme of the Fall Faire will be "children," commentary on the controversial issue of logging in the Argenta watershed. Eggs and books wait patiently for pick-up.

There are notices about tai chi, cob building workshops, ecofeminism, drumming and the Global Living Project. A birthday message celebrates Argenta's Leos. Articles, quotes and magic formulae offer insights into various mysteries. Bodywork, deep-tissue work and chainsaw work are all advertised. Dwarf bunnies, homemade ice cream and black walnut–wormwood tincture can be purchased. Bob wants people to know that he will be baking bread on Tuesday; place your order below. And if you have taken the chainsaw, please return it to the centre, and remember: God is watching you.

I am reminded of what Hugh Herbison had said the day before, that Argenta is surprisingly similar today to the way it was in the 1970s. Its economic underpinnings are different—less self-sufficiency, more government assistance. Making a living can be "a very dicey thing." But neighbourliness is still evident, as are a sense of trust and concerns for the environment and how kids should be brought up. There is a willingness to work through the inevitable disputes in consensual fashion. "People still come here because they like the community," Herbison had remarked. "They still choose Argenta for idealistic reasons."

The late 1960s, when the first baby boomers were turning twenty, was a time for celebrating, not settling down. Most utopian undertakings associated with the counterculture in B.C. got rolling in the early 1970s. But at least one notorious communal endeavour started before then. The Lasqueti Island colony founded by Ted Sideras derived much of its fame from Alan Edmonds' before-and-after articles, written for *Maclean's* and *WEST* magazines in, respectively, 1970 and 1991. A rather grotesque thriller, *The Dance of Shiva,* by William Deverell, at one time the colony's lawyer, also contributed to its cult status.

Ted Sideras, born in Wisconsin, was living in Medford, Oregon, when he decided that there was more to life than the material rewards he was enjoying as the owner of an employment and credit-checking agency and a restaurant. Aged forty-five, he sold up, headed north and bought thirty-two hectares of land on Lasqueti, the most isolated of the large islands in the Strait of Georgia. His manager, George Orton, moved too, and they brought their families with them. It was 1967, the year the hippie movement achieved international prominence—the year of the "summer of love."

Other relatives joined them, as did several young Lasqueti Islanders. Sideras apparently welcomed seekers after non-material bliss. Word of his sanctuary spread fast on the underground grapevine and, only two years later, almost fifty people were camped on the property, half Americans and half Canadians.

Sideras seemed an unlikely leader. Journalist Edmonds described him as "stoop shouldered, crinkle-eyed, minus a few front teeth" with a "wind-roughened face fenced by a moth-eaten beard." Photos reveal a man with a vaguely academic air, hair combed over a balding pate, wearing heavy, dark-framed glasses. He reminded Edmonds of Woody Allen.

When Edmonds showed up, in 1970, he found fifty-four gum-boot-clad men, women and children living in tents, eating in a plastic-walled mess hall and helping construct Stone House. This rough-hewn mansion, its shingle-clad upper section supported by walls of the plentiful native rock, held six two-room suites on the second floor, plus a cavernous living room and more bedrooms and bathrooms on the ground floor. But so many people flocked to Sideras Place that, even when Stone House was finished, half of them still had to live under canvas.

Sideras appeared to be paying the bills for this experiment, with others throwing in whatever money they could. A teacher was appointed and children attended rudimentary classes. The communards were not compelled to help build Stone House. Lack of compulsion was part of the appeal. "After a while," Sideras told Edmonds, "they find no demands of any kind are made on them, and you see them beginning to relax...doing things they want to do and have to be done anyway—cooking, or cutting down trees, or the laundry, or helping with the house. It's real nifty to see."

Edmonds liked Sideras, and his *Maclean's* article approved of the Lasqueti goings-on. There were no drugs in evidence, no orgies, no religious mania. Everyone seemed happy. He spent three days on Lasqueti and ended up comparing Sideras and his "family" to those early Christian ascetics and martyrs who preferred the solitude of the desert to the marvels of Roman civilization. But Edmonds was not given the entire story; he wasn't told about The Asking, for instance, where commune members went off alone to seek God's will and bring messages back for Sideras to ponder.

In his retrospective, what-went-wrong piece for *WEST,* Edmonds told a disturbingly different tale. Things had changed fast at Sideras Place. The growing influx of people was more than either the pocketbook or patience of its patron could bear. In late 1970, Sideras sold the house and moved the family—eighty strong by this time—to Calvert Island further north, where they lived as squatters.

Lasqueti is remote, but it's not that far off the beaten track. There's a passenger ferry and a village with some facilities. It's less than two hours away from the urban temptations of a town such as Nanaimo. But Calvert is a different degree of island. On B.C.'s central coast, eighty-five kilometres north of Port Hardy, it definitely has no ferry— or anything in the way of amenities. No store, few people; just mosquitoes and muskeg and rainforest.

On Calvert Island, everything fell apart. Sideras retreated to his tent in a funk. Many people now had guns, and threatening encounters with hunters and fishermen were reported. The police had to fly in and remove a young colonist who had suffered some kind of mental breakdown.

Lawyer Deverell had been hired to wrangle a note from the provincial government allowing the colonists to remain on Calvert. Deverell considered Sideras "the most normal, worldly person, but there were strange vibrations," according to Edmonds. Some ex-colonists felt that their leader had a strange, pseudo-hypnotic power over the group. "God, that man had a magic tongue," one reported. "On Lasqueti, everyone was docile and content," said Deverell. "But on Calvert they seemed zombie-like."

Deverell's 1984 *Dance of Shiva* featured the murders of twenty-one cult members at Om Bay, a mythical commune in the northern Strait of Georgia. Om Bay had "a lot of the Sideras place in it," the author told Edmonds. But no murders ever took place at Lasqueti, or at Calvert. Sideras and Orton became the focus of a trial that made the local front pages, but the killings they were charged with concerned cows, not humans. The cattle-rustling caper didn't come to light until 1972, when a Lasqueti landowner finally noted that his Hereford herd was considerably smaller than it should have been. The family had left Calvert Island earlier that year, evicted by the government after Deverell's negotiations had failed. Sideras, with about twenty of his inner circle, was living in Vancouver.

Commune members had arranged to buy several cows to supplement their food supply. They were accused of taking several dozen more than they had paid for, after being told by Orton that "the cows are given by God." Sideras was acquitted for lack of evidence, Orton because the testimony against him came from an accomplice. Sideras was soon in the news again: the father of a commune member, believing his son was under some kind of demonic control, threatened him. After these fiascos, the dwindling family bought land at Kingcome Inlet in 1973, another isolated spot on the B.C. coast, and homesteaded there until only eight adults remained. In 1976, Sideras and Orton and their families moved to Fiji. Today, their whereabouts is unknown. Stone House burned to the ground in 1987.

Edmonds felt his original article may have contributed to the downfall of Sideras Place. The *Maclean's* piece didn't mention the commune's location, but it was reprinted in the United States and Europe, and about two thousand people wrote letters of enquiry. Edmonds sent them on to Lasqueti. For twenty years, he wrote in *WEST,* he'd believed he had "carelessly helped kill a way of life before it could take root and perhaps become an example to us all." Perhaps.

The Lasqueti Commune was rural, apolitical and tragic. Its essence was "like gossamer," according to its founder. "When you try to touch it, define it, it vanishes." Its antithesis among early B.C. intentional communities was the Campus Residence Co-operative Association, more commonly known as the New West Co-op, which also started life in 1967. The New West Co-op—urban, politically conscious and successful enough that it still flourishes today—was everything Sideras Place could never be.

New West was "the oldest housing co-op in B.C. and one of the most durable intentional communities in the province," according to its resident historian, Jim Bowman, writing in a 1978 *Open Circle* newsletter:

> At different times the co-op has oriented toward laissez-faire hip-pyism and New Left radicalism, but it has matured to become a non-ideological, rationally organized comfortable home. Its twenty-five members encompass a wide range of ages, occupations and personality types. They choose to live communally because it is a more efficient way to utilize human and economic resources, and because the social stimulation of communal life is satisfying. Openings for new members seldom appear but people are welcome to add their names to the short waiting list.

There is no echo of New Norway or New Jerusalem in New West. The co-op was nicknamed after its Lower Mainland home town of New Westminster. The Campus Residence Co-operative Association was formed by students and faculty from nearby Simon Fraser University. With loans from the Central Mortgage and Housing Corporation and the B.C. Central Credit Union, they bought and renovated a pair of side-by-side, three-storey Edwardian houses and later gained control of a third building. Residents called them the "three sisters." Rents were established, a group of current and former students moved in, and the great social experiment began.

The counterculture journal *Communities* asked Bowman to co-ordinate a special section on British Columbia for a 1979 issue. He did some of the writing, as well, and his article on New West notes that residential co-ops sprang up near many Canadian universities in the late 1960s. In fact, Toronto's Campus Residence Co-operative Incorporated, after which the New Westminster group was named and modelled, had been operating co-ops at the University of Toronto since 1936. Their most famous venture was Rochdale College, an experimental "free university" named, in turn, after the birthplace of the co-operative movement, an English town where a group of flannel weavers opened a co-op store in 1844. The Toronto Rochdale, a sinister concrete polyhedron, opened in 1968 and closed seven years later after a deluge of negative, drug-related publicity.

New West also got off to a rocky start. Bowman described an early purge of "mystics" and "dopers" by a vociferous faction of "politicals," who turned the co-op into a base for campus activism and made it a cell in a network of underground revolutionaries. Other early residents, such as former *Georgia Straight* and *Vancouver* editor Bob Mercer, remember the co-op as less polarized and more chaotic, a "beehive" that they nevertheless belonged to and felt part of. This radical phase, claims Bowman, ended quickly after it was discovered that certain "politicals" had misappropriated co-op funds, leaving the association with a serious deficit. New West rallied by loosening entrance qualifications in order to attract more members.

The early 1970s saw an almost comical round of

One of three Edwardian houses— the "three sisters"—on Queen's Avenue in New Westminster that make up the New West Co-op, still going strong after thirty years of operation. (Andrew Scott)

power struggles. First, a charismatic "middle-aged divorcée" with "a knowledge of group dynamics and psychology" took control. Her reign involved "a series of group LSD sessions," according to Bowman, "which led to a feeling of group identity." She was outmanoeuvred, and "a community worker with a penchant for politics" eventually emerged as top dog. The co-op then started helping emotionally disturbed teenagers, who also became residents.

By the mid-seventies, a leaderless system of organization had been worked out, using committees and rotating chairpersons. Cooking, food shopping and cleaning duties were assigned at weekly meetings. The clanging of an old cowbell indicated that the communal evening meal was ready. In 1979, Bowman reported a co-op population of three children and twenty-four adults, the latter ranging in age from eighteen to sixty-six. Most shared two- and four-bed rooms. "They had great parties, especially at Halloween and New Year's," recalls Vancouver writer John Masters, who lived there because he "believed in the concept." Bob Mercer considers that the co-op was a beneficial place for people to learn to solve problems by consensus, rather than by calling in experts. Its fatal flaw? "We almost never solved any of our problems."

New West's weakness as a community was its mutability. Only a few residents saw their membership as a long-term commitment. The rest were transient. Masters feels that the co-op had "lost its revolutionary edge by the mid-1980s" and become more of "a cheap place to live." In 1979, Jim Bowman wrote that New West's emphasis "on understanding people, on social dynamics and the moral concept of sharing provides an important interpersonal support network to counter the impersonality of city life." Today, he is an archivist at Calgary's Glenbow Museum. After nine years at the co-op, he says, "I was a bit concerned that I might end up like your stereotypical old hippie, unable to adjust to modern life. I decided it was time to move on and seek a profession."

Jim Bowman donated a box of alternative-community periodicals and correspondence to Special Collections at the University of British Columbia library. It is an archive of optimism, not only so far as settlements were concerned, but also with regard to health collectives, food co-operatives, community media, education facilities and social action groups. To leaf through the papers is to experience the power of positive thinking. Just the names of the various groups are enough to transport the reader back twenty years, so well do they reflect a vanished era.

Scattered along the B.C. coast were the Rising Spirit Centre and Steven's Farm (Fulford Harbour); Mother's Vision, Springridge and People Share (Victoria); Moonstar Family (Hagensborg); Bright Farm and Sydney Banks Spiritual Foundation (Ganges); Maurell Island Co-op; Refuge Cove Co-op; Catface Community (Tofino); Syzygy and The Shire (Hornby Island); Living Water Estate (Abbotsford); Silverhill Community and His Land (Mission); Treefrog (Mayne Island); Zero Holdings (Shawnigan Lake); Last Frontier (Courtenay); and Rainbow Family (Cortes Island). Vancouver, of course, was home to many communal ventures: Demeter Village, Saturna Heavyweight Aggregate, Maya House, Beshara, Waterfront Co-op, Turning Society, Holy Order of Many, Cosmic Debris, Arica House, Inner Symmetrics.

The B.C. Interior was well represented, with Swamp Hollow and Genesis (Lumby); Jubilee Traders (Harrogate); Gestalt Community (New Denver); The Farm (Queens Bay); The Rock (Rock Creek); Kootenay Brotherhood (Boswell); Pepperland (Williams Lake); New Joy Farm (Wycliffe); Min Opah Monastery (Quesnel); Caravan Theatre Farm (Armstrong); Human Family (Ashcroft); Bodhi Farm and Castle Mountain (Christina Lake); Applespring (Lillooet); Sunbird (Golden); and Yasodhara Ashram (Kootenay Bay).

Some groups, such as Vancouver's Clear Springs and Cook's Farm Collective in Victoria, started in the city and moved out of town; Clear Springs went to Nelson and Cook's to Galiano. Others stayed in the city. The Community Alternatives Society, a prominent organization examined in more detail in the next chapter, found the best of both worlds: a Vancouver base with an offshoot in the country. Many visions never materialized; the Bowman papers are littered with air castles and utopian dreams. But thousands of people, certainly, were involved in B.C.'s back-to-the-land movement.

The transition from urban to rural life could be precarious—and hilarious: Redlands, for instance, migrated from Vancouver to Whaletown on Cortes Island and posted a newsletter bulletin offering to bring oysters to the Interior to trade for fruit. A second, hasty notice disclosed that the commune "may have been wrong about having oysters ready by August; it seems that after spawning time they are off-tasting for awhile."

For the first half of its short, four-year existence, *Open Circle* went by the name of *Rain and the Rhinoceros,* an obscure reference to a Thomas Merton essay, in which Merton contrasted the condition of modern man, portrayed as a savage rhinoceros in Eugene Ionesco's famous play, with the free, God-given rain. The rain part, at least, made sense for B.C. Responsibility for the quarterly newsletter rotated among coalition members, as did the job of organizing quarterly "conferences." The host community traditionally included a brief overview of its own origins, struggles and goals.

Thus, for instance, we learn that Locus, in Sooke, was trying "to build a small centre where we would live and also provide a service to people ... a place for people who needed it to come and participate in a 'new' way of living, thinking, relating." Hoping to survive from the sale of crafts and garden produce, its members planned a communal workshop, believed in innovative architecture and low-energy technology, and pledged to observe themselves "in order to become more aware of the effects of our chosen behaviour upon each other, immediate community, society and world."

Workshare Farm, by contrast, owned fifty-five hectares near Cherryville. Rope hammocks and "wood heaters" were manufactured, and new members had to ante up $2,000, for which they would receive "a balanced vegetarian diet and comfortable shelter" and be paid three dollars a week for a clothing allowance. There were only three "voting members" at Workshare; "others will not get a vote until/unless they decide to devote their lives to the Community and are accepted by the membership." The community's goal was "to create a classless society by requiring an equal amount of time to be spent on community work by members (the quota has recently been raised to fifty hours per week for members and thirty-five for visitors)."

Workshare started its Sunday meetings with "a Socialization Session in which we express any feelings which might have begun to build up during the week, with the idea that if our comrades know that certain things hurt our feelings that they will be inclined to think twice before doing these things." Members believed that "people conditioned in Capitalist Society are sick." The farm's principles, which "no one has been able to persuade us to relax," included "vegetarianism, communal child raising, abstaining from drugs and pollutants" and "creating an equilibrium between production and consumption," all essential, apparently, for the creation of a "just society."

A wonderful assortment of community mini-profiles can be gathered from the pages of *Rain and the Rhinoceros*. Yalakum owned a house in North Vancouver and six hectares of land near Lillooet. Members planned to produce pottery. Ambado was "building slowly towards a commune" near Cherryville. There were fourteen people on less than a hectare, the property of one of the group. They did, however, have a "verbal contract" that "nobody owns the land." Primal Point, which sought "independence from the present social system," boasted twenty-two people and 1.5 hectares on Galiano Island, but were desperate for more space. Lee Creek Community owned a bus, a lumber truck, tractors and seventy-eight hectares at Chase, operated a sawmill and staged festivals throughout the summer. They were "potters, carpenters, artists, musicians, wood carvers, farmers and log builders."

Grindrod Community consisted of eight people living in a house on a productive, sixty-five-hectare farm near Enderby. They were "trying to equalize work loads and diminish sex roles," striving to "create a community which works by providing a better living environment rather than existing on the basis of a specific religion, philosophy or ideology." A seven-person commune on Mayne Island had woodworking, pottery, airbrush, darkroom and sewing facilities, which they had "opened up for the use of the community." They were a "labour resource centre" for "people with odd jobs needing fulfillment." Stonetree's ten members wanted to complete the purchase of 250 hectares close to Castlegar and admitted that "the financial pressures on the group at the moment are uncomfortable."

There were places you wished you knew more about, such as Space Feather Family and Common Good Co-op from Enderby, Kosmunity from Procter, Center of the World Beautiful at Kootenay Bay and the Bar None Farm in Summerland. But all that remained of many undertakings were obsolete phone numbers and addresses in fading mimeographed mail-outs. Most communities were temporary and melted away; most communitarians moved on to other endeavours. Coalition correspondence was usually conducted on a first-name basis, making it difficult to track participants down. Full names could often be as evocative as those of the communities represented: Owl Swan, Hopi Sprout, No Guns, Boreal Chickadee.

Several groups left melancholy messages before they disappeared. "Legally, we will still be a co-operative for another year because of a mortgage we hold, but in reality the members have all disbanded and gone their separate ways," wrote Harmony Farmstead of Grand Forks. "Personally, it was a disappointment, but at the same time it was a worthwhile venture and a learning experience." For Vancouver's Pacific Life Community, there were "many emotional ties…when we had our last meeting many tears and sighs were shed. The revolution in our hearts still grows."

For a few unlucky individuals, communal life was devastating rather than disappointing. In *The Eden Express,* Mark Vonnegut, son of novelist Kurt Vonnegut, Jr., chronicled with great insight a frightening descent into schizophrenia, most of which took place at a commune on Powell Lake near the pulp-mill town of Powell River. A mescaline trip that never ended saw him committed to a New Westminster psychiatric hospital. One aspect of Vonnegut's illness, a crazed insistence on nudity, could be seen as an impaired echo of the familiar Doukhobor protest, designed to remind onlookers that unfettered simplicity was at the heart of a true spiritual life.

Another book about a B.C. commune, *Apple Bay,* by Paul Williams, describes a year in the lives of a dozen young back-to-the-landers, most of them from California. The place names are fictionalized, but the action probably takes place at Galley Bay on Desolation Sound north of Powell River, where an isolated farm harboured, at times, as many as a hundred people. Galley Bay was notorious with local yachtsmen, for whom the sound has long been a prime recreation site. Unclothed maidens would swim out to nearby vessels and cadge cigarettes from gawking skippers or entice speedboat owners into letting them practise a little nude water-skiing. *Apple Bay,* however, is a diary of sexual experimentation, personal conflict, tension and jealousy; few idyllic moments are portrayed.

The entire life-and-death cycle of one group was instructively chronicled in the CICC newsletters. This was An Alternate Community, which had its origins in a Vancouver Free University class on intentional settlements. The class decided to put into practice what it had learned, and in 1975 about thirty people leased six hectares from a young couple who had already made one haphazard attempt to start a commune on their Lumby property. Their goal was "a large 500-plus community, self-sufficient with industries, school, etc."

Savings and possessions were pooled. Meals were communal. Decisions were made by consensus. There were lots of ideas for generating income: demolition work, making canoes and snowshoes, a woodworking shop, a bakery. "All was meetings and political consciousness-raising and communal enterprise for a year," wrote one participant. But by 1976, the community was "in a state of crisis." Attendees at a CICC conference confessed their need "to escape from the situation for a few days." Half the members had left. The collapse was blamed on "the frantic schedule to get practical things done to ensure the group's physical survival, such as preparing crops for winter." This frenzy had "overtaken anything higher which might unite the group on an emotional level."

A neighbour offered another view. "Any time which was not spent working was spent planning, organizing and discussing work— Garden Collectives, Food Collectives, Vehicle Collectives, Tool Collectives, Collective Collectives, work weeks, person work weeks, person work days, lists, charts, schedules, calendars, agendas, organization, *ad nauseam infinitum,* etc., etc. Good Grief! The Alternative Bureaucracy. New and improved, more complex—guaranteed to bewilder the inexperienced observer."

The outpost disbanded. The owners of the land, indefatigable in their quest for the ideal community, soon found new romantics to move in. Their colony, one reported to *Open Circle,* was "forever changing."

Fantasy Farm at Enderby dealt with similar problems. In 1976, it was "in the process of letting all the practical work go." Commune members would then "concert all their energy into unifying as a group, even though it seemed probable they would have to buy their winter food supplies." The Ochiltree Organic Commune objected to this approach. "We become unified as a group by practical action," they responded. "We put our energy into working with animals and the land, which in turn brings us closer to our true livelihood."

Livelihood was, indeed, the biggest problem facing most of B.C.'s alternative communities. Those that could come up with adequate funding—through outside employment, group industries or rich uncles—survived. Those that couldn't, didn't. Government helped out, as it had done eighty years ago. In the 1890s, free land and a budget for roads were the incentives; in the early 1970s, it was handouts in the form of Opportunities for Youth (OFY), Local Initiatives Program (LIP) and other types of grants.

OFY-funded enterprises mushroomed all over the province, providing communitarians with jobs and upright citizens with grounds for complaint. Roberts Creek and Sechelt became a hotbed for both. News reports revealed that twenty members of the Legal Front Commune, General Store and Funny Food Farm were using public largesse "to turn a garage into a community tool-pool and car-repair teaching centre." And that was just the beginning: there were plans for a craft shop, organic-food market, restaurant and free school. The Crowe Road Commune was "developing self-sufficiency for urban young people through learning crafts, vegetable gardening and stock raising." Bayview was a "rural commune providing free meals and places to stay for transient youth." All three, according to hostile locals, were a waste of tax dollars and bound to attract unwanted, long-haired visitors.

The Texas Lake Community, between Hope and Yale, was organized as an official nonprofit society. It operated a successful hostel in an old motel as a source of income. The commune's twelve inhabitants pooled all earnings and received a dollar a day plus a clothing allowance. They also planted trees, fought fires and managed goats, ducks, bees, chickens and an organic garden. One member reported to *Open Circle* that "essentially we live together…to help each other grow. Sometimes it works and sometimes it doesn't. Sometimes we just evolve from crisis to crisis."

The commune, which eventually purchased fifty hectares on the East Kettle River north of Rock Creek, where it hoped to run a spiritual retreat and conference centre, became a charter member of the Turtle Island Land Stewardship Society. Turtle Island, now known as TIES Canada (Turtle Island Earth Stewards), started as another CICC initiative, designed to allow communities to preserve their property for some specific, permanent purpose—as wilderness, for instance, or as rural farmland. Linnaea, a 135-hectare farm commune on southern Cortes Island, also joined the land trust.

Another group that solved the livelihood conundrum was Earth

Seed at Nelson. With a nucleus of three people, and "an assortment of others who come and go, and look upon the farm as home," the commune specialized in tree planting—as did many others. Earth Seed was "managing to construct its own buildings, grow much of its food, become involved with community-oriented work in Nelson, attend to relationships within the group, advance through growing in spiritual and meditative areas, have spare time for enjoyment and relaxation and at the same time remain financially solvent." No small achievement. "This community appears to most definitely have its act together," *Open Circle* enthused.

Besides acting as a resource directory and communication network for B.C.'s alternative settlements, CICC also worked out, after endless discussion, a series of principles and goals for members. Among them were "non-exploitative social and work relationships" and "non-hierarchical decision-making." The coalition aimed to replace private land ownership with "social control" (land trusts, stewardships, collective ownership and government leases). It hoped to develop a strong "collectivist economy through bartering and exchange" and connect groups needing people with people looking for groups. Ultimately, it sought to create "a new and separate category within the existing land act for intentional communities."

In 1979, shortly before it evaporated, the CICC reported a membership of eighty "communities and communitarian organizations." Of the forty-three classifiable settlements, thirty-three were rural and ten urban. Twenty were described as "co-operative living arrangements whose purpose is mainly economic or social," ten were New Age spiritual communities and three were political activist groups. The report concluded on a sombre note that the number of people living "in community" in B.C. seemed to be in decline.

The idealistic and mostly cheerful conversations carried on in the pages of the CICC newsletter were frequently interrupted by the dissenting voice of the Ochiltree Organic Commune, located northeast of Williams Lake. We have heard this voice once already, protesting Fantasy Farm's plans to relinquish agricultural work. Ochiltree took exception also to the strident tone of Workshare Farm's mission statement, which claimed that vegetarianism was a crucial underpinning for a "just society."

Vegetarianism—and many other New Age practices—were the result of "straight thinking," according to this confrontational group of Marxist-Leninists. Conflict first flared at a CICC conference in early 1977. It was customary for participants to contribute food to these events, and host Texas Lake had requested vegetarian donations. Ochiltree brought meat. "Some discussion followed," commented the newsletter. The dead animal flesh was eventually accepted, and the magnanimous Texas Lakers even thanked Ochiltree for precooking it, "as they wouldn't have wanted it in the kitchen." The various communes worked hard to appreciate one other, and the Sunday night jam found "the Ochiltree carnivores and the Texas Lake carrot crunchers getting it on together like one big happy family."

Jerry and Nancy LeBourdais, who had moved from Vancouver to the Cariboo in 1971, were the founders of the rebel commune. In 1975, with a group of friends, they set up camp on a piece of Crown land known as Borland Meadow and dedicated themselves to animal husbandry and organic gardening. "Expect to get to know our animals," declared their publication, *In Defense of Nature*. "The animals keep on giving. Taking from the earth only what they need to sustain their lives and giving back to the best of their ability. They are teaching us this." Each issue, as promised, contained a farmyard fable, featuring Percheron horses, goats, leghorn chickens, Rooter and Ripear the pigs and Douglas McWool, a Dorset sheep. The stories sometimes ended with the butchering of a beloved beast.

There were many aspects of the CICC that Ochiltree could not condone. Its criticisms became relentless. Healing circles were "part of a phoney, metaphysical bullshit philosophy that promotes passiveness and self-love." The commune was down on land trusts, as they perpetuated "the private property syndrome," and against tree-planting, which provided support for the forest industry. Monogamy was "an extension of private property." Even eloquence was suspect. "Some of us have to learn not to write that way," explained *In Defense of Nature*. "Our writing style is simple, and we hope direct." But Ochiltree didn't want to give up on its fellow communitarians—not yet, anyway—and made a gracious offer to host the May 1977 gathering.

At the start of the muddy, seven-kilometre hike into Borland Meadow, attendees were met by a sign stating that "this road leads to revolution." The meeting was not a total success. "The only meat available was supplied by Ochiltree," complained the commune. "The same goes for the coffee. As usual both were consumed with gusto.... We suggested the raw foods workshop make a salad for lunch—they didn't." Not surprisingly, Ochiltree soon left the coalition. "We have to rid ourselves of all the bourgeois philosophy that places the interests of people ahead of mother nature's, e.g. food faddism, vegetarianism, mysticism and spiritualism.... CICC has not gone anywhere since its inception—it remains fossilized."

The militant commune pursued a very different affiliation—with the disenfranchised native street people of Williams Lake, known as the Troopers. Ochiltree agreed to help the Troopers set up a large market garden and co-op store on the Sugar Cane reserve just east of Williams Lake. The garden prospered and became a small farm. At the Williams Lake Fall Fair, the Troopers were able for the first time "to rub elbows with the townspeople in a proud way." They won recognition for their vegetables and cured hams and took home a blue ribbon for their pigs. A government grant was soon secured to expand the operation.

At first the Ochiltree activists discouraged alcohol at Sugar Cane in an attempt to rehabilitate the Troopers. But this approach only reflected a "whiteman headspace." Subjecting themselves to rigorous self-criticism, commune members discovered they were still affected by residual straightism and decided to join the Troopers when they passed the bottle round. They changed their co-op store policies. "The people want white rice, white sugar, white flour, and pop and candy," they noted. "If we didn't stock these things we wouldn't be serving them. We don't teach the people, we learn from them." They also sold cut-rate vanilla extract, which the Troopers consumed for a cheap high.

The combined energies of the radicals and the Troopers began to attract the attention of many different authorities. The RCMP kept a close eye on the unholy alliance. Town officials wished they would just disappear. Health and agriculture inspectors objected to pigs being fed with supermarket waste. Other co-ops were aghast at the vanilla extract sales. Eventually, in 1979, the government grant was cancelled and the Troopers forced to leave Sugar Cane. Ochiltree, outraged, changed its name to the Troopers Commune and published its own little red book, *The Revolutionary Hippy Manifesto*. "There are no greys within the revolution," members declared, "just black and white, right and wrong. Revolution is total change."

The commune rented a house in Williams Lake, operated a hostel, and much to the chagrin of mayor and council, began to participate fully in the cultural life of the town. A float, for instance, was entered in the Williams Lake Stampede parade. This consisted of a flat-deck truck driven by a Trooper with a number of other Troopers on the back, including the Troopers Goodtime Band. The truck was decorated with the Troopers' symbol—a clenched fist and Indian drum—and a sign that said TROOPERS WELCOME YOU TO WILLIAMS LAKE—OUR TOWN. "We played the kind of music most people like to hear at stampede time," the commune paper reported. "Of course, we had our annual queen, an elder from Alkali who proudly displayed her chest banner, 'Miss Trooper 1980.'"

Because of its reputation for farming and gardening expertise, the commune was offered several pieces of land to till. Troopers put in large gardens on the Toosey reserve at Riske Creek, fifty kilometres west of town, and at McTaggart Meadow northwest of Toosey. A plot became available at Glendale, just outside Williams Lake, then another at Rose Lake to the northeast, where the LeBourdais family had started out in 1971. Although still deeply involved with the Troopers, the group changed its name again, to the Cariboo Organic Commune. In 1985, members were forced off their Borland Meadow base after an eighteen-month eviction battle.

Today, the commune goes by the name of CEEDS, short for Community Enhancement & Economic Development Society. Its fifteen full-time members, native and white, still include Jerry and Nancy LeBourdais and are based at Horse Lake, near the town of 100 Mile House. They operate four small rented farms in the South Cariboo. Street people continue to fluctuate between Williams Lake and these properties. CEEDS is attempting "to change the disastrous present-day methods of agriculture," says its listing in an intentional-communities directory. "We are ecologists deeply concerned with and actively working in the defense of Mother Nature.... Our deeds do match our words."

Not far from Horse Lake, on the edge of 100 Mile House, an assortment of buildings clusters around a rustic, sixty-year-old lodge. Aging barns and an organic garden rub shoulders with apartments, private homes, an auditorium, dining room, offices, tennis courts, outdoor swimming pool and antique log chapel. This is the heartland of the Emissaries, an association of more than a thousand individuals, nearly five hundred of whom live together in eight communities in North America and England. Wealthy and patrician, the sect has been relatively rudderless since the death, in 1988, of its charismatic leader, Martin Exeter.

If CEEDS is either black or white and nothing in between, then one might colour the Emissaries grey. They espouse a middle-of-the-road spirituality: ethereal, unfocused, surprisingly difficult to pin down. A favourite saying often accompanied Exeter's rather stern portrait in sect literature: "The truth is true and all is well; unconquerable life prevails." One can easily imagine the Troopers' response to such a platitude. It's ironic that the two groups operate within a ten-minute drive of each other. They are as different in style and appeal as it's possible to be.

Formed in the 1940s, and with spiritual roots that go back even further, the Emissaries are the longest-lasting, largest and most unlikely of B.C.'s recent communal experiments. The sect's transformations mirror both the promise and the dark undercurrents of post-war life. Like CEEDS, the New West Co-op and Argenta, the Emissaries are still very much in existence, but may have peaked in vitality and influence. They provide a fitting conclusion to a chapter on New Age settlements and a transition point for examining utopian activity today. Certainly, the community has undergone profound change since Martin Exeter arrived in the Cariboo from England in 1930.

The young lord was only twenty-one when he was sent out to manage his family's six-thousand-hectare Bridge Creek Ranch, acquired in 1912 by his father, the fifth Marquess of Exeter. There was no town at that time. 100 Mile Lodge, a historic former gold-rush hostelry located on the estate, was the ranch's centre of operations. Some of B.C.'s choicest rangelands were once owned by wealthy British aristocrats, though few had much direct involvement with their spreads. Martin Exeter, by all accounts, enjoyed the exotic cowboy life and didn't shrink from physical labour. He moved into his primitive new home and threw himself into learning the cattle business.

The Exeter pedigree was ancient and blueblooded. William Cecil, lord high treasurer and chief adviser to Queen Elizabeth I, was a direct ancestor. Martin Exeter, or Lord Martin Cecil, as he was formally known, was born and raised in Lincolnshire at Burghley House, one of Britain's most famous mansions. The marquesses of Salisbury, occupants of Hatfield House in Hertfordshire, formed another branch of the Cecil family. For someone with Exeter's background, staying at dilapidated 100 Mile House must have been as challenging as camping in the Gobi Desert.

By the late 1930s, Exeter had become a respected rancher. He was married—to Edith Csanady de Telegat, an aristocratic young Hungarian woman he had met before moving to Canada—and the couple lived in the newly constructed 100 Mile Lodge, which was a hotel as well as the focal point of the ranch. Exeter had somehow developed an interest in the occult and spiritualism, reading books on the Rosicrucians and the work of Kahlil Gibran. The writings of Lloyd Meeker, an American visionary who called himself Uranda, made a deep impression on him, and Exeter arranged for Meeker to give a series of public talks in Vancouver in 1940.

Meeker taught that within each individual dwelt an aspect of an invisible, animating life force, the source of all being, which he called the spirit of God. To be "attuned" to this spirit was to know love and happiness. Life's problems resulted from a lack of attunement and could only be dissolved by turning one's heart and mind into pure channels for divine energy. Meeker had been spreading his message, which had similarities to certain Doukhobor and Quaker beliefs, since the early 1930s. And like Brother XII shortly before him, Meeker received his inspiration—and much useful information, which he faithfully scribbled down—from an intense vision. In 1940, he founded a church, the Emissaries of Divine Light, "to assist in the spiritual regeneration of the human race."

While his teachings were designed to harmonize thought and feeling, Meeker also sought to promote a parallel effect on a physical level. He devised a chiropractic remedy, similar to Chinese *qi gong* healing or therapeutic touch. By moving his hands over various organs, he believed he could realign a patient's energy without touching the body. A number of chiropractors were attracted to the sect, and "attunements" are still an important part of Emissary practice.

Meeker became Exeter's guide and mentor, and they formed a

close relationship. The British lord and his wife would travel by car to Colorado, where Meeker had established a base at Sunrise Ranch, near Loveland. Soon, Exeter was acting as Meeker's deputy in the church organization. In 1948, he donated some land at 100 Mile House to the church and formed a community of half a dozen lodge and ranch employees. Within a decade this modest group had grown fivefold.

In 1954, Meeker died in an air accident. Exeter took over leadership of the Emissaries, commuting by small plane between 100 Mile House and Sunrise Ranch, where fifty or more people now lived. Eight years later, a new community, Green Pastures, was established in New Hampshire. Courses on the "art of living" became part of the Emissary curriculum at all three centres. A dynastic 1967 marriage united Michael Exeter, Martin's only son, and Nancy Rose Meeker, Lloyd's eldest daughter. The sect multiplied rapidly in the late 1960s and 1970s as hundreds of young seekers found refuge in its undemanding rhetoric and highly structured communal environment.

100 Mile House was also expanding. A nearby sawmill and a strong demand for lumber had created many jobs in the area in the 1950s and 1960s. A secular community, which sprang up on land leased from the ranch, was incorporated as a village in 1965. When

Historic 100 Mile Lodge, a former gold-rush inn, as it looked in 1929, the year before Martin Exeter moved in and made it the headquarters for the Bridge Creek Ranch. (BCARS A-03898)

the Exeter family offered to sell the leased lands, controversy erupted over the price, which villagers claimed was exorbitant. Conflicts between sect, ranch and town were kept to a minimum by Ross Marks, a staunch Emissary and former Bridge Creek manager who served as mayor of 100 Mile House for twenty-one years.

Emissary influence on the town was undeniable. The sect built a modern new hotel, the Red Coach Inn, and ran at least fifteen businesses, including a bakery, electronics and building-supply stores, the local newspaper, a gas station and a real-estate agency. Elsewhere in B.C., communities were established and properties purchased in Prince George (a house called The Willows), the Fraser Valley (a fifty-hectare estate named Edenvale) and Vancouver (FourWinds, a regal Shaughnessy mansion). The Emissaries also owned a large organic farm and orchard in Kamloops called Riverbend and many other businesses and properties.

At its zenith in the mid-1980s, worldwide membership may have totalled over three thousand, with about a thousand adherents in B.C. Approximately one-quarter of them lived communally. New settlements were started in California, Oregon, Indiana, Ontario, England, South Africa, Australia and France. Dozens of nonresidential centres were created. The spiritual influence of the Emissaries extended far beyond the various communities, touching the lives of tens of thousands of individuals. Exeter and his followers had achieved an extraordinary success.

The sect held extensive global holdings, including an eight-seat jet and hotels in England and South Africa. A publishing unit cranked out a torrent of pamphlets and books. Emissaries branched into all sorts of nonprofit ventures: a Whole Health Institute, an Association for Responsible Communication and an outdoor adventure school. They worked with universities and school boards to sponsor workshops on multiculturalism and environmental stewardship.

Up to 140 people lived communally at 100 Mile House, with another 35 or so at Edenvale. Residents were employed within the community or worked at Emissary businesses and received a stipend unless they chose to keep their finances private. They ate together and attended twice-weekly addresses by Martin Exeter, which would be recorded and transcribed, then used by the other groups. Although women could theoretically choose any type of work, they were encouraged to perform traditional domestic duties and subordinate themselves to the men in the group.

Exeter was the unquestioned leader. He is portrayed in sect literature as benevolent, though ex-Emissaries have described him as cold and aloof. Exeter would not tolerate dissent; non-conformists were asked to leave. He consolidated control by appointing his son and son-in-law—and Lloyd Meeker's children and their spouses—to important positions. "Such obvious nepotism was tolerated and rationalized" by the wider fellowship, according to long-time Emissary Anne Blaney, now general manager at the 100 Mile community. "It was futile to challenge the power structure," she wrote in a candid recent essay on community life, "because that meant challenging Martin, and that would have been like challenging God."

In 1988, when Exeter died, the Emissaries were thrown into turmoil. Michael Exeter assumed the nominal leadership, but things just weren't the same. Although articulate and competent, Michael did not have his father's overpowering aura. He was not distant and godlike; other members, who had lived alongside him and watched him grow to manhood, had a hard time perceiving him as a figure of authority.

A power struggle ensued. Dark clouds of bitterness and acrimony began to swirl about the Emissary communities, obscuring the divine light but bringing into the open much that had previously been hidden. The sect's patriarchal, hierarchical structure and feudal rites of succession were criticized, especially by female communitarians. "The spell was broken," commented Anne Blaney. "Twenty-year friendships ended in grief."

Reports of sexual misconduct surfaced. "If a woman was married," a former Emissary told me confidentially, "it was almost taken for granted that her husband could carry on relationships with other women. She would be expected to accommodate herself, and if she couldn't, then the attitude was that there must be something spiritually wrong with her." Community members, including many older people who had spent their entire adult lives within the Emissary fold, started leaving in droves.

Emissary enrollment today has declined by two-thirds or more. Four of the international communities have disbanded. About fifty people remain at 100 Mile House, fifteen at Edenvale and a mere half dozen or so at The Willows and FourWinds. Colorado's Sunrise Ranch has become the headquarters and main settlement for the sect. Except for the chickens, farm animals that used to be part of the scene at the 100 Mile community have been sold. The organic garden is now a private enterprise owned by one person. Residents find employment where they can and pay rent to the sect, which still owns four hectares of land around the lodge. Martin Exeter's speeches no longer form the basis for spiritual gatherings, and Michael Exeter, though still part of the organization, has retreated from the limelight and moved to California. The Bridge Creek ranch continues under his private ownership and control; other family properties are held in trust.

"Today," wrote Blaney, "we resemble a neighbourhood more than a spiritual community." Committees and boards are elected rather than appointed, and fresh policy is slowly evolving through consensus rather than by decree. The sect has dropped "divine light" from its name. Its spiritual platform, never sharply defined, has become wholly eclectic, its mission statement broadened "to promote holistic values in living and stewardship for the earth."

At 100 Mile House, members are content to try "to bring an integrating influence into human affairs." Their unobjectionable goal is "to make this community a setting in which people may increasingly know the magic of their presence on earth." Despite ongoing problems, B.C.'s Emissaries felt stable enough in 1996 to renew a tentative recruitment campaign. An advertisement in Vancouver's *Common Ground* magazine sounds a familiar, age-old refrain. "We have openings," it announces, "and are looking for men, women, couples and families who are interested in living in spiritually based communities."

WWW.UTOPIA

Intentional Communities in B.C. Today

Community isn't a place. It is a feeling
among people of wanting to be together.
—Bob Brown, *Communities Directory*

If you type "utopia" into an Internet search engine, you will find websites dealing with architecture, software design, jewellery, science fiction, shopping malls and sex. You'll note that Victorian futurist Edward Bellamy is once again in vogue at the virtual Centre for Utopian Studies, where gigabytes of information on literature, film and art can be retrieved. You can visit surrealistic on-line collectives such as Youkali, a mythical island and artists' retreat with a Hawaiian flavour, or the Sprawl, a metropolis of data named after a notion from a William Gibson novel. Cyberspace, which lends itself to purely imaginative constructions, seems an ideal environment for those who would envision utopia.

For flesh-and-blood creations, keying in "intentional communities" is a better way to search the net. You will shortly be led to the web pages of the Fellowship for Intentional Communities (FIC), a U.S.-based network that has published *Communities* magazine since 1972 and acts as the global pulse of the alternative-settlements movement. Here you can learn about the Kansas scholar/technicians of Skyfire; Earth Re-Leaf in Hawaii ("a co-op farm network/play organization"); the Free-the-Land New York City Squatters' Community; California's Dancing Rabbit, dedicated to a sustainable environment; Spiricoasis, now forming in Toronto and intent on "personal and planetary brilliance"; and Lichen—a group of "organisms living and growing together for mutual benefit" in Oregon.

Many communities connected with the Fellowship are large and long-established. Arden Village in Delaware was founded in 1900 and has a population of 550. Five hundred live communally at Chicago's Jesus People U.S.A., and thousands more occupy dozens of other Christian colonies; the 360 worldwide settlements of the Hutterian Brethren alone have more than forty thousand residents. In the U.S., several large ashrams—Ananda in California, Satchidananda in Virginia, Kripalu in Massachusetts—have flourished for decades; scores of similar retreats thrive in India and elsewhere. The seven North American "anthroposophical" settlements based on the theories of Rudolf Steiner are part of a global network. Israel's 270 kibbutzim vary in size from twelve to fifteen hundred people; all are communal. Maharishi International University in Iowa and the Methow Centre of Enlightenment in Twisp, Washington, have ambitious community plans for thousands of individuals.

Stephen Gaskin's famous Tennessee commune, The Farm, founded in 1970, is still going strong with two hundred members. Christiania in Copenhagen, Europe's most notorious squat, has lasted twenty-five years and now has a thousand inhabitants. India's Auroville—a "universal township" founded with much fanfare near Pondicherry in 1968—is home to eight hundred and continues to expand. Other well-known groups include Scotland's Findhorn Foundation, formed in 1962, with 140 residents; Riverside in New Zealand (1941, 75 people); Arcosanti, Arizona (1970, 75); Padanaram, Indiana (1966, 160); Shannon Farm, Virginia (1974, 90); Twin Oaks, Virginia (1967, 100). And the list goes on.

So it only makes sense that, in addition to its magazine, the FIC should also publish a hefty and fascinating guide to actual settlements, called the *Communities Directory*. The 1996 edition describes 620 groups, many of which are at a formative stage, and 260 related "resource" outfits. These, of course, are only the groups that wish to be publicized; the total number of intentional communities worldwide is difficult to estimate, but must be several thousand at least. An editorial states that "we are in the midst of the biggest wave of inquiries about community and announcements of new starts in twenty years." The directory has twenty-eight listings for Canada, with eleven from B.C.

Some of B.C.'s entries we have met before. The Emissaries at 100 Mile Lodge are looking for "those who resonate with the art of rebuilding." The Kootenay Co-operative Land Settlement Society reports thirty-one residents and considers itself part of the larger alternative community of Argenta. And CEEDS—"we are still part of the hippie back-to-the-land movement"—hangs in at Lone Butte near 100 Mile House. Another group, Cardiff Place in Victoria, will be described in greater detail later in this chapter.

Avalon, now forming, is somewhat specialized. Its four members live in Clearbrook but hope to relocate to the mountains "before the turn of the century" and offer year-long training in neo-pagan witchcraft, herbalism, hunting and "wildcrafting." Bamberton is not specialized at all; this proposed townsite on Vancouver Island has been kicking around for years. At Tofino, the twenty-three members of the Crow Circle Collective are establishing a "clean sustainable culture" on eight hectares. OUR House in Victoria is a community youth project.

Two B.C. ashrams are mentioned in the directory. The Salt Spring Centre in the Gulf Islands is an ashtanga yoga retreat under the direction of Baba Hari Dass. The centre's eleven members also run an alternative school and offer such healing treatments as massage and reflexology. Kootenay Bay's Yasodhara Ashram, guided by Swami Radha, has provided courses on various kinds of yoga since 1966. Fifteen people live at the sanctuary and manage a small farm. The final settlement listed is Vancouver's Community Alternatives Society. The more you learn about this successful collective, the more you wonder why there aren't others like it.

Jan Bulman, Kaz Takahashi and I are relaxing in the comfort of pod nine's living room when I ask why Community Alternatives hasn't been more widely imitated. Morning sunshine streams in through the windows, and banging can be heard outside, where carpenter and pod inhabitant Ian McMeekin is engaged in some building repairs. Joe Schofield, a spiky-haired university student, emerges from his room and pulls up a stool at the kitchen counter. Bulman shrugs at my question and shakes her head. "We didn't think we were trying anything unique," she says. "I thought people would model designs after us but nobody leapt to do it. The usual response was: that's really interesting but I couldn't live like that."

The design in question, if not unique, is certainly unconventional. Rather than endow their three-storey Kitsilano building with the usual mixture of private, self-contained apartments and minimal public areas, the society's founders opted instead for lots of common facilities and nine multi-bedroom units. All have spacious kitchens, living and dining rooms, decks and several bathrooms; four have three bedrooms, two have four bedrooms and three have eight bedrooms. The inhabitants of each unit share a communal evening meal and many participate in a building-wide potluck dinner on Saturday nights.

Residents describe their living quarters as pods because "unit" sounds too institutional and "apartment" too cold. They want to be close, not apart, explains Bulman, a former social worker and mother of four grown children. To foster a sense of togetherness, generous work, recreation and common zones, including a library, darkroom and sauna, are built into the plan. Airy ground-floor courtyards and a roof patio add finishing touches. Community Alternatives is more than a housing co-operative; it's a hundred-room urban village. It even has a rural pod: a four-hectare organic farm located sixty kilometres east in the Fraser Valley near Aldergrove.

The society got its start in the mid-1970s. A dozen or so founders decided to form what they now call "a value-based community." The values in question were to be egalitarian, intergenerational, co-operative and non-sexist. Decision-making would be consensual. All community development would be based on sound ecological principles. Naturally, the non-sectarian group joined the Coalition of Intentional Co-operative Communities. A 1975 issue of *Rain and the Rhinoceros* reported on a meeting that society members held with Norm Levi, minister of human resources in B.C.'s left-of-centre New Democratic government. Levi had spent five years on an Israeli kibbutz, and he wanted to help the province's co-operative settlement movement to grow. His interest turned out to be premature; the NDP were turfed from office shortly after the meeting and nothing came of it.

The Community Alternatives vision began falling into place in 1977, after an attempt to lease a large tract of agricultural land near Fort Langley fell through. Members lived co-operatively in Vancouver, naming their rented accommodations Nasaika Won and Nasaika Too after the Chinook word for "people-place." They hoped to convert a downtown warehouse into living and commercial space but instead purchased the Fraser Common Farm near Aldergrove—now pod ten—with pooled funds. At around the same time, the Kitsilano Area Planning Council decided that co-op housing should be developed for a site on West Second Avenue, where a row of derelict homes was slated for demolition. Out of several applications, the society's proposal was chosen. The dream was about to take material form.

Five years earlier, in 1972, the federal government had decided to encourage an innovative, affordable form of city housing: the urban co-operative. People of varying economic means would cohabit. They would buy shares in their building but not be able to sell those shares for profit. They would pay rents based on income levels and work together to manage their affairs and pay off their mortgages. For the next twenty years, start-up funds, low-interest loans and other subsidies and guarantees were offered through the Canada Mortgage and Housing Corporation. By 1992, when a change in policy restricted CMHC money to low-income projects only, seventeen hundred co-ops with sixty thousand units had been born from coast to coast.

Very few of them boasted pods. At least one other complex—Juniper Co-op, also in Kitsilano—was built on the multiple-bedroom plan, but only the Community Alternatives gang was able to turn its building into a true island of unity. Society members, for example, formed a special bond over the issue of solar heating. As CMHC would not agree to fund anything so adventurous, they were forced to find an extra $18,000 bank loan and install much of the plumbing, basement water tanks, heat-exchangers and forty-four solar roof panels themselves. The CMHC stance was probably justified, as the solar system only worked for about ten years and is presently in mothballs. But, as Jan Bulman pointed out, "it was a powerful example of our concern for renewable energy and self-sufficiency."

Another example of that concern is "edible landscaping"—the grape trellises, vegetables and herbs that adorn the co-op grounds. Then there is Beulah, a huge rotary composter enthroned in the basement, which the co-op hopes to market to other housing complexes. These elements, wrote David Beers in a *Western Living* magazine profile, marked Community Alternatives as "a model for the coming communal ecotopia."

A gulf between this idealistic, untried model and real life soon became apparent. "Living here," one inhabitant told Beers, "requires a shitload of emotional work." Or as Bulman put it more delicately in an account she wrote for a book on communal living around the world: "We place a high value on commitment to work problems out amicably, not retreat from conflict but hang in and communicate until an agreement is reached."

The way Community Alternatives bridges all gulfs is to hold meetings—lots of meetings. Members spend about twelve hours a month talking and sometimes battling in order to reach consensus on everything from the composition of the annual budget to the installation of a bicycle rack. A leadership team of four or five people organizes and chairs all assemblies and special events for a six-week cycle, then a new team is appointed. Besides business and membership meetings, there are also "process" meetings, where the exigencies of communal life are discussed, or "processed," until problems are temporarily smoothed away.

Co-op gatherings are not all serious. The schedule posted at the time of my December visit features a Hanukkah potluck dinner, a Santa Lucia festival with a candle parade and feast, a big winter solstice party and talent night, a mummers performance and a New Year's Eve bash. But there are also business and process meetings to attend, and the latter has a bruising agenda: develop a mission or vision statement and reach consensus on how consensus should be defined. It promises to be a long session.

Consensus is most difficult to find when money or membership is involved. The co-op requires all members to disclose their income, assets and liabilities. An annual budget is devised, each person makes a financial pledge—which can vary from $200 to almost $700 a month—and meetings are held until pledges and budget coincide. "New members," Bulman admits, "are often paralysed by this process." But somehow it always works out.

Between city and farm, Community Alternatives has a current population of forty-five, including eight children. Ages range from one to sixty-six. There are only two nuclear families, one at Aldergrove and one occupying their own four-bedroom pod in Kitsilano. About twenty people are full members, with shares in the co-op and a say in all decisions. The remaining adult residents are either rent-paying students or undergoing a four-month "exploring period" to see if communal life appeals to them. "There's more turnover than we'd like," explains Kaz Takahashi, who is retired from a career as a public-health nurse. The way of the pod is not for everyone.

But for many long-time residents it is the only way. "Living here has changed me," Takahashi reflects, "allowing me to work with people in a new way." For Jan Bulman, the co-op is "a little bit of heaven." Both women point to shared celebration as a high point of collective living. For instance, a number of accomplished musicians live in the complex and impromptu performances are common. For ten years, a thirty-five-person gospel choir practised there. An Easter sunrise gathering at the farm is a popular event, and summer and winter solstices are traditionally honoured with dance, theatre and feasting. "We're an easy bunch to party with," says Bulman.

In a pod, one can be close to life's important transitions. People have been married—and separated—there; children have been born. A seventy-five-year-old co-op member, dying of cancer, wanted to leave the hospital and spend his final days at home. His fellow communitarians acceded to his wish and cared for him round the clock. "We're like a small village," another member told a *Vancouver Sun* reporter. "I think this is the way most people in the world live. We support each other in many, many ways."

Life in small villages can have a dark side also, and Community Alternatives is no exception. A child in the co-op was sexually abused by one resident. The community expelled the man and saw him sent to jail. The meeting process—often frustrating and slow, sometimes confrontational and abusive—has prompted members to leave. Personality conflicts and relationship problems are not uncommon. Every so often, when things get bad enough, a great "shuffle" occurs, with people moving from pod to pod in an attempt to re-establish harmony and social equilibrium.

Over the years, a set of "guiding principles for desirable behaviour"—also known as the "community ode" ("code" sounded too bureaucratic)—has evolved. Fourteen "respects and responsibilities" try to mark out the boundaries for personal conduct, encourage honesty and openness, and ensure that meetings and work parties are well attended. An elaborate system of conflict resolution has been developed; if "self-empowerment contracts," consults with an "accountability committee," and "hear and clear" sessions fail to solve problems, a "community action meeting" can be convened and a member evicted—something that has happened only once.

The co-op has supported a number of commercial ventures. A video-production and editing collective uses one space in the building; a dozen computer-sharing individuals and their office paraphernalia occupy another area. Folk from Community Alternatives started Isadora's, a popular co-operative family restaurant on Granville Island. They created Mountain Muffin Works, a bakery and coffee shop, in order to provide employment for a member's son who is mentally disabled. The co-op even provides its residents with a dental plan.

Another ambitious community initiative is the Glorious Garnish and Seasonal Salad Company. This enterprise, based at Fraser Common Farm, employs three co-op members and markets specialized organic produce to upscale restaurants. As I drive down the winding gravel road to Fraser Common on a soggy winter's day, the farm is not looking its cheeriest. Even so, I can see from the ordered rows of stubble in the neatly maintained fields that serious quantities of vegetables are raised here.

Susan Davidson greets me from the henhouse, and four-year-old Isabelle Wicklund proudly shows me the brown eggs that several dozen brown chickens are busily producing. In an adjacent greenhouse, Davidson and her co-workers are trying to raise some of the exotic herbs and edible flowers—such as johnny jump-ups, lemon licorice, wild sorrel, pineapple sage, mizuna, baby kale and New Zealand spinach—that they grow outdoors in warmer weather. The idea is to supply their famous salad mix on a year-round basis. But low light levels and incessant moisture are making it difficult to cultivate many varieties in the dark depths of December.

Over herb tea in the huge kitchen of the farmhouse, where four co-op members and two children currently live, Davidson talks about the success of Glorious Garnish. Annual sales of carefully washed and sorted gourmet greens peaked near $300,000 in the early 1990s, but cheap imports and the decline of the tax-deductible business lunch have hurt business recently. The company also sells produce at farmers' markets. Community shared agriculture (CSA) is another goal: city dwellers agree to purchase, in advance, a share in a farm's harvest, then receive organic produce—including fruit, berries, nuts, vegetables and herbs—throughout the year.

Back in Kitsilano, urban co-op members face challenges, too. The building's envelope has deteriorated—a common problem for apartment complexes in B.C.'s damp coastal climate—and rot has set in. Expensive repairs must be budgeted for and carried out. The stability of the membership is a concern for long-term residents. A balance must be struck between young and old, poor and not-poor, robust and delicate. Some are drawn to Community Alternatives because it can be a sanctuary, others because they want to put ideas into action. The embrace of the co-op has so far managed to include introverts and extroverts, though some people worry about maintaining an adequate core of active members.

Children find that Community Alternatives is like living in an enormous family home with dozens of aunts and uncles—lots of fun, in other words. Even awkward teenagers, who must sometimes find the co-op relentlessly public, often do well here; if connections with parents get too intense, they can move temporarily to another pod. I think back to Brother XII's fantasy of preparing the way for the births of future world leaders; if only he'd chosen a co-op as a social model, rather than a cult.

Adult members describe co-op life as stimulating, rich with social discourse, new ideas and a sense of belonging. They like being part of a social experiment that really seems to work. "People get more out of their lives when more people are involved in their lives," says Jan Bulman. "I love Community Alternatives and hope one day, far hence, to die here."

Groups of individuals must have been getting together deliberately for millenia to solve their housing needs. If the solutions were at odds with prevailing social conventions, those individuals were likely to be dismissed as radicals or misfits. It's easy to ridicule the social experiments of the past, especially when they make us feel uncomfortable—as the prospect of co-operative, closely scrutinized contact with other people often does. The experiments of the recent past, which touched our lives directly, are the easiest of all to disregard. But the yearning for a deep human connection is part of our nature. Today's recipes for social intimacy attempt to combine territory explored by such groups as Community Alternatives with hard-nosed, end-of-the-century economic realities.

One innovative approach to creating more satisfying communities is illustrated by WindSong, located at Walnut Grove near Fort Langley. Superficially, little distinguishes this housing development from its shiny 96th Avenue neighbour to the west. To the east, it's true, a stream runs through a marshy chunk of bottomland. Fenced off and surrounded by new subdivisions, this beaver-dam meadow looks like a diorama in a drive-by museum: part of an exhibit on how things used to be. But it will remain a natural haven because it is part of WindSong.

The pitched, elaborate greenhouse roof soaring above the complex itself is also unusual. WindSong has a hybrid look and feel: half mall, half apartment building. As one steps through the front door and stands in the airy, heated atrium, one can see into a dining room, where three or four people are sitting around a table talking. In an adjacent room, children play under an adult's watchful eye. Another well-lit office is obviously being used for crafts demonstrations. A room with a big television and a number of sofas has been taken over by teenagers. Double doors on either side of the Common House, as the central atrium is called, lead to two unheated, glassed-in, pedestrian corridors, where individual homes are located.

WindSong is a cohousing project, the second one in Canada. It is not co-operative housing and has not been designed with low-income tenants particularly in mind. Strata-titled units are financed and owned in the usual manner. One, two and three-bedroom townhouses are the norm—nary a pod in sight. But WindSong's shared, common features, including the optional communal meals that are part of the cohousing philosophy, distinguish it sharply from other developments. No two cohousing projects are alike, due to the infinite number of variables that members can choose from. As more cohousers turn vision into reality, pods and other unorthodox living arrangements may well appear on the scene again.

These designed neighbourhoods take their name from a 1988 book, *CoHousing: A Contemporary Approach to Housing Ourselves,* by Kathryn McCamant and Charles Durrett. The authors studied collaborative housing in Denmark, where the idea started thirty years ago. They coined the term "cohousing" and went into the business of helping North Americans build similar alternatives. Today, twenty-five projects have been completed in Canada and the U.S., and two hundred in Europe; hundreds more are on the drawing boards. Canada's cohousing starts are all in B.C. so far. Cardiff Place in Victoria was the national guinea pig in 1993, then WindSong in 1996. A third example, Quayside in North Vancouver, is expected to open in 1997.

The Victoria venture got a jumpstart when its founders were able to purchase a seventeen-unit, two-building condominium complex that had already been designed and had received zoning approvals. McCamant and Durrett, based in Berkeley, advised the group on adapting the layout, and the developer agreed to join the buildings, convert the ground floors to communal use with a dining room, kitchen, guestroom, playroom, lounge, laundry and workshop, and construct an outdoor playground. Four-storey Cardiff Place, adorned with dormer gables and scraps of pseudo-half-timbering, fits into the scale of its genteel Fairfield neighbourhood well.

With fewer than thirty inhabitants, it's a small project by cohousing standards. The thrice-weekly communal meals that are part of the Cardiff Place formula, and attended by most of the residents, are not quite as onerous to prepare as they are at larger developments. The

At WindSong, B.C.'s second completed cohousing complex, Cathy Ringham keeps an eye on Kieran Griffiths, left, and Gareth Ringham under the glass roof of one of the project's two pedestrian corridors. (Andrew Scott)

cohousing idea appeals primarily to low- and middle-income singles, couples and families, plus the elderly and people with special needs. Cardiff Place, for instance, has attracted a number of single mothers with children. "We wanted a place where we know our neighbours," says its listing in the *Communities Directory*, "where it is safe to raise our kids, and where there are people of diverse ages and occupations."

WindSong is not in the 1996 directory because its ninety-six residents only began opening their thirty-four front doors in July of that year. As resident Alan Carpenter tours me around the building, he compares the benefits of cohousing with the disadvantages of other forms of development, most of which, he maintains, have a sterile, cookie-cutter ambience. Whether people live in townhouse terraces, condominium highrises or detached subdivision homes, few get to know their neighbours or have much input into the design and construction processes that affect them so vitally.

With cohousing, everyone knows everyone else because they've been working together for several years to bring a common goal to completion. "WindSong has a real richness of community," says Carpenter. "There are genuine connections between neighbours." He points out some of the many small but important elements that can be incorporated to help a sense of community grow. Kitchens and ground-level porches, for instance, face the glassed-in "street," so that homemakers can watch children and take in social activity. Indoor "gathering nodes" and outdoor gardens and play areas foster spontaneous get-togethers and casual conversations. Like most cohousing groups, WindSong residents went to great lengths to ensure that their design would be environmentally friendly.

I meet some of those residents, mostly youngish mothers with preschool-aged youngsters, in the dining room where they are drinking coffee. Cathy Ringham tells me that she and her family lived in a traditional housing complex but didn't feel at home there. "Everything was too perfect; everyone was keeping up with the Joneses." But this, she says, waving her hand around at the Common House, "this is what we've been searching for."

Sue Collerman and Maureen Butler agree. They like the fact that there are lots of kids around. They like the balance that WindSong offers between privacy and community. They feel good that several disadvantaged residents—a woman with a physical disability, for instance, and a blind man—have quickly and happily adapted to this new home. But their feet remain on solid ground. "We'll always experience some difficulties," reflects Butler. "A few people's balloons will be popped," says Ringham.

All three women are articulate and practical, qualities that cohousing residents tend to develop as they go through the design and construction processes. WindSong's founders spent five years agreeing on a plan, securing construction loans and brainstorming with architect Davidson Yuen Simpson and builder Northmark. They learned how to compromise. To keep costs down and free up funds for common areas, they opted to do without dishwashers and ensuite bathrooms.

Units are fairly small, ranging from 65 to 155 square metres; residents claim that because of the shared facilities they don't need quite as much room. Even so, the cost of those facilities tends to make cohousing slightly pricier than other similar-sized forms of housing. At WindSong, one-bedroom-plus-den homes sold for $150,000, while three-storey, four-bedroom models were $265,000. Monthly strata fees must reflect such expenses as heat and light for the 560-square-metre Common House.

Is cohousing just another style of planned community for the affluent? Early projects in Denmark were disparaged as "dentists' communes." The movement's proponents admit that more attention needs to be paid to affordability. Disorganized, inexperienced cohousing groups can run up bills by making design changes or taking too long to decide what they want. Cost overruns bedevilled several early U.S. efforts—and WindSong, as well. But as the cohousing infrastructure grows, as consultants and "facilitators" gain expertise and architects and builders become used to the concept, start-up periods should shorten and prices decline.

Governments could help cohousing become a genuine option for people of all income levels, according to its advocates, by offering low-interest building loans and assisted mortgages. But many enthusiasts are not waiting around for official support. "We're not government-financed in any way," a Cardiff Place founder told Adele Freedman, the *Globe & Mail's* architecture critic, "so a lot of assistance starts happening among group members. People help each other by giving flexible second mortgages." Residents claim that their costs of living are reduced by sharing childcare and home-office expenses, communal meals—and anything else they can think of.

Despite the high level of trust and co-operation that must be built before a project can succeed, cohousing groups don't usually define themselves as intentional communities. In the WindSong dining room, Sue Collerman flinches when I use the phrase. "I think the people who are attracted to this place don't like to be pigeon-holed," she says. "Intentional communities have a common belief focus," Alan Carpenter suggests. "Our members' belief systems are quite diverse. I prefer to describe what we have here as an intentional neighbourhood design."

One major difference between WindSong and Community Alternatives concerns the degree of obligation that members are under regarding communal duties. WindSong operates on a "team" basis. There are teams for kids' activities, meals, chores, common-area use and governance. During the start-up period, different ones were required, including a "sweet" team, whose mandate was to organize entertainment. But no one is compelled to join a team. Although the entire enterprise would instantly founder without constant volunteer activity, no one is compelled to do anything. "It's always a choice," says Carpenter.

Like Community Alternatives, WindSong members spend much time in meetings—but only if they choose to, of course, which most do. They also rely on consensual decision-making. Cohousing groups have traditionally used a system of coloured cards to aid this process. During discussions, the cards are used to ask questions (yellow), answer questions (green), make comments (blue) or indicate problems (red). The true power of this system is revealed when members vote. Yellow then stands for uncertainty, green for approval, blue for indifference and orange for grudging acceptance. But red means disagreement, and as long as a red card is showing, consensus is blocked and the deliberations must continue.

Because the kitchen in the common dining room has yet to be finished, WindSong residents have been holding potluck meals on weekday evenings. Eventually, responsibility for communal dinners will be rotated—again, on a volunteer basis—and participants will pay a modest meal charge based on the cost of the food. The logistics of cooking for thirty or more people sounds daunting to me, but Carpenter is confident that the group will handle it in style, as other cohousers have done. Meal planning, preparation and clean-up might take most of an afternoon and evening, I'm told, but each household ideally will only have to do it about once a month.

Can groups of total strangers, dissatisfied with existing housing choices, bond together to form more productive, satisfying communities? That appears to depend on the strangers. If they're committed and willing to make the effort, and can develop the personality prerequisites of tolerance, patience and friendliness, cohousing could have an unprecedented impact on the shape of our neighbourhoods. Architects, builders and planners will be paying careful attention to the movement. But cohousing is not just about the living quarters people want: it is a contemporary return to the way of the village—to deeper human links, decentralization, grassroots power and harmony with one's surroundings.

Alan Carpenter sees a strong, pent-up demand for better neighbourhood designs. This demand, in fact, has pushed him forward into a new career. A former developer, he is now working fulltime as a cohousing consultant, and helped coax North Vancouver's Quayside project into being. Quayside will feature a number of new twists, including four strata-title units and one rental suite that will be offered to low-income purchasers or tenants at twenty percent below market price—made possible by profits from the rest of the development. Carpenter promises that B.C. will be seeing further innovations in future plans. "The more cohousing groups there are," he assures me, "the better the world will be."

Co-operative communities and neighbourhoods in B.C. today are not just a feature of urban or suburban life. The cities may be more desperate for alternatives, but settlements in rural areas are also trying to redesign themselves. The most striking evidence of these backcountry transformations can be found in the efforts of B.C.'s First Nations.

If the Nisga'a people of the Nass valley in northern B.C., for instance, were listed in the *Communities Directory,* they might describe themselves as "re-forming." The communal society they enjoyed before early European explorers and traders appeared had an enviable social unity and spiritual cohesiveness. Today, the Nisga'a are at the forefront of native-rights negotiations in Canada and have reclaimed considerable control over their culture and health and education services.

The back-to-the-land movement of the 1970s took many of its ideas, especially in the realms of environmental stewardship and worship, from an imagined way of aboriginal life. The word "tribe" was commonly used to describe the social groupings of the period; a column called "Tribes" that ran in the *Georgia Straight,* Vancouver's venerable alternative weekly, served as a bulletin board and clearing house for information about B.C. communes.

An aboriginal way of life, in B.C. as elsewhere, means small, language-related communities in control of specific regions of land: river valleys and watersheds, for example. The Nisga'a, in their valley fastness, have the exact geographic requirements and approximate numeric strength that Plato thought was necessary for the development of an ideal community: five thousand people, living self-sufficiently from the resources of a single valley system. A setting and a small population are about all *The Republic* and the Nisga'a have in common. But it's satisfying to consider that, at the time Plato was dreaming up *The Republic,* with its woodsmen and farmers, the Nisga'a were busily harvesting ocean and forest half a world away.

In 1975 I first visited that maritime, evergreen ecosystem, following the dirt road along the lower Nass to where it petered out at a floating dock. A few fishing boats and dinghies were tied up, and cars and trucks were parked in a clearing. North, across the river's mouth, lay the village of Greenville, completely beyond my reach. And further west, at the back of beyond, the little community of Kincolith sat on its beautiful pebbled beach next to the inlet that leads to the ocean.

I returned to the great lava beds near the other two Nisga'a villages, Aiyansh and Canyon City. This eerie landscape, the result of an eighteenth-century volcanic eruption (Canada's most recent), was fascinating to explore, and you could camp nearby. The valley seemed very quiet to me; hardly anyone was about. I wanted to go to Canyon City, where the lava flow constricted the Nass River to a narrow rocky gorge and a suspension bridge had been thrown across for pedestrians. The community perched on the far edge. I walked to the centre of the bridge and looked down at the rapid current, but Canyon City was so silent and still I could not step into it.

The atmosphere felt very different two decades later. There's now a vibrancy to the valley, an upwelling of energy. A bridge across the lower Nass has brought a good gravel road to Greenville—or Laxqalts'ap, its Nisga'a name. Another bridge is nearing completion at Canyon City (or Gitwinksihlkw). Proud new totem poles stand over three of the villages, and at the carving shed beside the old suspension bridge, Alver Tait is finishing another pole. The lava fields and volcano have been preserved as parkland, and a steady trickle of welcome visitors is passing through.

A chain of events, introduced at Metlakatla, the first intentional community described in this book, comes full circle with the Nisga'a people. Although the Tsimshian and the Nisga'a are different nations, they are neighbours and share a related language. The model developed at Metlakatla by William Duncan was also instituted by his successors—men such as William Collison, Robert Tomlinson and James McCullagh—at Kincolith and Aiyansh.

Today, several religious organizations remain active in the valley, but in a humbler way than they did a century ago. Many Nisga'a are Christian. But traditional Nisga'a art, music and dancing are also resurgent. Rod Robinson, for instance, executive director of the Nisga'a Tribal Council, receives his inspiration from both sources and

Kincolith, an isolated Nisga'a community at the mouth of Nass Bay, was one of several nineteenth-century "model native villages" based on the example of Metlakatla. (Edward Dossetter; author's collection)

sees no contradiction between the two. In fact, he draws parallels between Christian beliefs and the Ayuukhl Nisga'a—his people's ancient code of laws and customs. "The code instructs us not to use strong language, not to insult those who oppose us," Robinson explains in *Nisga'a: People of the Nass River.* "We are taught to respect everyone's way of life. Share our land, yes. But never give it away."

Tensions do exist, however, between traditional and western ways. And nowhere are they felt more acutely than at isolated Kincolith, or Gingolx—still, with its oversized Anglican church, referred to as the "holy" village. I spend three days at Kincolith, enjoying the magnificent scenery and talking to people. During my stay, I hear many echoes of Metlakatla. More than half the villagers are Anglicans, and many belong to the Church Army, an Anglican offshoot modelled on the Salvation Army, where members assume such ranks as captain, lieutenant and sergeant-major.

Alcohol abuse is still a problem at Kincolith. "Sometimes we go round the whole village praying for the drinkers," one resident tells me. I am sure that the drinkers sometimes go round the whole village, too, expressing their feelings for those who pray. It is as if I have stumbled into an ancient wheel of suffering—those who drink and those who pray, inextricably entwined, locked in a vicious, endless cycle of Duncanesque "shaming and correcting."

"When they first formed this place, a lot of our traditional values were lost," assistant band manager Alvin Nelson tells me. "They weren't given as high a priority as they were on the upper Nass." There are no poles in Kincolith; the village is better known for its fifty-member brass band than for its ceremonial regalia. Old values are returning, though. In 1993, a dance troupe was established; a year later, dancers from all four villages performed together for the first time in Prince Rupert. A road will begin to sneak around the rugged shoreline of Nass Bay towards Kincolith in 1997. By 1998, when it should be completed, Kincolith will likely participate in more of the traditional activities that are reuniting the people of the valley.

Recent Nisga'a land-claim progress has also had a rejuvenating effect on the region. Since 1881, when Sim'oogit Sganisim Sim'oogit led the first Nisga'a negotiating team to Victoria and was rudely rebuffed, the inhabitants of the Nass have waged a ceaseless struggle to manage their own lands, inspiring other First Nations, also. "As we have said many times, we don't want to secede as a separate state or sell the land," vows Robinson, "but we do want to control its use. We will work with the governments and resource industries, yes, but we will make the important decisions."

The 1995 land-claim agreement in principle gives the Nisga'a two thousand square kilometres of land in their beloved valley, logging rights, a share of the Nass River salmon run, broad powers of self-government and $190 million in cash. It is interesting that the two First Nations at the head of the line-up for claim settlements, the Nisga'a and the Sechelt, both have deep connections with early coast missions. (The pioneering Roman Catholic Oblate Order of Mary Immaculate established "model" villages at Sechelt and North Vancouver in the 1860s.) Perhaps some of the old missionary tenacity rubbed off on these regions. Duncan, for instance, was an early champion of sorts for aboriginal land claims, even if the rest of his program had its flaws.

The Nisga'a achieved control of their education system twenty years ago. "There is no more effective way to undermine a culture than to destroy its language," says elder Bert McKay in *Nisga'a*. "In residential schools, our children were made to feel ashamed of being Indian."

Kincolith's recently constructed boat harbour symbolizes the new spirit alive today in the Nass Valley, where traditional Nisga'a customs co-exist harmoniously with Christian beliefs. (Andrew Scott)

Today, in School District 92, Nisga'a language instruction is compulsory from kindergarten to grade seven and an elective in grades eight to twelve. It is also an accredited language at B.C.'s post-secondary institutions. School District 92 was the first native-run district in Canada, created in 1977.

The Nisga'a approach to land-claim negotiations reminds me of what Lester Peterson had said was the aim of the Cape Scott settlers: "to form a colony which could be very much like the modern municipality, in which you'd have your own local laws in a framework of federal and provincial laws." It reminds me, too, of cohousing consultant Alan Carpenter's "intentional neighbourhood design." Decentralization and local control over resources is the direction most aboriginal people want to move in. It is also the preferred direction of the world's ecovillagers. They agree: we should once again become a network of tribes.

Perhaps there is a final irony here. At one time, Europeans imposed their notion of an ideal community on aboriginal people. Today, after nearly 150 years of damage has been done, most Canadians admit that this approach was misguided and wrong. With a chance to start again where they left off in the nineteenth century, B.C.'s native people have an opportunity to teach the rest of us about self-sufficiency and how to create a better society. The utopian flame, it seems, flickers constantly in human nature. The urge to rehabilitate our communities, to improve the ways we live together, continues to make itself felt in the lives of British Columbians.

BIBLIOGRAPHY

Books

Akrigg, G. P. V., and Helen B. Akrigg. *British Columbia Place Names.* Victoria: Sono Nis, 1986.

Alapuro, Risto. *State and Revolution in Finland.* Berkeley: University of California, 1988.

Andersen, Doris. *Evergreen Islands.* Sidney, B.C.: Gray's, 1979.

Anderson, Aili. *History of Sointula.* Sointula, B.C.: Sointula Centennial Committee, 1958.

Anderson, Charles P., Tirthankar Bose, and Joseph I. Richardson, eds. *Circle of Voices: A History of the Religious Communities of British Columbia.* Lantzville, B.C.: Oolichan Books, 1983.

Andreae, Johann. *Christianopolis: An Ideal State of the 17th Century.* Translated and introduced by Felix Emil Held. Oxford: Oxford University, 1916.

Arctander, John W. *The Apostle of Alaska: The Story of William Duncan, of Metlakahtla.* New York: Fleming H. Revell, 1909.

Bacon, Francis. *Essays, Advancement of Learning, New Atlantis and Other Pieces.* New York: Odyssey, 1937.

Bellamy, Edward. *Looking Backward, 2000–1887.* London: Routledge & Sons, 1888.

Berton, Pierre. "The Strange Case of The Brother, XII." In his *My Country: The Remarkable Past,* 100–21. Toronto: McClelland & Stewart, 1976.

_____. "The Spirit Wrestlers." In his *The Promised Land: Settling the West 1896–1914,* 66–100. Toronto: McClelland & Stewart, 1984.

Blaney, Anne. "Hard Fall to Accountability." *Shared Visions, Shared Lives,* ed. Bill Metcalf, 130–41. Findhorn, Scotland: Findhorn Press, 1996.

Boaz, Franz. *Geographical Names of the Kwakiutl Indians.* Columbia University Contributions to Anthropology, vol. 20. New York: AMS Press, 1969.

_____. *Kwakiutl Tales,* vol. 2. New York: Columbia University Press, 1910.

Bowman, Phylis. *Metlakahtla—The Holy City!* Prince Rupert, B.C.: P. Bowman, 1983.

Brown, Justine. *All Possible Worlds: Utopian Experiments in British Columbia.* Vancouver: Transmontanus/New Star, 1995.

Bulman, Jan. "Love-Puddlers and Social Activists." *Shared Visions, Shared Lives,* ed. Bill Metcalf, 40–51. Findhorn, Scotland: Findhorn Press, 1996.

Calder, Frank. *Nisga'a: People of the Nass River.* Vancouver: Douglas & McIntyre/Nisga'a Tribal Council, 1993.

Cameron, Silver Donald. "The Children of Terror." In his *Seasons in the Rain: An Expatriate's Notes on British Columbia,* 181–98. Toronto: McClelland & Stewart, 1978.

Campanella, Tomasso. *The City of the Sun*. Berkeley: University of California, 1981.

Campbell, Kenneth. *North Coast Odyssey: The Inside Passage from Port Hardy to Prince Rupert*. Victoria: Sono Nis, 1993.

Canada. *Official Handbook of Information Relating to the Dominion of Canada, 1897*. Ottawa: Department of the Interior, 1898.

Cherrington, John A. *The Fraser Valley: A History*. Madeira Park, B.C.: Harbour, 1992.

Cole, Douglas. *Captured Heritage: The Scramble for Northwest Coast Artifacts*. Vancouver: Douglas & McIntyre, 1985.

Communities Directory: A Guide to Co-operative Living. Rutledge, Missouri: Fellowship for Intentional Community, 1996.

Dawson, George Mercer. *Notes and Observations on the Qwakiool People of the Northern Part of Vancouver Island and Adjacent Coasts*. Fairfield, Washington: Ye Galleon, 1973.

_____. *Report on a Geological Examination of the Northern Part of Vancouver Island and Adjacent Coasts*. Montreal: Dawson Brothers, 1887.

Derry, T. K. *A History of Modern Norway, 1814–1972*. Oxford: Clarendon, 1973.

Deverell, William. *The Dance of Shiva*. Toronto: McClelland & Stewart, 1984.

Downs, Barry. *Sacred Places: British Columbia's Early Churches*. Vancouver: Douglas & McIntyre, 1980.

Drucker, Philip. *Northwest Coast*. Berkeley: University of California, 1950.

Ewashen, Larry A., and Koozma J. Tarasoff. *In Search of Utopia: The Doukhobors*. Castlegar, B.C.: Spirit Wrestlers Associates, 1994.

Faa, Eric. *Norwegians in the Northwest*. Victoria: Runestad, 1995.

Fish, Gordon. *Dreams of Freedom*. Sound Heritage Series, no. 36. Victoria: Provincial Archives of B.C., 1982.

Foster, Chris. *One Heart, One Way: The Life and Legacy of Martin Exeter*. Denver: Foundation House, 1989.

Fourteenth Biennial Convention Centennial 1894–1994: Sons of Norway, Bella Coola Valley, B.C. Bella Coola, B.C.: Skjonne Dal Lodge #7-142, 1994.

Friesen, John W., and Michael M. Verigin. *The Community Doukhobors: A People in Transition*. Ottawa: Borealis Press, 1989.

Graham, Ron. *God's Dominion: A Sceptic's Quest*. Toronto: McClelland & Stewart, 1990.

Hansen, Gwen. *The Quatsino Chronicle, 1894–1995*. Port Hardy, B.C.: Quatsino Archives Association, 1996.

Holt, Simma. *Terror in the Name of God*. Toronto: McClelland & Stewart, 1964.

Kopas, Cliff. *Bella Coola*. Vancouver: Tenas Tiktik, 1970.

Kosachova, Nataliya G. "The Doukhobors." In *Russian Canadians, Their Past and Present (Collected Essays)*, ed. Tamara F. Jeletzky, 11–47. Ottawa: Borealis Press, 1983.

Landale, Zoe. *Harvest of Salmon: Adventures in fishing the B.C. Coast*. Saanichton, B.C.: Hancock House, 1977.

Larsen, Karen. *A History of Norway*. Princeton: Princeton University, 1950.

Lawrence, J. C. *A Brief History of the Sooke District: The South-West Coast of Vancouver Island from Metchosin to Bamfield.* Sooke, B.C.: Sooke and North Sooke Women's Institute, n.d.

McCamant, Kathryn, and Charles Durrett. *CoHousing: A Contemporary Approach to Housing Ourselves.* Berkeley: Habitat, 1988.

MacIsaac, Ron, Don Clark, and Charles Lillard. *The Devil of De Courcy Island: The Brother XII.* Victoria: Press Porcepic, 1989.

McKelvie, Bruce A. *Magic, Murder and Mystery.* Cobble Hill, B.C.: 1966.

Malloff, Marjorie, and Peter Ogloff, eds. *Toil and Peaceful Life: Portraits of Doukhobors.* Sound Heritage Series, vol. 6, no. 4. Victoria: Provincial Archives of B.C., 1977.

Meilleur, Helen. *A Pour of Rain: Stories from a West Coast Fort.* Victoria: Sono Nis, 1980.

Merton, Thomas. *Raids on the Unspeakable.* New York: New Directions, 1964.

Mumford, Lewis. *The Story of Utopias.* New York: Peter Smith, 1941.

Murray, Peter. *The Devil and Mr. Duncan: A History of the Two Metlakatlas.* Victoria: Sono Nis, 1985.

_____. *Homesteads and Snug Harbours: The Gulf Islands.* Ganges, B.C.: Horsdal & Schubart, 1991.

Neering, Rosemary. *Down the Road.* North Vancouver, B.C.: Whitecap, 1991.

Nichols, Sheila, ed. *Maple Ridge: A History of Settlement.* Maple Ridge, B.C.: Canadian Federation of University Women, Maple Ridge Branch, 1972.

Norris, John. *Strangers Entertained.* Vancouver: B.C. Centennial Committee, 1971.

Nugent, Walter. *Crossings: The Great Transatlantic Migrations, 1870–1914.* Bloomington: Indiana University, 1992.

Oakley, Stewart. *The Story of Denmark.* London: Faber & Faber, 1972.

Oliphant, John. *Brother Twelve: The Incredible Story of Canada's False Prophet.* Toronto: McClelland & Stewart, 1991.

Ormsby, Margaret A. *British Columbia: A History.* Toronto: Macmillan, 1958.

Peterson, Lester. *The Cape Scott Story.* Vancouver: Mitchell Press, 1974.

Popoff, Eli A. *Stories from Doukhobor History.* Grand Forks, B.C.: Union of Spiritual Communities of Christ, 1992.

Rasporich, Anthony W. "Utopia, Sect and Millenium in Western Canada, 1870–1940." In *Prophets, Priests and Prodigals: Readings in Canadian Religious History, 1608 to Present,* eds. Mark G. McGowan and David B. Marshall, 213-41. Toronto: McGraw-Hill Ryerson, 1992.

Scott, Jack David. *Four Walls in the West: The Story of the British Columbia Penitentiary.* New Westminster, B.C.: Retired Federal Prison Officers' Association of B.C., 1984.

Solway, Jeff. *Canadian Alternatives in 1975: A Movement Maturing.* Ottawa: Secretary of State, 1976.

Tarasoff, Koozma J. *Plakun Trava: The Doukhobors.* Grand Forks, B.C.: MIR Publication Society, 1982.

_____. *Traditional Doukhobor Folkways: An Ethnographic and Biographic Record of Prescribed Behaviour.* Ottawa: National Museums of Canada, 1977.

Tarasoff, Koozma J., and Robert B. Klymasz, eds. *Spirit Wrestlers: Centennial Papers in Honour of Canada's Doukhobor Heritage.* Hull, Quebec: Canadian Museum of Civilization, 1995.

Thiering, B. E. *Jesus and the Riddle of the Dead Sea Scrolls: Unlocking the Secrets of His Life Story.* Toronto: Doubleday, 1992.

Usher, Jean. *William Duncan of Metlakatla: A Victorian Missionary in British Columbia.* Ottawa: National Museum of Canada, 1974.

Vonnegut, Mark. *The Eden Express.* New York: Praeger, 1975.

Wellcome, Henry S. *The Story of Metlakahtla.* London: Saxon, 1887.

Wild, Paula. *Sointula: Island Utopia.* Madeira Park, B.C.: Harbour, 1995.

Wilde, Oscar. *The Soul of Man Under Socialism.* Boston: Crescendo, 1969.

Williams, Paul. *Apple Bay, or Life on the Planet.* New York: Warner, 1976.

Wilson, Edward Arthur. *The Aquarian Age.* Akron, Ohio: Sun, 1927.

_____. *Foundation Letters & Teachings.* Akron, Ohio: Sun, 1927.

_____. *Unsigned Letters from an Elder Brother.* San Diego: Concord, n.d.

Wilson, Herbert Emmerson. *Canada's False Prophet.* Richmond Hill: Simon, 1967.

Wittke, Carl. *We Who Built America.* Cleveland: Western Reserve University, 1939.

Woodcock, George. "Harmony Island: A Canadian Utopia." In *British Columbia: A Centennial Anthology,* ed. R. E. Watters. Toronto: McClelland & Stewart, 1958.

_____. *Ravens and Prophets.* Victoria: Sono Nis, 1993.

Woodcock, George, and Ivan Avakumovic. *The Doukhobors.* Toronto: Oxford University Press, 1968.

Wuorinen, John. *A History of Finland.* New York: Columbia University, 1965.

Periodicals

Beers, David. "Close for Comfort." *Western Living* 22 (Dec. 1992): 66–68+.

Bekker, Bertold. "Wonders Around Cape Scott." *Daily Colonist,* 20 Dec., 1919, 21.

Bjork, Kenneth O. "Bella Coola." *Americana Norvegica* 3 (1971): 195–222.

_____. "The Founding of Quatsino Colony." *Norwegian-American Studies* 25 (1972): 80–104.

Bowers, Vivien. "Friends in Argenta." *Beautiful British Columbia* 38 (Fall 1996): 34–39.

Bowman, James. "Campus Residence Cooperative Association." *Communities* no. 36 (Jan./Feb. 1979): 34–35.

_____. "Coalition of Intentional Cooperative Communities." *Communities* no. 36 (Jan./Feb. 1979): 47.

Brown, Justine. "Nowherelands: Utopian Communities in B.C. Fiction." *B.C. Studies* 109 (Spring 1996): 5–28.

Dawson, Will. "Quatsino Village." *B.C. Outdoors* 26 (March/April 1970): 54–58.

Doig, Ivan. "The Tribe that Learned the Gospel of Capitalism." *The American West* 11 (March 1974): 42–47.

Dunnett, Ryan. "Argenta." *Communities* no. 36 (Jan./Feb. 1979): 45–46.

Edmonds, Allan. "Would You Give up $25,000 a Year to Find 'Peace' Doing Chores in an Island Commune?" *Maclean's* 83 (Aug. 1970): 36–41.

_____. "Paradise Lost." *West* 3 (June 1991): 58–67.

Fougner, Ivar. "The Founding of Bella Coola, a Norwegian Settlement in B.C." *Canadian Magazine of Politics, Science, Art and Literature* 23, no. 6 (1904): 529–36.

Freedman, Adele. "Togetherness for the Nineties." *Globe & Mail,* 13 Sept. 1994, D1.

Gray, John. "Seven Families *Really* Got Away from It All." *Maclean's* 74 (7 Oct. 1961): 33–34+.

Grescoe, Taras. "With the Best of Intentions." *Georgia Straight* 28, no. 1407 (1994): 15–23.

Jamieson, Eric. "Cape Scott an Ill-conceived Providence." *Canadian West* 10 (Winter 1987): 132–39.

Kolehmainen, John. "Harmony Island: A Finnish Utopian Venture in British Columbia." *B.C. Historical Quarterly* 5 (April 1941): 111–23.

Kopas, Leslie. "Growing up in Bella Coola." *Raincoast Chronicles* 4 (1973): 18–23.

Kristjanson, Gus. "Icelandic Settlement on the Northern B.C. Coast." *Icelandic Canadian* 30, no. 1 (1971): 22–26.

Landale, Zoe. "The Home Team." *Western Living* 25 (May 1995): 67–70e.

Lawrance, Scott. "Sointula: Saltfish and Spuds Utopia." *Raincoast Chronicles* 4 (1973): 12–17.

_____. "Buddhist Columbia." *Raincoast Chronicles* 2 (1973): 15–17.

Leidl, David. "Live (With) Thy Neighbor." *B.C. Business* 24 (Nov. 1996): 29–33.

Mealing, F. Mark. "On Doukhobor Psalms." *Canadian Literature,* no. 120 (1989): 117–32.

"Ochiltree Commune." *Communities* no. 36 (Jan./Feb., 1979), 42–44.

O'Hagan, Howard. "The Weird and Savage Cult of Brother XII." *Maclean's* 73 (23 April 1960): 22–23+.

Oliphant, John. "Just Who was Brother Twelve." *Beautiful British Columbia* 35 (Summer 1993): 14–22.

_____. "My Search for Brother Twelve." *Step* 2 (1991): 32–39.

Scott, Andrew. "Bizarre History is Alaska Town's Trump Card." *Georgia Straight* 30, no. 1487 (1996): 21–22.

_____. "Kincolith: 'Place of Scalps.'" *Beautiful British Columbia* 37 (Winter 1995): 14–19.

_____. "Sointula, British Columbia: Harmony Island." *Equinox* 10 (March/April 1991): 89–107.

Stainsby, Mia. "From Commune to Community." *Vancouver Sun,* 19 Aug. 1995, C1–2.

Stevenson, Judi S. "Metlakatla." *Beaver* 44 (Aug./Sept. 1986): 35–41.

Thatcher, Dave. "100 Mile House: Emissaries of Divine Light." *Communities* no. 36 (Jan./Feb. 1979): 39–41.

Todd, Douglas. "The Utopians." *Vancouver Sun,* 2 Dec. 1989, B3.

Trower, Peter. "The Temptations of a Safe-Cracking Preacher." *Vancouver* 15, no. 7 (1982): 46–50+.

Tryggvason, Gustaf, and Nina Jobin. "The Icelanders in British Columbia." *Icelandic Canadian* 25, no. 4 (1967): 62–65.

White, Howard. "Bringing the Indians to Their Knees/Metlakatla." *Raincoast Chronicles* 4 (1973): 24–37.

Whiteley, Mary. "Unsettled Settlement." *Beaver* 20 (Summer 1962): 4–9.

Wild, Paula. "Sointula: Malcolm Island Utopia." *Canadian West* 6, no. 4 (1990): 132–38.

Wilson, J. Donald. "Matti Kurikka: Finnish-Canadian Intellectual." *B.C. Studies* 20 (Winter 1973/74): 50-65.

Young-Bateman, Nick. "Cape Scott." *Westworld* 1 (May/June 1975): 30–31+.

Other Sources

Bonney, I. Dean. "Bella Coola Colony." Report for B.C. Dept. of Education, 1953. Victoria: B.C. Archives and Record Service.

British Columbia. *Sessional Papers*. Victoria: 1894, 1897–99, 1913–18, 1921.

Dane, Bernard. "Cape Scott." Unpublished typescript, 1972. Victoria: B.C. Archives and Record Service.

_____. "San Josef Valley." Unpublished typescript, 1972. Victoria: B.C. Archives and Record Service.

Fougner, Ivar. "Diary of Ivar Fougner, April 8, 1892–December 30, 1915." Transcribed by J.R. Castilio. Unpublished typescript. Victoria: B.C. Archives and Record Service.

Helland, Andreas. "Pastor Christian Saugstad." Luther League Federation. Victoria: B.C. Archives and Record Service.

Peterson, Lester. "Cape Scott and Gibsons: Autobiography." Unpublished typescript, 1963. Vancouver: City Archives.

Saugstad, R. "My Memoires." Unpublished typescript, 1971. Victoria: B.C. Archives and Record Service.

Smith, Leonard L. "An Ethnohistorical Comparative Study of Scandinavian Colonization on Northern Vancouver Island, British Columbia: The Norwegians at Quatsino and the Danes at Cape Scott/San Josef Valley, 1894–1913." Master's thesis, University of Victoria, 1983.

Viken, Torliev. "Account of the First Settlement in Bella Coola Valley" (in Norwegian). *Norrona* 41, nos. 22–23, 25 (1950). Typescript translation. Victoria: B.C. Archives and Record Service.

INDEX

Bold entries refer to photographs.

Mountainview Doukhobor Museum, 113–14, **115,** 124
Murray, Peter, 22

Nakumgilisala, 76–78
Nanaimo, 96, 98–101, 141, 146, 150–52, 156, 170
Nass Bay, 29, **207**
Nass Valley, 23, 25, 205–10, **209**
Nels Bight, 69–70, 77
Nelson, 123, 132, 162–63, 166–67, 175, 181
Nelson, Nels, 74, 76, 80
New Denmark, New Brunswick, 73
New Denver, 134, 175
New Harmony, Indiana, 13, 99
New Hungary, Saskatchewan, 14
New Iceland, Manitoba, 14
New Jerusalem, Saskatchewan, 14, 172
New Metlakatla. *See* Metlakatla, Alaska
New Norway (Nye Norge), 62, 66, 172
New Settlement, 126
New West Co-op (Campus Residence Co-operative Association), 172–74, **173,** 185
New Westminster, 172–73, **173,** 178
New Zealand, 28, 144, 192, 198
Neyahshnawah, Chief, 25
Nisga'a, 15, 25, 205–10, **207, 209**
Nissen Bight, 77
Nogar, Thomas, 56, 65
Nordstrom, Christian, 54–57, 62
Nordstrom, George, 55
Norway, 43, 48–49
Norwegian immigrants, 9–10, 14, 43–46, 48–64, **53, 59, 63,** 67, 72, 86–87, 89, 97, 99
Nova Co-operative Society, 54–55
Noyes, John Humphrey, 99
Nuxalk, 45, 47, 54, 58, 60, 64

Ochiltree Organic Commune (Cariboo Organic Commune, CEEDS, Troopers Commune), 16, 159, 179, 181–85, 193
O'Hagan, Howard, 143
Okanagan, 50, 52
Oliphant, John, 143–44, 150, 154, 156–57
Oliver, Frank, 122
Oliver Wolcott (ship), 35
100 Mile House, 157, 184–90, **187,** 192
Oneida, New York, 13, 99
Ontario, 14, 188
Ooteshenie, 124–25
Open Circle, 160, 172, 176, 179–81
Orton, George, 169, 171
Osland, 14
Ottawa, 35
Owen, Robert, 13, 99

Pacifism, 114, 118, 121, 130, 134
Painter, Roger, 152, **155,** 156
Pass Creek, 127
Permaculture, 11, 17
Peterson, Lester, 83, 85, 87, 89, 210
Pirates Cove (Gospel Cove, The Haven), 151–52, 155–57
Plato, 13, 206
Pobirokhin, Ilarion, 117
Pollard, Mary, 162, 167
Popoff, Eli, 138
Port Alice, 62, 66
Port Chester, Alaska, 37
Port Hardy, 66, 170
Port McNeill, 93–94
Port Simpson. *See* Fort Simpson
Powell, Dr. Israel W., 35
Powell River, 178
Prevost, Captain James C., 23
Prince George, 163, 188–89
Prince Rupert, 14, 19–20, 62, 157, 208
Princess Louise (ship), 53–54, 62
Princess Maquinna (ship), 65

ABOUT THE AUTHOR

Andrew Scott has published more than 600 non-fiction articles on a wide range of topics. His work has appeared in *Equinox, Discovery, Maclean's, enRoute, Vancouver, Beautiful British Columbia, Raincoast Chronicles, Melbourne Age, New Zealand Herald,* and numerous other magazines and newspapers. He is a former editor-in-chief of *Western Living* magazine, senior editor of the *Globe & Mail*'s city magazine network (*WEST, Toronto,* and *Montreal*) and publisher of *Alaska Airlines Magazine.* In 1994, he received a National Magazine Gold Award for personal journalism. He has won three Western Magazine Awards as an editor and four as a writer, including awards for travel (1986), science and technology (1995) and best article from British Columbia (1994). Scott, who lives in Halfmoon Bay, B.C., also writes a monthly column about tourism for *The Georgia Straight.* This is his first book.